GREAT PERSONALITIES
OF THE NEW TESTAMENT

By the same author:

GREAT PERSONALITIES OF THE OLD TESTAMENT
AMAZING DEAD SEA SCROLLS AND THE CHRISTIAN FAITH
A BIBLIOGRAPHY OF THE DEAD SEA SCROLLS 1948-1957

Great Personalities of the New Testament

THEIR LIVES AND TIMES

by

WILLIAM SANFORD LaSOR

FLEMING H. REVELL COMPANY

To
HENRY SNYDER GEHMAN
AND
OTTO A. PIPER
this work
is gratefully dedicated

Preface

"NAMES MAKE NEWS," we are told, and likewise persons make history. We believe in a personal God who has dealt, even as He deals today, with persons. This book is an effort to tell the story of the founding of the Christian Church by recounting the stories of some of the key personalities.

In my first volume, *Great Personalities of the Old Testament,* I attempted to tell the story of God's redemptive activity through Israel His chosen. At that time I mentally determined to carry on this method for the whole story of His redemption—but one step is all that can be taken at a time. The publishers have had sufficient confidence in the idea, based on their experience with the first volume, that they have encouraged me to take the second step, for which I am indeed grateful. It is highly unlikely that future critics will debate, as they have done in the case of Luke, whether it was my intention to add a third volume. But to save them from useless discussion, let me say that this is my hope and purpose, the Lord willing.

Why have I chosen just these persons and omitted others? This, of course, is an author's prerogative. When a scholar publishes a dictionary of biography or a book about all the men and women of the Bible, he cannot omit any. But when an author attempts to tell a story, he selects only those characters and events that are necessary. That is why Luke omitted from Acts the works of most of the Twelve Apostles; that is why he failed to tell of the expansion of the Church into Egypt and the East: he had his sights on Rome. When I started to plan this work, I sketched in outline form the story I wanted to tell, and then worked through the New Testament characters who would serve as the means of telling that story. Why did I omit Matthew and include Mark, Luke, and John? The answer is simple: Matthew added nothing to my story that was not already included; on the other hand, if I had used Matthew and omitted any one of the others, the loss would have been, for my purpose, greater than the gain. Another author would have done it differently—that is the wonderful truth of the human race: we are not all alike. I could write this story because no one else had done it exactly this way; and another author will come along and write yet another story because I have not done it the way he would like to have it done.

These studies, for the most part, were presented to the Embassy Class of the First Baptist Church, Montebello, California, and recorded electronically. In editing them for publication, I have tried to preserve the informal and interpersonal style of the spoken word. Let me express here my appreciation of the splendid Christian fellowship we enjoyed and the gracious hearing I received during the weeks of this ministry.

A word about the dedication of this volume is in order. Professors Henry Snyder Gehman and Otto A. Piper are my teachers and friends. From them I first learned to be interested in history and the philosophy of history; from them I learned something of scholarly care and the critical approach to Biblical problems; from them I learned, above all, to be tolerant of views with which I do not always find myself in agreement. That I did not learn more is my fault, not theirs. For two decades and more I have cherished the friendship of these men of God. I cannot assume that they will always and everywhere agree with me, but I know that I can expect from them the same spirit of Christian love in disagreement that they have tried to inculcate in all their students.

For the transcribing of the tapes and the typing of the manuscript I am indebted to Miss Louise Hoffman, Miss Dolores Loeding, and my beloved wife. For her experienced and careful reading of the proof, I wish to thank Mrs. Anne Kimber. For the encouragement to undertake this series and to prepare it for publication I am indebted to my good friend Dr. Frank S. Mead, Editor-in-Chief of the Fleming H. Revell Company.

It is my sincere desire and prayer that this work will help you to know these personalities—not just to know about them—and that as you come to know them as friends you will come to know better the God they serve.

WILLIAM SANFORD LASOR

Fuller Theological Seminary
Pasadena, California

Contents

Contents

GREAT PERSONALITIES
OF THE NEW TESTAMENT

CHAPTER I

The Fullness of Time

IF YOU WERE going to launch a world-wide movement, when would you do it? You would probably wait until the political factors were just right. The ideal time would be when there was no war, and when communication was easy to all parts of the world. You would wait until the cultural factors were right. You would desire a minimum language barrier. You would look for ease in the spreading of ideas. And if the movement you were to launch happened to be a religious movement, you would feel that even the religious scene needed to be prepared.

In the letter to the Galatians, Paul says, "But when the time had fully come"—or as it is in the King James Version, "when the fullness of the time was come"—"God sent forth his Son, born of woman, born under the law, to redeem those who were under the law, so that we might receive adoption as sons" (Galatians 4:4f). In other words, Paul is saying that the advent of Jesus Christ occurred at that moment of history that could be described as "the fullness of time."[1] Jesus Himself suggested that the fullness of time had come when He began His public ministry with the words, "The time is fulfilled, and the kingdom of God is at hand" (Mark 1:15).

It is fitting as we begin our series on the Great Personalities of the New Testament that we try to understand something of the significance of this concept, *the fullness of time*. God works in history. God is the Lord of history. These sayings are so commonplace that they have become clichés. Yet in a very real sense these commonplace sayings are true. For centuries God had been preparing the world for the advent of the Redeemer. Without ever being aware of it, nations moved on and off the scene, fulfilling the parts that were determined for them: is this not what Paul was trying to tell the learned men of Athens (cf. Acts 17:24-26)? Only one nation in the world had

[1] For a stimulating discussion of "the fullness of time," see Otto Piper, *God in History* (New York: The Macmillan Company, 1939), pp. 1-40.

13

an intimate acquaintance with God and knew something of His purposes: that was the nation Israel. But it is written very clearly in the pages of the Old Testament that Israel was not the only nation in which God was active or through which God was bringing to pass His purpose. Through His prophets He made it very clear, as indeed He had done in the first promise to Abraham, that all of the nations of the world were involved in His redemptive activity (cf. Genesis 12:3; Isaiah 60:1-3).

All the nations of the world were involved—how?[2] Students of the Bible are familiar enough with the Egyptians and the Assyrians, the Babylonians and the Persians, and the parts they played in the divine plan. But the story of the Old Testament ends approximately in the middle of the fifth century B.C. It is a gross mistake to suppose that God's activity ended at that same time and did not begin again until the annunciations of the births of John the Baptist and Jesus of Nazareth. Some of the most important preparation of the world was taking place in the centuries between the Old Testament and the New Testament.

The political preparation. Instead of thinking of the Biblical world as spreading over parts of three continents, think of it as a geographical and cultural entity bordering on the eastern half of the Mediterranean Sea. Because of the mountains that extend across the northern portion from the Alps to the Himalayas, and the desert that stretches across the southern portion, plus the desert and seas of the eastern portion, communication between those parts of Europe, Asia, and Africa that border on the Mediterranean was far less difficult than communication to the remaining parts of any of the continents. This single area is the Bible world. Yet, it is still true that there are three distinct parts of the Bible world. There were Asiatics, Europeans, and Egyptians (to the last of which should be added, of course, the Libyans, Ethiopians, and others). Although the Egyptians were of great importance in the earlier portion of Old Testament history, by the time of the last centuries before Christ Egypt was no longer of primary importance. The struggle was between the Asiatics and the Europeans.

---

[2] I have tried to show something of the historical activity of God in my previous volume, *Great Personalities of the Old Testament* (Westwood, N.J.: Fleming H. Revell Company, 1959).

It is possible to trace a shift of power, first from the Semitic peoples in Asia to the non-Semitic, and specifically to the Indo-European peoples in Asia; then from the Asiatic Indo-Europeans to the European Greeks. The night Babylon fell before the forces of Cyrus the Great the hegemony of Semitic empires came to an end. When Darius the Third was conquered by Alexander the Great, the world-empires of the Asiatic peoples came to an end and the world-empires of the Europeans began. Since that time, only twice in history have Asiatics seriously threatened the supremacy of the European powers: first in the time of Mohammed, when the Islamic forces spread across northern Africa and into the Iberian Peninsula, only to be stopped by Charles Martel at Tours (A.D. 732); the second time when Genghis Kahn[3] swept westward into Europe to the Dnieper River in the early thirteenth century A.D. Both of these attempts, it will be noted, are considerably later than the time of Christ, and both of them failed.[4]

The rise of world empires is undoubtedly part of the political preparation employed in the idea of the fullness of time. At the end of the third millenium B.C., Sargon of Akkad had ideas of world empire when he called himself, "king of the four quarters of the earth." But this amounted to little more than a self-conferred honorary degree. The idea, however, seems to have been present in the minds of rulers who succeeded him, and at last in the days of the second Assyrian Empire it began to take on reality. Tiglath-pileser I (c.1118-1078 B.C.) provided considerable stimulus for its development, but the carrying out belongs really to the dynasty of Tiglath-pileser III (c.745-727 B.C.), including Shalmaneser V (c.727-722 B.C.), Sargon II of Assyria (722-705 B.C.), and Sennacherib (705-681 B.C.).[5] The Assyr-

[3] Pronounced jĕng'gĭs kän'—it is a common mistake to pronounce the first g hard.

[4] This is of course not to imply the superiority of the European over the Asiatic, nor for that matter over the African. The historian knows that there is no assurance that the European empires (or powers, as we now call them) will continue to maintain a relative supremacy in the world; in fact, the decline of the West was apparent to some historians years ago. But to discuss this would be to get away from our present purpose.

[5] It is debatable whether this succession of kings should be called a dynasty. According to most scholars, Sargon was a usurper of the throne; on the other hand, van der Meer lists him as a brother of Shalmaneser V (cf. P. van der Meer, *The Chronology of Ancient Western Asia and Egypt* [2d ed.; Leiden: E. J. Brill, 1955], p. 76). Unfortunately, van der Meer does not document this, and I have been unable to find the record in which the relationship is expressed.

ian empire was indescribably cruel, and maintained its grasp not so much by means of wise and efficient government as by sheer brute force. With the destruction of Nineveh in 612 B.C., it was replaced by the Babylonian empire of Nebuchadnezzar; but this empire was doomed to fall even before it arose, for it had come into existence by a coalition of powers and was unable to maintain the loyalty of its allies.

The Medo-Persian empire came into being by the destruction of Babylon in 539 B.C., and proceeded to establish a system of government which should have furnished sufficient cohesion to hold together an empire stretching from the Aegean Sea to the Indus River and including Egypt. But the Medo-Persian empire probably overextended itself by attempting to subdue the Scythians along the Danube, and later by attempting to conquer Athens and other parts of Greece. At the same time, we must recognize the fact that another power had arisen that was able to conquer the Medo-Persian empire.

Alexander the Great of Macedon had come to the throne and succeeded in whipping together the peoples of Greece, who had hitherto shown no remarkable unity. Moreover, he had established an ideal which struck fire. Quickly he moved across the world of his day, conquering the Medo-Persian empire and attempting even to extend its boundaries. Alexander died young, before the empire was really unified, and he bequeathed his empire to his four generals who soon reduced it to four and then three parts. By the end of the fourth century B.C. it would seem that the idea of world empire had come to an end.

This, however, was not to be. A new power had arisen in the west which, after it had overcome its only western rival, Carthage, on the northern coast of Africa,[6] turned its attention to the east, and by 63 B.C., Rome had taken over the lands of the eastern Mediterranean. While it is true that the Roman empire did not reach its greatest extent until the rule of Trajan (A.D. 117), it is also true that Roman rule extended over enough of the world of Jesus' day that it could be called "the whole world" (Luke 2:1).

The Romans were able to give to the world that unity and strength of government which was necessary for peace and for the rapid spread of the gospel. *Pax Romana* (Roman peace) was not only an ideal; it was a fact. Perhaps for the only time in the history of the world there

[6] In the three Punic Wars, 264-241, 218-201, and 149-146 B.C.

was an extended period of universal peace. If Jesus Christ had come into the world one hundred years either side of the actual time of His advent, the story, from the historian's point of view, would have been far different. Alongside *Pax Romana* was *Lex Romana* (Roman law). The Roman empire in some way had learned to balance local autonomy and central authority, the rights of individuals and the rights of the state. So well was Roman law developed that the legal systems of the western world are largely drawn from it.

We would not suggest that there were no problems. In order to maintain peace, the Roman empire had a standing army of a quarter-million men. True, the citizen army maintained by conscription had been replaced by a professional army. But armed forces are expensive, and taxes were imposed in the forms of customs, excise, inheritance, and sales taxes, usually collected by men who bought the office as a concession and then charged what they could get. Once every fourteen years a census or poll-tax was levied. These things were sources of annoyance and an occasional riot. But all-in-all, it was a time of peace and prosperity.

The cultural preparation. The empires which had preceded that of Alexander the Great were dead. It would not be possible to speak of a continuing Babylonian or Persian ideal, or any other. But the ideal of Alexander the Great, with the establishment of the Roman empire, was far from dead. That ideal can be summarized in one word: Hellenism. While this term can be used, and has been used, to cover many things, it will help us to think of it as the desire to give to the world the best of Greek life and thought. Alexander wanted to establish all over his empire centers of Greek culture, libraries that would house Greek writings, theaters that would present Greek drama and music. Cities named "Alexandria" sprang up all over the empire, and anyone who travels in the Near East will be duly impressed by the magnificence and geographical extent of Greek ruins. The library in Alexandria, Egypt, possessed over 500,000 volumes, and this was not the only library in the empire, for when it caught fire, Antony gave to Cleopatra 200,000 volumes from the library at Pergamum as replacement. It was Alexander's ideal also that a common language should unite the empire, and, of course, that would be Greek. One of the most dramatic ways in which Alexander attempted to put into effect his ideal was a mass wedding ceremony, held at Susa (one of the capitals of the Medo-Persian empire), where Alexander and his generals, and ten thousand of his soldiers, attempted to symbolize the marriage of Europe and Asia by taking Persian wives.[7] In some ways Alexander's expedition could be looked upon as scientific, somewhat as was Napoleon's expedition to Egypt many centuries later. Alexander took with him scholars, historians, geographers, and botanists. He built a fleet of ships at the mouth of the Indus River which was to explore the coast of the Persian Gulf; and he had other ideas which were considerably in advance of his day.[8] And the most completely Hellenized part of the empire outside Greece itself was Syro-Palestine![9]

When the Roman empire achieved supremacy, it is fortunate, or we prefer to say, providential, that there was no spirit of pan-Romanism. No effort seems to have been made to overthrow the Hellenistic ideals, to replace the Greek language with the Latin, or to develop an indigenous Roman culture. To expect the world to adopt a second universal language so soon would be to expect the impossible. Greek continued to be the language of the empire for several centuries. Moreover, the Romans were imitators rather than originators. Their art is largely Greek art, and other elements of their culture owe much to the Greeks who preceded them. Rome made a different type of contribution to the culture of the world; perhaps we could say it was more practical. Hellenism was an ideal. *Pax Romana* and *Lex Romana* were not ideals, they were realities; and because they were realities, the Hellenistic ideal was able to take even firmer root than it had, and the unity of which Alexander dreamed was realized in the Roman empire. Roman roads tied the empire together; Roman ships plied the lanes

---

[7] Arrian, *Anabasis of Alexander*, 7.4.4-8; Plutarch, *Life of Alexander*, 70.2. It is true that Alexander's soldiers conducted a burning and looting expedition, and some scholars have little sympathy with Alexander's pan-Hellenic ideal; cf. A. T. E. Olmstead, *History of the Persian Empire* (Chicago: University of Chicago Press, 1948), pp. 519-523. The attitude of Ghirshman, reminding us of Voltaire's words ("Alexander had built more towns than other conquerors had destroyed"), is a moderating viewpoint; cf. R. Ghirshman, *Iran* (Pelican Book A239; Harmondsworth, Middlesex: Penguin Books, 1954), pp. 212-219.

[8] S. Vernon McCasland has pointed out that this expansion of Greek influence had been under way for a long time and that Alexander's conquests only gave an impetus to it; cf. "The Greco-Roman World," in *The Interpreter's Bible* (New York: Abingdon-Cokesbury Press, 1951), vol. 7, p. 75. It is nevertheless true that the impetus was needed and Alexander provided it.

[9] Cf. John Pentland Mahaffy, *The Progress of Hellenism in Alexander's Empire* (Chicago: University of Chicago Press, 1905), p. 97.

of the Mediterranean; the Roman postal system made rapid communication possible; Roman citizenship not only protected the rights of individuals who were citizens, but made possible widespread travel. At the same time, the principle of colonial home rule added a sense of significance and individual value.

But a sense of human value can cause trouble! When a slave, or an ex-slave, suddenly realizes, "I, too, am a man," he can cause all sorts of difficulty for those who want to be masters. Slavery was a great problem in the Roman empire. It has been estimated that one-third to one-half of the entire population were slaves. Life was cheap. A master who was displeased with the way his slave served the table could throw him to the fish. A mistress could permanently disfigure her servant whom she caught brushing her hair. Emperors might send hundreds, even thousands, of slaves into the arena to engage in mass slaughter—just for entertainment! But others were thinking about these things. If human life has value, how can it be destroyed so easily? When life is cheap, immorality is rampant. In particular, immorality of a sexual nature is encouraged when human beings are insignificant. Roman writers have left us full, frank, and disgusting accounts of their day.[10] But Roman writers were also rebelling against such conditions. Cicero's orations against Catiline in 63 B.C., once known by every schoolboy Latin student, are only one example that could be cited.

There is a nobler side, even in fallen man, for which we ought to thank God. Men were grappling with serious matters. They did not always come up with the right answers, but they were making interesting suggestions. We still study their philosophies and find much of value in them. This is not the place to discuss them; I simply want to point out one fact: when God was ready to send His Gospel into the world, there were men who were ready to give it serious consideration.

The religious preparation. The four and a half centuries between the close of the Old Testament and the advent of Jesus Christ were

---

[10] For a graphic resumé, amply documented, see David R. Breed, *A History of the Preparation of the World for Christ* (New York: Fleming H. Revell Company, 1893), pp. 403-430. More restrained is McCasland's treatment, *art. cit.,* in *The Interpreter's Bible,* vol. 7, pp. 80-84. Paul refers to this condition in Romans 1:18-32.

years of great experience for the Jewish people. At the beginning of
the sixth century B.C., they had been carried from Judah to Babylon
in captivity. In 538 B.C., Cyrus the Great had granted to them the
opportunity of returning to their land. Not all Jews, however,
returned; as a matter of fact, some estimates of the number of Jews
who seized the opportunity are as low as ten per cent.[11] Those who
remained in exile made a new home for themselves. That home was
the world. Such Jews were the "Diaspora," or the Jews of the Dispersion.[12]

Several things happened to the Jewish people in the Dispersion. For
one thing, they developed a world view. Too long had they associated
their God merely with the land of Palestine. By the rivers of Babylon
they had wept because they had thought they could not sing the Lord's
song in a foreign land (see Psalm 137:1-4). But now they had come
to realize that the world was the Lord's. They not only could sing the
Lord's song in foreign lands—they could even translate the song into
foreign languages! In Babylon and the Mesopotamian region, as well
as in the land of Egypt to which Jews had migrated in the time of
Jeremiah and possibly earlier, Aramaic became the language of the
Jewish people. Jews gradually spread to other parts of the world, and
began to speak the Greek language. As their knowledge of the original
Hebrew language decreased, it became increasingly necessary to have
an explanation of the meaning of the Scriptures. Interpretations in
Aramaic were at first preserved in oral form only, known as Targums,
but later these were standardized in written form. Likewise Greek
translations of the Old Testament Scriptures were made, which were
far more significant for the New Testament period than were the
Aramaic Targums.

Perhaps that statement needs a word of explanation. The reason
why the Greek translations were important can be explained by the
fact that the Jewish people were undergoing, consciously or uncon-
sciously, a process of Hellenization. If they were not all participating
in the games in the stadium—some indeed going so far as to have
the visible signs of circumcision removed by an operation—at least
their vocabulary was being expanded with Greek ideas. When the

[11] See my *Great Personalities of the Old Testament*, p. 174-183.
[12] Cf. F. J. Foakes Jackson and Kirsopp Lake, *The Beginnings of Christianity*
(London: Macmillan and Co., 1922), vol. 1, pp. 137-168; and Robert H. Pfeiffer,
History of New Testament Times (New York: Harper & Brothers, 1949), pp.
166-196. The latter has an excellent bibliography.

Hebrew Old Testament was translated into Greek, Hebrew words that had narrow meanings were often translated by Greek words that had broader meanings. Key theological terms had to be translated by words that had various nuances and connotations not present in the original. It could not possibly be otherwise. Our words are integrally part of our culture. When two cultures merge, the language has to become richer.[13] And the Jews had entered the Hellenistic stream of culture. The old wineskins were already being stretched; the new wine would require new wineskins. It is highly doubtful that Paul could have preached his gospel in the Gentile world if he had been limited to the concepts of the Hebrew Old Testament, and certainly impossible if he had been limited to the Hebrew language.

Another feature of the Dispersion was the development of the synagogue to serve as a partial substitute for, and later to take the place of, the temple at Jerusalem. While Jews lived in the land of Palestine, it was possible to fulfill literally the law requiring attendance at the annual feasts. When, because of distance, this could no longer be fulfilled, the synagogue provided a means of religious expression. It also provided a means of community, so that the Jews of the Dispersion continued to use the Scriptures of the Old Testament, and to a lesser and modified extent they preserved the elements of worship. It does not need to be argued that the preachers of the gospel found their first steppingstones into the Gentile world in the synagogues scattered throughout that world.

We could devote an entire study to the development of the Messianic expectation among the Jews, but here it is enough to point out that the hope that the day of deliverance was at hand was burning brightly. A whole literature was being produced centering largely about this theme.[14] False messiahs had arisen and would continue to arise for another century.

Nor was this sense of expectation limited to the Jews. There was

[13] One very familiar illustration is our own English language, which after the Norman conquest absorbed many French words to take care of new cultural elements. For example, Anglo-Saxon words were sufficient for the kitchen and barnyard, but French words were needed for the dining room, prepared food, and eating utensils (cf. *pig—pork, ox—beef, stool—chair; table* and *napkin* were additions, but not *knife* and *fork*).

[14] Cf. Charles F. Pfeiffer, *Between the Testaments* (Grand Rapids: Baker Book House, 1959), pp. 121-124; the entire book will provide an introduction to the intertestamental period. For a more detailed study, cf. Robert H. Pfeiffer, *op. cit.,* 561 pp.

in the Gentile world a sense of dissatisfaction with existing religions, and alongside this an expectation of something better. The Greeks had climbed Mount Olympus and found no gods there. The Latin writers Tacitus and Suetonius record the expectation of a powerful king.[15] All over the Gentile world many were becoming proselytes to Judaism, and it seems reasonable to suppose that it was the Messianic hope rather than the Mosaic law that was appealing to them.

This, then, is the fullness of time. God had prepared His world. Politically it was at peace under a stable government. Culturally it was united in the Greek language and the Hellenistic ideal. And the Jews, the people of God, scattered throughout the world, had at last come to the threshold and were ready to enter in to fulfill the promise made to Abraham, that they not only should be blessed, but that they should also be a blessing to the nations of the world.

[15] Tacitus, *History*, 5.13; Suetonius, *Vespasian*, 4.

CHAPTER II

John the Baptist

JESUS ONCE SAID, "Among those born of women none is greater than John" (Luke 7:28). If you go through the teachings of Jesus and note particularly the things He has to say about John the Baptist, you will probably be surprised at the unusually strong statements. Yet we frequently overlook John the Baptist. We know much about Paul and Peter and John, and less about some of the other Apostles. But what do we know about the Baptist? Some men can tell us that he wore a camel's hair coat, and that he lost his head when a drunken king made a rash promise to a dancing girl—usually they know her name— and that is about all. We confuse John the Baptist with John the Evangelist, and we are often not sure which John is referred to as we read the Scriptures.

I would like to try to correct that. If Jesus placed such a high estimate on John the Baptist, I think we should try to learn more about him.

John the Baptist and the Old Testament. John is the link between the Old and New Testaments. Jesus accepted this link. We shall see the significance, I trust, before we are finished.

The story of the birth of John is in itself startling. "In the days of Herod, king of Judea, there was a priest named Zechariah, of the division of Abijah; and he had a wife of the daughters of Aaron, and her name was Elizabeth" (Luke 1:5). Both of them were of priestly families, devout, "walking in all the commandments and ordinances of the Lord blameless. But they had no child" (Luke 1:6-7). Perhaps in our western society it is a little bit difficult to understand just how deeply the Semitic world felt childlessness. It was often looked upon as a curse, and was considered sufficient reason in some places for a man to divorce his wife and take another. Zechariah and Elizabeth prayed about the matter.

One day, as Zechariah was fulfilling his duty in the temple—as I understand it, it was given to each priest to minister in the temple and light the sacred fire once in his lifetime—the aged priest had a vision. An angel said to him, "Do not be afraid, Zechariah, for your prayer is heard, and your wife Elizabeth will bear you a son, and you shall call his name John" (Luke 1:13). Notice the devotion of the father and mother! They were continuing to pray for a son, even though they were past the prime of life. Is that not what the angel's words mean, for why else would the promise of a son be connected with the words, "your prayer is heard"?

The child was to be filled with the Holy Spirit. He was to bring joy and gladness not only to the family into which he was to be born, but to other people as well. He was to "turn many of the sons of Israel to the Lord their God . . . to turn the hearts of the fathers to the children, and the disobedient to the wisdom of the just, to make ready for the Lord a people prepared" (Luke 1:16-17). All the power of inspired prophecy was to be in him, for the Holy Spirit who inspired the prophets of the Old Testament was to come upon a human being once more that he might speak the word of God. All the hopes of a brighter tomorrow that had been hidden in the hearts of these people for several centuries were to be realized because of this child that was to be born.

There was no breach with the past. God was not saying, "I am through with My people. Those Scriptures that you have been reading for generations and that religion you have been following are now abolished, and We are going to start something new." Some may present Christianity as a breach with the past, but that is not the truth. Rather, God is saying, "We are continuing the old in the new. The same Spirit that came upon the prophets is going to come upon this child, and because of this fact, the people are going to be ready when I send My redeemer into the world."

And so "the time came for Elizabeth to be delivered, and she gave birth to a son" (Luke 1:57). This was just a little while before Jesus was born—perhaps six months. When the child was circumcised, they wanted to name him Zechariah after his father, but Zechariah, who had been dumb from the day of the vision in the temple, wrote, "His name is John." With that, his voice was restored, and he spoke the great song (the *Benedictus*) that includes the words: " 'You, child, will be called the prophet of the Most High; for you will go before the Lord to prepare his ways, to give knowledge of salvation to his people in the forgiveness of their sins, through the tender mercy of our God, when the day shall dawn upon us from on high to give light to those who sit in darkness and in the shadow of death, to guide our feet into the way of peace.' And the child grew and became strong in spirit" (Luke 1:76-80). This was the one who would later be known as the "Forerunner."

Christianity does not repudiate the Old Testament. It does not say that the Bible begins with the Gospel of Matthew. Christianity says that the Scriptures of the Old and New Testaments are the word of God. Jesus expressly said that He had not come to abolish the Old, but to fulfill it (cf. Matthew 5:17). John the Baptist rightly bridges the two; he is the prophet of the Old and the forerunner of the New.

John the Baptist and Judaism.[1] Judaism was in its formative period, and at that time was a house divided. In the New Testament we hear of the Pharisees and the Sadducees; there were also other factions not mentioned by name. Herod, who sat upon the throne, was an Edomite and could scarcely claim to be a Jew. The prophetic voice had been silent: the famine of the word of God that had been promised by the prophet (Amos 8:11). For centuries no prophet had spoken in Israel, and in the place of prophetic religion there had settled down upon the nation a curious mixture of formalism and rationalism and separatism. Not that these were all found in the same place: that is why I called it a house divided.

There were the Pharisees, the purists, who held to the letter of the law. Jesus was critical of the Pharisees, and pointed out that they were not instrumental in the redemptive work of God in the world. They had failed to bring men to realize that God was seeking to free them; rather they were binding men to a bondage that was far more rigid than God had ever intended. They were making men children of hell and not sons of heaven. They had reduced the glorious religion of the Old Testament to a system of ritual and rites and ceremonies, to things that should be done and things that should not be done, to tithes that should be given and tithes that were not required. They had paid attention to garden herbs, and ignored the more important matters of the Law (see Matthew 23:1-36). Fortunately, Judaism was able to break the bonds of Pharisaism and move beyond it.

[1] For a Jewish estimate of John the Baptist, see Josephus, *Antiquities,* 18.5.2.

Then there were the Sadducees, the old conservatives. That will strike some as a strange label, but a careful study of the Sadducees will justify it. They were the dead conservatives, so dead that they repudiated any notion that had come along since the time of Moses. They were not interested in the rest of the Old Testament, and if they did not find it in the Law, they wanted nothing to do with it. They were not only the starched traditionalists, but worse, they were hardened by rationalism. Having set down the lines within which truth as they understood it must conform, they had rationalized it until there was very little spirit left, and very little place for God's Spirit to work. They had taken over the priestly caste (the priests were the sons of Zadok, or Zadokites, which is probably the derivation of the name "Sadducees") and they sought to dominate the religious life of the nation.[2]

The Jewish historian, Josephus, mentions a third sect of Judaism, namely the Essenes. As I understand this movement, it was composed of those who had rejected the dead ritual of the Pharisees, who had grown tired of the starched conservatism of the Sadducees, and who sought the answer in asceticism. The Essenes wanted to get away from the world, to live in the desert, to have no part in the Jerusalem religion but rather to have their own true religion. The famous Dead Sea Scrolls were being produced in the century or so before the birth of John the Baptist. Most scholars working on the Dead Sea Scrolls are convinced that they were written by Essenes or by those very closely allied to Essenism.[3] The Qumran literature makes it quite clear that there were Jews who looked upon the Jerusalem priesthood as wicked, who repudiated the rest of Judaism, and who formed a separatist movement.

There were other divisions in Judaism, in addition to these three, but these will suffice to make the point that Judaism was no longer a single people worshiping God in God's way, but a set of factions, filled with suspicion, distrust, and hostility, so that it was possible to throw the Sanhedrin into a turmoil just by mentioning the word "Pharisee" (cf. Acts 23:6-10).

[2] It is difficult to evaluate the source material on the Sadducees, since it has come down to us only through Pharisee eyes and the New Testament. But the picture is much the same in these sources, and reasonably reliable. The new material added by a study of the Dead Sea Scrolls, in my opinion, strongly confirms this view.

[3] See my *Amazing Dead Sea Scrolls* (revised edition; Chicago: Moody Press, 1959), pp. 177-189.

Where does John fit into this? Well, John was apparently an ascetic, who drank no wine nor strong drink (Luke 1:15) and who was in the wilderness until "the day of his manifestation to Israel" (Luke 1:80). His food was vegetarian, or nearly so (locusts and wild honey), and his clothing was coarse (Mark 1:6). He was apparently not one of the Pharisees, and certainly not one of the Sadducees. He has often been identified as an Essene, and as often this has been denied.[4] Recently, he has been identified with the Qumran group.[5] Now, Qumran was certainly one of the few places in the wilderness of Judea capable of supporting life. John and the Qumranians both traced their origin to the priestly line. Both practised baptism. Both were ascetic. Both claimed Isaiah 40:3 as their keynote.

But on the other hand, there are important differences. The Qumran group was esoteric: only for those initiated into the group. There is nothing like this in John's preaching. The attitude of Qumran was to withdraw from the world. John, on the other hand, went back to the world to preach a message of repentance. The Qumran message was to withdraw from the world in asceticism. This certainly was not John's message. Rather, he said, in effect, "Conform your life to your faith in the world. Bring faith and life together." The soldier, asking what he should do, was not told to give up his military life; he could still be a soldier. The tax collector could still be a tax collector. The king could still be a king. But whatever he was, his service was to be rendered in accordance with the will of God. Finally, the Qumran group was waiting for a Messiah yet to come. John the Baptist was proclaiming that the Kingdom of God was present.[6]

John the Baptist and the world. One day, John left the wilderness to go to preach to the sinful world. Luke gives us the date. I suppose if you could ask the seven persons who are named what was

[4] For the identification, cf. K. Kohler, "Essenes," in *Jewish Encyclopaedia* (New York: Funk & Wagnalls Co., 1903), vol. 5, esp. pp. 231-232. For a thorough discussion of the opposite viewpoint, see J. B. Lightfoot, *St. Paul's Epistle to the Colossians and to Philemon* (London: Macmillan and Co., 1875), pp. 158-179.

[5] Cf. Jean Steinmann, *Saint John the Baptist and the Desert Tradition* (tr. M. Boyes; New York: Harper & Brothers, 1958), 191 pp.; but see also Millar Burrows, *More Light on the Dead Sea Scrolls* (New York: Viking Press, 1958), pp. 56-63.

[6] Several points here have been drawn from the very lucid discussion by Robert B. Laurin, article "John the Baptist," in *Baker's Dictionary of Theology* (Grand Rapids, Mich.: Baker Book House, 1960), p. 299.

the most important thing they had done in life, you would receive all sorts of answers; but so far as Luke was concerned, they were significant for dating the beginning of the ministry of John the Baptist: "In the fifteenth year of the reign of Tiberius Caesar, Pontius Pilate being governor of Judea, and Herod being tetrarch of Galilee, and his brother Philip tetrarch of the region of Ituraea and Trachonitis, and Lysanias tetrarch of Abilene, in the high-priesthood of Annas and Caiaphas, the word of God came to John the son of Zechariah in the wilderness" (Luke 3:1-2). It is almost as though John is saying, "Now I'm not sure which one of these men will be remembered, so I shall list seven and hope that one turns out to be significant." Fortunately, we know that the fifeenth year of Tiberius Caesar was about A.D. 27 or 28. It may have been a sabbatical year; if so, that would explain why the Jews were able to go to the Jordan in great numbers to hear this prophet.

John's message is a striking one. It has three major points.

First, the Kingdom is here.[7] To the Jews, the hope of the Kingdom was no mere academic subject to be discussed in theological schools, and perhaps to be preached by fanatical preachers. It had become their very reason for existence. How long had they hoped? A thousand years? Two thousand? They had hoped for glorious deliverance when Moses led them out of Egypt, but soon they were longing for something better than the wilderness hardship and the endless manna. They had hoped for a place in the sun when they got their first king. When he failed, they hoped David would be the one. Then David's son. And then the hope seems to have turned into a vague dream. David's son—would David's son never come? And suddenly, here comes a man out of the wilderness to proclaim that the Kingdom is here!

That called for an investigation, and Jerusalem sent its representatives. "Who are you?" they asked; and he confessed, "I am not the Messiah." "Then are you Elijah?" "I am not." "Are you the prophet?" "No." "Then who are you? Let us have an answer for those who sent us." "I am the voice of one crying in the wilderness, 'Make straight the way of the Lord,' as the prophet Isaiah said" (cf. John 1:19-23).

[7] For a clear discussion of the Kingdom, see George Eldon Ladd, *The Gospel of the Kingdom* (Grand Rapids, Mich.: Wm. B. Eerdmans Publishing Co., 1959), 143 pp.

Just a voice—but what a voice! And what a message! "The Kingdom of Heaven is at hand!" If I could tell you today that the Kingdom of Heaven is here and all our troubles are over, all fears of war, all hatred and class struggle, all famine, sickness, and death, are forever ended, I would feel that I had the greatest privilege given to man. But it is not that easy!

The Jews had figured that when the Kingdom came, all Jews would be blessed, and all Gentiles would be put where they belonged. The prophets had tried to teach the people of God better than that. They tried to show that judgment begins at the house of God, that God was letting down a plumb line in the midst of Israel (Amos 7:7-9). Before there can be a Kingdom there must be righteousness. When Jesus began to lay the axe at the root, they protested: "We are Abraham's children." Abraham's children!—God can turn stones into Abraham's children (cf. John 8:39-40). The only heritage that counts in the Kingdom of God is spiritual heritage.[8] The Kingdom is here, and this means that the house of God, the people who have lived in the light of the revelation of God for these many years, will now have to face the judgment of God.

The New Testament says the same thing to us who are Christians. Judgment must begin with the house of God. We who have had the revelation most clearly are certainly going to be judged most severely. (See Romans 2:1-24; James 3:1-18.) If that disturbs your complacency, thank God that you have a Saviour who is able to keep you through it. But don't suppose for a minute that you are going to escape! There will be no man in heaven who has not had to stand before the judgment seat of God. And all those in heaven will be there because the blood of Christ has covered their sins.

With such a stern message, it is only logical that the people should ask, "What shall we do?" Listen to what John tells them. He does not say, "Attend the services more regularly; give tithes more faithfully; pray more earnestly." Rather, he says, "He who has two coats, let him share with him who has none; and he who has food, let him do likewise" (Luke 3:11). If the Kingdom of God is here, it is time to begin living like members of the family of God. Tax collectors said,

---

[8] Even the command, "Be baptized," would underscore this, for baptism among the Jews had been only proselyte baptism, i.e., for Gentiles, and John is in effect saying, "You are the same as Gentiles; you must be baptized." See W. F. Flemington, *The New Testament Doctrine of Baptism* (London: S.P.C.K., 1953), p. 16.

"What shall we do?" John did not say, "Leave your job, you puppets of Rome!" He said, "Collect no more than is appointed you." Soldiers asked him, "And what shall we do?" How many times this verse has been overlooked by well-meaning Christians who seek to force non-violence on the world. John did not say, "Get out of the army; you cannot be a member of the Kingdom and bear arms!" No; rather, he said, "Rob no one by violence or by false accusation, and be content with your wages" (cf. Luke 3:12-14).

I suppose King Herod asked him one day, "What must I do?" It is clear that John told him, for later Herod had a guilty conscience about John. Herod had been responsible for the imprisonment and death of John, because John had told him, "It is not lawful for you to have your brother's wife" (cf. Matthew 14:1-12).

When the Kingdom comes, it is time to set our lives in order, for the coming of the Kingdom means the coming of judgment.

The third part of John's message was, "Repent!" The word, as everyone knows, means to turn around, change your attitude. Psychologists tell us that it is impossible in certain mental conditions for a person to be helped until first he decides he wants to be helped. They can do nothing with an alcoholic until the alcoholic definitely wants to be cured. That is why modern psychology puts so little emphasis on counsellor advice, and so much stress on client self-analysis and determination. First, there must be a change of attitude. Even so, before God can help us, we must repent.[9]

Repent! The things you are doing that cannot stand before judgment must go. You will have to make up your mind to do things in God's way, if you want to live in God's kingdom. Be baptized! Let your repentance be publicly declared. Take your stand in the world for God and His Kingdom. Bring forth fruits worthy of repentance! For after all, men will judge you, and not only you, but the Kingdom you represent, by your fruits.

John the Baptist and his followers. John won many followers, and they loved him. Some of them became Jesus' first disciples (John 1:35-42), but there were others who never followed Jesus. The teacher

---

[9] I am aware that some will insist that man can do nothing at all, not even repent, unless God's Spirit moves him. It is possible to be so logical as to be un-Biblical! I am glad that when they asked John, "What shall we do?" he did not say, "Wait until the Spirit moves you to repent."

is not always able to influence all his students. John taught his disciples to pray (Luke 11:1). He taught them to fast (Matthew 9:14). But more than religious acts, he taught them a religious attitude. They developed a tremendous loyalty, so much so that when Jesus put a question to the rulers about the source of John's baptism, they feared to answer because of the people (Matthew 21:25-26).

The ministry of John lasted possibly only six months. But twenty years later there were disciples of John the Baptist at Ephesus (Acts 19:1-7), and probably at Alexandria (Acts 18:24-25). There are still disciples of John the Baptist in the world; a few years ago I visited some of them in the silversmiths' bazaar in Baghdad.[10]

One wonderful day it was John's privilege to point to Jesus and say to his followers, "Behold, the Lamb of God, who takes away the sin of the world!" All his life was lived for that moment. From then on, it was, "He must increase, but I must decrease" (John 3:30).

[10] For a brief discussion and bibliography for further study, see my *Amazing Dead Sea Scrolls*, pp. 203-206.

CHAPTER III

Mary the Mother of Jesus

WHEN THE ANGEL Gabriel was sent from heaven to Nazareth, he greeted Mary with the words, "Hail, thou that art highly favored" (Luke 1:28, KJV). Elizabeth greeted her with the words, "Blessed are you among women"—or it could be translated, "You are the happiest of all women" (Luke 1:42).

In some areas of the Christian Church there has developed a body of fantastic superstition and tradition covering over the beautiful humanity of Mary until she appears as no one who ever lived on earth. In reaction against this fantasy, the rest of the Church has largely ignored her. It seems to me that we ought to recognize that she is the only woman in history chosen by God to be the mother of the God-man, Christ Jesus. She is unique. We should study Mary to find out what we can learn from her blessed nature, what examples we can use for our own spiritual growth, and what elements of womanhood there are that should be emulated by Christian women everywhere.

Mary and God. The angel addressed her as one who is highly favored. She was God's choice to be the mother of Jesus. Why? When you read the first chapter of Luke, let your mind wander back over the prophecies of the Old Testament that foretold the coming of a deliverer into the world. Think about God's choice of a people: it was the twelve tribes, the nation, the Jewish people, that God had chosen. Therefore, it had to be a Jewess who would be the mother of the child to be born (cf. Isaiah 9:6). I have heard that every Jewish woman in the world had the fond hope that she might be the mother of the Messiah. My mother never had that hope, nor did any other Gentile woman. That hope belonged to the Jewish people. Mary was one of the chosen race.

The coming redeemer had to be of the line of David. There are two genealogies of Jesus in the New Testament, one in Matthew, the other in Luke. Some scholars believe the one is Mary's, the other Joseph's; other scholars believe that both are Joseph's. Both go back to David. Whether Mary's genealogy is given in the New Testament, I do not know; but I believe that Mary was of the Davidic line, for the Scripture tells us that Jesus was born, according to the flesh, of the seed of David (Romans 1:3), and Jesus' human nature was not derived from Joseph, for Jesus was born of the Virgin Mary.

Girls married very young in that time and place, and tradition tells us that Mary was in her early or middle teens. She was a devout girl, and had been steeped in the Scriptures. We become aware of this fact as we listen to the beautiful words of the *Magnificat* that came from her lips (Luke 1:46-55). Every home has a Bible today, but that was not so when Mary was a girl. The Scriptures were hand written on large leather scrolls. I was called upon once to examine a scroll of the Pentateuch (the five books of Moses), and it was necessary for two of us to unroll it on the floor of a large room; I have no idea how long the scroll was. Imagine trying to study from such a Bible! the only practical way to use it was to keep it rolled on rollers, in a synagogue, and to work consecutively through it, in the manner in which some churches today have a lectionary with lessons from the Gospel and the Epistle. The student of the Scripture, since he would have access to the word of God only in the *Bêth ha-Sêpher,* committed large portions to memory, and when he wished to discuss a given matter, he would string together passages that were relevant. Even so Mary must have stored Scripture in her memory, for the *Magnificat* is composed entirely of parts of the Bible. The word she had indeed kept in her heart, and when the time came that she burst into a paean of praise, it came out spontaneously in the words of Holy Scripture.

There was no immorality in Mary. There was nothing that would make questionable the Saviour's birth. This is necessarily implied by God's choice of her. And yet there would be shame. When Mary asked the angel, "How can this be, since I have no husband?" (Luke 1:34), it was not, in my opinion, a question of doubt. Rather, the question was asked in a sense of awe—and perhaps in the back of Mary's mind there was also the question, "What will I tell people, since I have no husband?" Soon she must have asked herself, "What will I tell Joseph, the man I love, the man I am engaged to, the man I am planning to marry? What will I tell him when he learns that I am going to have a child, and he is not the father?" There would be shame. But Mary was brave enough to endure the shame and reproach, for her conscience was clear. And so she gave her consent: "Let it be to me according to your word" (Luke 1:38). Some call her the Mother of God;[1] she calls herself the handmaid of the Lord.

Mary and Joseph The picture of Mary and Joseph is not given to us in so many words in the Bible. Rather, we have to put it together from the first two chapters of Matthew and the first two chapters of Luke, and then we have to let our sanctified imagination think about some of the things that must have happened in the relationship between Joseph and Mary which the Holy Spirit has not seen fit to record.

We do not know much about Joseph. We do not know his mother's name, and in view of the problem of the two genealogies, we are not even sure of his father's name. There is a tradition that he was much older than Mary—but I am not sure that there is sufficient reason for accepting that tradition. For one thing, it seems to be part of the effort to support the concept of the perpetual virginity of Mary. According to this view, Mary never had any normal marital relations with Joseph, never had any other children besides the virgin-born Jesus. This would involve, of course, an equally unnatural celibate life for Joseph. But if Joseph had been previously married, if he had already raised a family, and if he had married Mary, at God's bidding, only in order that the child to be born would have a legal name and an honorable home, then, it is suggested, the concept of Mary's perpetual virginity does not involve Joseph. In effect, Joseph would look upon the girl Mary as a daughter rather than as a wife. In my estimation, this is an unworthy line of reasoning that belittles the Biblical view of marriage contrary to the explicit teaching of the Apostle (I Corinthians 7:2-5) and elevates the concept of virginity contrary to the Hebrew ideal of womanhood blessed in childbearing. A second reason for thinking that Joseph was an old man is suggested by the implication that he died between Jesus' twelfth and thirtieth year.[2] But even so, this does not prove that Joseph was an old man. If Joseph had been twenty-five when he married Mary, and died when Jesus

---

[1] The term "Mother of God" (*theotókos*), although used earlier, was not adopted by the Church until the Council of Chalcedon in A.D. 451. The Council of Ephesus in 431 condemned Nestorius, largely for his opposition to the use of the term.

[2] Since he is never mentioned after the visit to Jerusalem.

was fifteen (these figures are only for the sake of example), that would have made him forty—and certainly there is nothing unreasonable in that figure. I see no valid reason to accept the tradition that Joseph was an old man when he married Mary.

Was he previously married? This question has been raised as part of the problem of "the brothers and sisters" of Jesus. In Matthew 13:55-56 (and also in other passages), the brothers and sisters of Jesus are mentioned. The simplest interpretation of the expression is the natural one: they were children of Joseph and Mary, born after the birth of Jesus. This seems to be the earliest interpretation in Christian literature. But with the development of the idea of the perpetual virginity of Mary, other explanations were put forth. According to Epiphanius of Salamis (died A.D. 403), the brothers and sisters were the children of Joseph by a former marriage. According to Jerome (c. 340-420), they were the children of Mary's sister, also named Mary, the wife of Clopas. Helvidius, who was a contemporary of Jerome, defended the natural interpretation, which was opposed by Jerome.[3] Once again I feel that the attempt to escape the clear meaning of Scripture (including the use of "until" in Matthew 1:25, as well as the expression "brothers and sisters") is based on an unworthy view of marriage, an unholy view of the conjugal relationship, and an unscriptural doctrine of the perpetual virginity of Mary.[4]

Joseph, we know, was a carpenter, for Jesus was known as "the carpenter's son" (Matthew 13:55). By the offering for Mary's purification, we know that Joseph was poor (Luke 2:24; cf. Leviticus 12:8), hence he knew what it was to work with his hands, to work for low income, and, later, to have the responsibilities of a large family.

[3] The three positions are usually identified by the names of these three protagonists: Epiphanian, Hieronymian, and Helvidian. It should be added that this is not a difference strictly following Protestant and Roman Catholic lines, for a number of Protestant scholars defend the Epiphanian view. For full discussions, see article, "Brethren of the Lord," in Hastings' *Dictionary of Christ and the Gospels* (New York: Charles Scribner's Sons, 1924), vol. 1, pp. 232-237; and J. B. Lightfoot, *Saint Paul's Epistle to the Galatians* (rev. ed.; London: Macmillan and Co., 1881), pp. 252-291.

[4] In the *Catholic Commentary on Holy Scripture* (New York: Thomas Nelson & Sons, 1953), the Roman Catholic position is presented clearly and concisely, together with representative bibliography, §§ 672-673. The tendentious nature of the position is revealed in the closing statement, "Such an explanation [Jerome's] is the only one which safeguards both the dogma of the perpetual virginity of our Lady and the tradition of the Church as to the perpetual virginity of St. Joseph" (§ 673e).

Somewhere along life's way he had become engaged to Mary. We must be careful not to read back into the account our western customs of courtship—and yet we must avoid the other extreme of picturing the match as an Oriental transaction between the parents.[5] The young couple probably rarely had more than a passing glimpse of one another; they almost certainly were never together alone. They had no opportunity to plan together and dream together, as we think is necessary. And yet true love did develop—perhaps it was truer than the romantic type we have come to know. Then it happened! The angel told Mary that she was going to have a child by the Holy Spirit. She probably stayed around Nazareth a while, and then, before people would suspect and set their busy little tongues to wagging, she went to visit her cousin Elizabeth.

I suppose that she had not told Joseph what had happened. But when the time drew near for Elizabeth to have her baby, it was necessary for Mary to return home. According to Luke 1:56, Mary was by that time three months pregnant, and was beginning to show, or soon would, that she was with child. And she would have to see Joseph! I think it was at that point that the annunciation to Joseph took place. Read it carefully: "When his mother Mary had been betrothed to Joseph, before they came together she was found to be with child of the Holy Spirit; and her husband Joseph, being a just man and unwilling to put her to shame, resolved to divorce her quietly" (Matthew 1:18-19). Engagement, according to Jewish law and custom, was tantamount to marriage, and could only be broken by giving a bill of divorcement. "But as he considered this, behold, an angel of the Lord appeared to him in a dream, saying, 'Joseph, son of David, do not fear to take Mary your wife, for that which is conceived in her is of the Holy Spirit; she will bear a son, and you shall call his name Jesus, for he will save his people from their sins'" (Matthew 1:20-21).

[5] The thoughtful reading of David and Vera Mace, *Marriage: East and West* (Garden City, N. Y.: Doubleday and Co., 1960; 359 pp.), will help us to see that there is much of real value in the customs of the East. On the other hand, the Talmud makes it clear that a couple could not be married without the girl's consent (*Kiddushim,* 2a), nor was marriage permitted between fiancés who had never seen each other (*Kiddushim,* 41a); the same source provided for the possibility that the man could make his own arrangements for marriage; it did not have to be contracted for by the parents.

Joseph woke from his sleep, and proceeded at once to take Mary into his home as his wife—note the important words—"but knew her not until she had borne a son" (Matthew 1:25).

Mary and Jesus. So Mary gave birth to a little boy. Her body had been the tabernacle for His in the fetal stage, and her tender mother's care provided His nourishment and protection when He came into the world. She was His mother. She probably taught Him the first prayers, kissed away the tears, bandaged the bumps and bruises. The record clearly shows that she did an excellent job in bringing up Jesus. Joseph, no doubt, made his contribution, too. But the earliest years are mother's years.

There was another side, however, a side that Mary would find hard to understand. The *Nunc Dimittis* of Simeon included the enigmatic words, "a sword will pierce through your own soul also" (Luke 2:35). We usually refer this to the time of the crucifixion. But I think that sword began to pierce Mary's soul long before Jesus' death.

There was the time, for example, when Jesus was twelve and the family had gone to Jerusalem. By that time there were other children in the family,[6] and Mary and Joseph had their hands full of responsibility. They probably traveled in caravan, the men and older boys in one part, the women and children in another. And on their way home, when they halted for the first night's rest, probably at some caravanserai, it was discovered that Jesus was not with them. So they turned back to Jerusalem, where they found Jesus three days later, in the Temple, in the midst of the doctors of the Law. Mary said to Him, "Son, why have you treated us so? Behold, your father and I have been looking for you anxiously" (Luke 2:48). There is a trace of anxiety in the words, and perhaps a trace of rebuke. Mary seems to imply, "You know that we had to look out for the younger children; you are old enough to take care of yourself. You should have stayed with us, and not forced us to come back to look for you."

Jesus answered, "How is it that you sought me? Did you not know that I must be in my Father's house [or, about my Father's business]?" Did Mary understand those words? Put yourself in her place. Twelve years and more ago, the angel had told her something of the mystery of the child to be born. But during those twelve years, unless we be-

[6] Regardless of the interpretation of "brothers and sisters of Jesus," all agree that there were other children in the home.

lieve the fantastic accounts in the apocryphal gospels, He had been just like any other child. There had been no indication that He was different. Now, suddenly to say, "I must be about My Father's business" —what did He mean? Did a sword stab Mary's heart as she thought, "Joseph is not His father; God is"?

One day, not long after Jesus had begun His ministry, some eighteen years later, Jesus and His first disciples came from Jerusalem to Cana of Galilee, and there was a wedding there. Jesus was invited, and His mother was there. Perhaps they were related to the family, for Mary seemed burdened about details that would hardly concern a guest. Suddenly, Mary reported to Jesus, "They have no wine" (John 2:3). That is a beautiful touch! Let your mind play over it a moment. Jesus was a guest: what business was it of His? Yet, Mary felt that her Son would share her feelings and the feelings of the host, for the refreshments had run out and the party was not yet over.

Jesus said to her, "Woman, what have you to do with me?" (John 2:4). That was a harsh word. And the harshness is not in the word "woman," for in the Near East that can be used as a term of proper address. It is in the words that follow that Mary must have felt the sword's piercing thrust. The words that Jesus used were very likely *mâ lî weḷēk*—"What [is there] to me and to you," or "What do we have in common?" It is the kind of question that you put to a person when you want to say, "This is my business and that is your business."

As I sense the implication—and the expression is quite commonly used—it carries a mild rebuke. It is as though Jesus were saying, "For thirty years, now, I have been your son, and an obedient one. But now there is a gulf between us. Now that I have started My ministry, the accomplishment of My Father's business, it is time that you learn your place and My place." Jesus, of course, did not enlarge upon the statement, as I have done. His mother would have understood, without this. Then He went ahead and did what she wanted Him to do, quietly, without drawing attention to Himself (John 2:5-10). But the schism was developing none the less.

Then one day, a few years later, when Jesus began to run into opposition, Mary started to worry about Him. She was afraid for His welfare, and she and His brothers sought to take Him away from the endless crowds (cf. Mark 3:21,31). Word was passed to Jesus, "Your mother and your brothers are outside, asking for you." And Jesus said, "Who are my mother and my brothers?" Then, looking at those who sat at His feet, listening to His teachings, He said, "Here are my mother and my brothers! Whoever does the will of God is my brother, and sister, and mother" (Mark 3:33-35).

Now look at one more scene. Jesus was on the cross, and a heart-broken woman was standing at the foot. It was her firstborn son hanging there. Among the last thoughts that Jesus had in His dying hours was one for His mother. When Jesus saw His mother standing along-side her sister and her sister's son John—the disciple whom Jesus loved —Jesus said, "Woman, behold your son!" and to the disciple He said, "Behold your mother!" (John 19:26-27).

Why did Jesus do that? Could it be that He was already looking forward to the time when a great multitude from every nation and race would be standing around the throne; when severed friendships would be eternally rejoined? Mary will be there—but what will be her relation to the Lamb? Was Jesus already thinking of that moment, when He said, "Woman, John is your son, now, and you are his mother"?

Some say that Mary is closer to Jesus than anyone else, therefore ask her to get Him to help you. Jesus says, "He that does the will of God is my brother, and sister, and mother." Jesus Christ, the Son of God, will have no earthly ties in heaven. There will be no special in-terests and no pressure groups. A woman, looking at Jesus one day on the road, thinking, I am sure, how wonderful it would be to have a Son like that, said, "Blessed is the womb that bore you, and the breasts that you sucked!" Jesus said, "Blessed rather are those who hear the word of God and keep it!" (Luke 11:27-28).

Mary and the Church. Mary was at the foot of the cross when Jesus was crucified. She needed a Saviour. To talk about the immaculate conception of Mary, to say that she had no sin, is unscriptural. The idea was built logically upon a false view of sin that says, if sin is in-herited, and Jesus was without sin, then His mother must also have been without sin. No, Mary was a sinner, too, and faced the same sinful temptations in life as any of us. She needed a Saviour. Christ died for her sins.

Mary was in the Upper Room, with the Eleven, and Jesus' brothers, and the women who had attended Jesus in His earthly needs (Acts 1:14). They were waiting for the Holy Spirit. Mary needed the gift of the Holy Spirit, just as we all do. She was no more divine, and no less human, than the six score on whom the Spirit came at Pentecost. What happened to her after that we are not told, except that she lived in the house of John the son of Zebedee. Did she move to Ephesus with him, when he went there years later? According to one tradition, she did, and died there; according to another, her death occurred at Jerusalem.[7]

Mary will be in Heaven, but not as Queen of Heaven, and not as Mother of God. She will be there as a ransomed sinner saved, not by the blood of the child she bore, but by the blood of the infinite One, as a member of the Church which God purchased with His own blood (Acts 20:28).[8] When we cast our crowns around the throne and sing our praises to the Lamb, Mary, too, will hail Him as King of kings and Lord of lords. When He takes His power and reigns, she will reign with Him—but as a member of the Church which will be His glorious bride.

Hail, Mary, favored of God and happiest of women! But she has deserved better than she has gotten from the Church. For she is a woman, not a goddess; redeemed, not redemptrix—for there is only one Mediator between God and men, the man Christ Jesus (I Timothy 2:5)—the woman chosen by God in the fullness of time to be the mother of His son.

[7] These are, as a matter of fact, competing traditions at present in the Roman Catholic Church. At Ephesus I found a strong feeling in support of the Ephesus tradition. The "Assumption of Mary," the most recent dogma of the Roman Church (officially promulgated November 1, 1950), is the belief that after her death, Mary's body was taken up to heaven, where she was crowned as Queen of Heaven. It is admitted in Catholic writings that "there is no reference in Scripture to either of these events," but that they are logically inferred from the Immaculate Conception, which in turn is inferred from the Motherhood of God, which also is without scriptural foundation. See *A Catholic Commentary on Holy Scripture,* § 86e.

[8] "God" certainly has better manuscript authority in this verse than "the Lord," and greater intrinsic probability (*lectio difficilior!*).

CHAPTER IV

Jesus the Son of Man

THE CHRISTIAN CHURCH has always been faced with the problem of
the nature of Jesus Christ: is He God, or is He man—or is He perhaps
something other? The Church has fully debated the subject, and
has given a clear answer. The answer sets forth four main points:
(1) He is truly God; (2) He is truly man; (3) these two natures
are not separate, but are truly one Person; (4) yet these two natures
are not merged into one, but remain without confusion.[1] The Church
has made it perfectly clear that He was not a man who became
God, but God who became man without losing deity. He was in
the beginning with God and was God, and then, at what human
beings would call a "point in history," He laid aside the glory which
He had with God the Father, and became fashioned as a man (cf.
John 1:1-4,14; Philippians 2:5-8). Yet these two natures are so perfectly united in one person that it is impossible to say, now He is
human and now He is divine; it is impossible to say, for example, that
as God He walked on the sea, and as man He fell asleep.

Sometimes the Church has stressed one of these natures, and sometimes the other. It largely depends on the trend of thinking of the
times. We are living in a day when the emphasis is on humanism,
with a corresponding stress on the humanity of Jesus. Hence the
Church, particularly that part which feels called upon to defend the
historic faith, has reacted by stressing the divine nature of Jesus.

This is as it should be. But sometimes when we stress the one, we
do it at the expense of the other. And in those churches today where
the deity of Christ is being defended so very zealously—as it should be!

---

[1] Historically, the problem unfolded a step at a time. The "Arian" heresy, expressed by Arius (A.D. c.265-336), denying the true deity of Christ, was condemned by the Council of Nicea in 325. The "Apollinarian" heresy (Apollinaris,
310-390), denying the true humanity, was condemned by the Council of Con-
stantinople in 381. The "Nestorian" heresy (Nestorius, died 451), asserting
that the two natures were distinct, was condemned by the Council of Ephesus in
431. The "Eutychian" heresy (Eutyches, first half of fifth century), asserting

—we sometimes forget that Jesus was also a man, a man like ourselves. This results in a serious loss. God could have come to earth as God, but for our sakes He came as man. He took upon Himself our likeness in order that we might have some benefit from the incarnation, and that benefit is lost if we think of Jesus only as the Son of God.

One of Jesus' favorite names for Himself was "Son of man." What did it mean? There was an apocalyptic movement in the Jewish world when Jesus came into the world, and the title "Son of man" was used in the literature of that movement. The "Son of man" was to come from heaven and take over the rule of this world. But what did Jesus mean by the term? It is obvious, as H. H. Rowley has pointed out,[2] that the term could not have been synonymous with "Messiah" in the popular mind, for in that case it would have been meaningless for Jesus to charge His disciples to tell no one that He was the Christ (Mark 8:30) when He was constantly using the term "Son of man" of Himself. The term "Son of man," was also a common expression meaning simply "human being." Jesus certainly used the term in that sense. He also, beyond any doubt, used the term in a messianic sense. In fact, I am convinced that it was Jesus' use of the expression, "Son of man," that has given it its fullness of meaning. But when the words first fell from His lips, they probably conveyed little more than the use of the first personal pronoun would have done.[3]

The human beginnings of Jesus. The birth of Jesus occurred in an unusual way. According to independent testimony,[4] both Joseph and Mary were disturbed by the annunciations of the birth, for, as both records state clearly, there had been no union between them (Matthew 1:18 and Luke 1:34). By the Holy Spirit, Jesus was conceived in the womb of an intact virgin, hence we say He was "born of the virgin

---

that the two natures became one, was condemned, along with the Nestorian, by the Council of Chalcedon in 451. Cf. W. G. T. Shedd, *A History of Christian Doctrine* (3d edition; New York: Charles Scribner's Sons, 1883), vol. 1, pp. 392-408; Ronald S. Wallace, article, "Christology" in *Baker's Dictionary of Theology,* pp. 120-121.

[2] In *The Relevance of Apocalyptic* (2d edition; London: Lutterworth Press, 1952), pp. 30-31.

[3] Whether the first use of "Son of man" was in Mark 2:10 or John 1:51 makes little difference; we could substitute "I" or "me" respectively without changing the meaning.

[4] The first chapters of Matthew and Luke cannot be assigned to "Q" for they are entirely different accounts.

Mary." This is the historic faith of the Church;[5] I wholeheartedly subscribe to it and defend it vigorously.

But when we have said that, let us remember that Jesus was born just as any other child. Once He was conceived in Mary's womb, the processes were the normal life processes. Mary carried the child as all mothers do. When the time came, she gave birth to the child as all mothers do.

Jesus was born in Bethlehem,[6] due to a census or poll tax that required Joseph to appear in his ancestral town. We do not know the year, and we do not know the day.[7] Yet the event was of sufficient importance that a star appeared, leading Wise Men from the East to worship the child-King (Matthew 2:1-2), and a king became so agitated that he caused the massacre of baby boys in Bethlehem (Matthew 2:16). The event one day changed the calendars of the world to read "Before Christ" and "In the Year of Our Lord."

Jesus grew up in Nazareth in Galilee. There were other children in the home. Four brothers are named: James, Joseph, Simon, and Judas; and there were also sisters (at least two; some think "all" means at least three—cf. Matthew 13:55-56). He lived a normal childhood; there is no place for the fantastic accounts we find in the apocryphal gospels. There we read that the boy Jesus made clay birds, then caused them to fly away; He stretched boards to the right length for Joseph; He carried water from the well in His cloak when He broke a pitcher; He made a salted fish come back to life. Even worse, we read that He cursed one teacher, ridiculed another, and struck dead a boy who accidentally bumped Him, until the parents of the city begged Joseph, "Take away that Jesus of yours from this place."[8] Such stories are fantastic! The Church, Protestant and Catholic alike, has repudiated

[5] Cf. J. G. Machen, The Virgin Birth of Christ (New York: Harper & Brothers, 1930), 415 pp.

[6] Cf. W. M. Ramsay, Was Christ Born at Bethlehem? (2d edition; London: Hodder and Stoughton, 1898), 280 pp.

[7] Dionysius Exiguus (died c.550) established the present calendar "Anno Domini," calculating the birth to have occurred in the year 754 A.U.C. (from the founding of the City of Rome). We now know that Herod died shortly after an eclipse of the moon which occurred March 12-13, 750 A.U.C., and Jesus was born prior to that, perhaps 748 or 749 A.U.C.—6 or 5 B.C. The birthday was set at December 25 in the fourth century, without historical basis.

[8] In the Gospel of Thomas (to be distinguished from the recent Coptic find at Nag Hamadi), The Ante-Nicene Fathers, A. Roberts and J. Donaldson, editors (Grand Rapids, Mich.: Wm. B. Eerdmans Publishing Co., reprinted 1951), vol. 8, pp. 395-404.

them.[9] There is no place for them historically or psychologically. When the time came for Jesus to take up His ministry, there is not the slightest indication that His fellow townspeople were either offended by His prior life or prepared for His miracles. They were simply amazed. "Where did this man get this wisdom and these mighty works? Is not this the carpenter's son?" (Matthew 13:54-55).

It was a poor home. Sometimes I get the feeling that incidental details in Jesus' teaching came from watching His mother. "Why don't you sew a new patch on that?" "Why don't you put the new wine in those old wineskins?" "Why are you sweeping the corners of the room so carefully?" "Why do you use only such a little bit of leaven?"

There would come a time when He would learn to read. Perhaps He was sent to the synagogue school.[10] He doubtless learned Aramaic, the common tongue, and Hebrew, the holy tongue; and, living in Galilee of the Gentiles, He probably learned some common expressions in Greek.

He loved the world of nature. He observed the birds, the flowers, the sower and his seed, the fisherman and his net, the clouds and storms, the stifling, blasting wind from the desert.

There was a saying, "Who does not teach his son a trade teaches him to steal." Joseph taught Jesus the carpenter's trade. He learned to work with His hands and arms until, I am sure, His hands were calloused and His arms were muscular. These paintings hanging in the museums of the world that make Jesus look like an emaciated weakling do not give the true picture! He could tramp the hills of Palestine with rugged men and keep up with the best of them.

He knew the Scriptures. He knew how to pray. He took part in the religious festivals, and it was His custom to attend synagogue on the Sabbath. When He visited Jerusalem in His twelfth year, perhaps for the *bar mitzvah* ceremony when He would take His place as a man in Israel, He amazed the doctors of the Law with His understanding and His answers. And He did not get those answers by being the Son of God! He got them by studying, just as you and I have to study. Then He went back to Nazareth with His parents "and he was obedient to them."

[9] Nevertheless they do hang on, in superstition, in ecclesiastical art, and often in anti-Christian writings.

[10] Elementary schools were started in Jerusalem by Rabbi Shim'on ben Shetach, c.75 B.C., but whether they had extended to Galilee by Jesus' day is not definitely known.

We know little of the eighteen years that follow, the "hidden years." We know that Jesus worked in the carpenter shop. It is quite probable that Joseph died, and that Jesus became the breadwinner of the family. We can be certain that He lived a perfectly normal life, from the reaction of the people; we can also be certain that He lived a perfectly pure life, from the reaction of God who said, "This is my beloved Son, with whom I am well pleased" (Matthew 3:17).

The beginnings of Jesus' ministry. One day, when John the Baptist had been baptizing for possibly six months, and the people were stirred to excitement by him, Jesus went from Galilee to the Jordan to be baptized by John. When John saw Jesus, he protested, "I need to be baptized by you, and do you come to me?" (Matthew 3:14). Did John know Jesus? John says, "I myself did not know him" (John 1:31). What was it then that made John protest? I think it was the clean appearance of One who had never sinned. At any rate, Jesus said, "Let it be so now; for thus it is fitting for us to fulfil all righteousness" (Matthew 3:15). I do not believe that Jesus was baptized in repentance for His own sins, for He had none; I believe He was baptized because He wanted to take His place with you and me. There was to be nothing to separate Him from the people He came to save.[11]

Following the baptism, John testified that he saw a dove descending upon Jesus, the sign that this was indeed the One for whom John was to prepare the way (cf. John 1:32-34).

Immediately, Jesus was driven into the wilderness to be tempted by the devil (cf. Luke 4:1-13). This deserves a study by itself; all we can do here is emphasize the fact that when Jesus was tempted, He was tempted as man; He faced both the subtle and the bold attacks of the Tempter in exactly the same way that you and I must face them. We get our ideas of sin hopelessly confused at times. We stress the fact that it is inherited, and we forget the fact that the greatest sin comes from our own hearts, our own wills. The great battleground of sin is in the human will. It is not the *temptation* that is sin, but what we will to do under temptation. It is not even the *deed,* but what we *will* to do. We may for one reason or another restrain the action; but the very fact that *we would like to do it* is sin. (Read carefully Matthew 5:21-

[11] On this, and on the temptations, see particularly G. Campbell Morgan, *The Crises of the Christ* (New York: Fleming H. Revell Company, 1903), pp. 107-210.

30.) When Jesus met the Tempter, He met him in the same freedom of will that you and I have as human beings. Moreover, Jesus faced the temptations under the worst possible conditions: in the wilderness, and alone.

I do not believe that Jesus' temptations ended at that time. Rather, I believe that He constantly faced temptation, for He "in every respect has been tempted as we are, yet without sinning" (Hebrews 4:15). On the last night of His earthly life, in the garden of Gethsemane, when He knew that He must drain the cup of death to its bitter dregs, He prayed in great agony, "My Father, if it be possible, let this cup pass from me" (Matthew 26:39). Not once, but three times He prayed this prayer. And every time He countered it with the prayer, "Nevertheless, not as I will, but as thou wilt." This was, in my opinion, the greatest temptation He ever faced: the temptation to save Himself. But He knew that if He saved Himself, He could never save others.

Jesus and His disciples. Somewhere I heard a saying, that if you would know a man, eat with him and sleep with him. Jesus ate and slept with His disciples. There are many teachers who get up in the morning, wash and put on their better clothes, go into the classroom or lecture hall and deliver their best lecture, and then go back home. Their students may never know how they live.

But Jesus did not teach that way. He did not get His disciples together for an hour or two a day in a lecture hall. He lived with them. They saw Him under all conditions: when He was hungry, passing through a field of grain; when He was tired, stretched out in the boat. They saw Him when religious officialdom prodded Him with sticky questions; they saw Him when a sinful woman washed His feet with tears of devotion because her sins had been forgiven. They saw Him bless little children; they saw Him drive money changers out of the Temple. They saw Him under every possible condition that could occur for about a year or more. Then one day Jesus said to them, "Who do you say that I am?" Peter spoke up, "You are the Christ, the Son of the living God" (Matthew 16:15-16). No man who has lived with me for a year is going to say anything like that about me—and I don't believe they will say it about you. But they said it about Jesus.

Jesus taught His disciples. Wonderful teachings! He used simple language, and drew upon familiar things for illustrations, and yet His teachings are so inexhaustible that men are still writing books about them, trying to get at the root of what Jesus taught. The subjects are of primary importance. Jesus is talking about God, about man, about sin and salvation, about righteousness and justice, about love and forgiveness. He is talking about the great central truths of life, the foundational matters on which all human relationships are built.[12] These are the things we need to know if we are to live together successfully in this world; and these are the things we must know if we are going to live with God in the world to come.

Comparisons are odious. I have had to study the scriptures of many other religions. It is impossible to get any real meaning out of the Bhagavad Gita unless some Hindu mystic explains it. When I studied the Qurân, my Arabic teacher assured me that it was impossible to understand it except in Arabic, and then only if you were an Arab. Even the apocryphal gospels of the Early Church present teachings, supposedly from Jesus, that are inconsequential. But when I read the Gospels, regardless of whether it is in Greek or in translation (and even the Greek is a translation of Jesus' original words), I know what Jesus is saying, and I know that it is significant. Little wonder that, when they listened to Him, they were astonished, "for he taught them as one who had authority, and not as their scribes" (Matthew 7:29). Little wonder that they said, "No man ever spoke like this man!" (John 7:46).

Jesus and His Father. Have you ever thought about Jesus and His Father? You probably have discussed the relationship between the First and Second Persons of the Trinity, but have you ever thought about the relationship between Jesus as a human being and His heavenly Father? In Philippians, Paul presents a subject that has evoked much discussion: theologians call it "kenosis." Speaking of Christ Paul says: "who, though he was in the form of God, did not count equality with God a thing to be grasped, but emptied himself, taking the form of a servant, being born in the likeness of men. And being found in human form he humbled himself and became obedient unto death, even death on a cross" (Philippians 2:6-8). This "emptying" is the kenosis. I do not pretend to know all that it means, but I am sure that it means at least this: while Jesus was in human

[12] One of the greatest books on this subject, in my opinion, is G. Campbell Morgan, *The Teaching of Christ* (New York: Fleming H. Revell Company, 1913), 333 pp. But, much as I value this book, having worked through it countless times, I feel it falls far short of exhausting the subject.

form He had the same relationship with God that you and I have as human beings.[13]

How did Jesus get along with God on this basis? It stands out clearly in the Scripture record: He pleased God. At the time of the baptism, that is, after about thirty years of life, He heard God say, "Thou art my beloved Son; with thee I am well pleased" (Mark 1:11). On the Mount of Transfiguration, when the public ministry of Jesus was all but over and He was about to set His face to go to Jerusalem, God declared again, "This is my beloved Son, with whom I am well pleased" (Matthew 17:5). Jesus could look His fellow men in the eyes and say, "which of you convicts me of sin?" (John 8:46), and He could stand before God and say unashamed and unafraid, "I always do what is pleasing to him" (John 8:29). He could pray, "Thy will be done," knowing that He would be happy with that will; when some of us pray "Thy will be done," I think we keep our fingers crossed!

On the last night of His earthly life, knowing that the next few hours would bring His death, He could say to God, "I glorified thee on earth, having accomplished the work which thou gavest me to do. . . . I have manifested thy name to the men whom thou gavest me. . . . I kept them in thy name. . . . I have given them thy word" (John 17:4, 6, 12, 14). He could look into His Father's face as He hung on the cross and say, "It is finished. . . . into thy hands I commit my spirit" (John 19:30; Luke 23:46).

This is how Jesus got along with God His Father. Do you want proof? Here it is: God raised Him from the dead. God has not raised anyone else from the dead.[14] But God, by the resurrection of Jesus Christ from the dead, said in effect, "This One does not deserve to die!" Therefore, Paul says, Jesus was "designated Son of God in power"—or it might be translated, "marked out as" or "declared to be the Son of God in power"—"by his resurrection from the dead" (Romans 1:4).[15]

[13] I did not say that He had *only* the same relationship. The mystery of His two natures, even though it may lie beyond our comprehension, enters at every point in His life.

[14] There have been other "resurrections," in which men and women, boys and girls, have been restored to this life, as recorded in the Scriptures. But none of them knew the resurrection by which they passed beyond death into the life of the world to come.

[15] The word *horisthéntos* has been variously translated, and is discussed extensively in commentaries on Romans. One thing it clearly can *not* mean is that

There is another nature about which we have said practically nothing: the divine nature of Jesus. Yet that was also manifest during His earthly life and ministry. We have not mentioned His knowledge of the innermost thoughts of men, nor His power to work miracles. These things were not used by Jesus to call attention to Himself, but only in the service of His fellow men. We have said far too little about His redemptive work, His substitutionary death, His resurrection and ascension, and His sending of the Holy Spirit. But these cardinal truths are so woven into the lives of the men and women yet to be considered, that we shall not ignore them. We have not mentioned the great purifying hope of the Church, the Return of Jesus Christ; that remains for another study.

We have confined our study to Jesus the man. He is the perfect man, the Adam who did not fall. He is the living proof that God's will is not impossible. If, in the judgment, Adam wants to stand up and say to his Creator, "You gave me something that could not possibly be done!" God can point to His Son who emptied Himself of His glory and took upon Himself Adam's likeness, who was tempted in all points as Adam was, without sinning, and God can say with finality, "He did it!"

But someone says, "I am not Adam; I inherited from Adam a fallen nature. I can't please God." Are you going to hide behind that excuse? God sent Jesus Christ into the world in order that we might hide behind Him and not behind Adam. In Christ that old man is crucified; you are a new man in Christ. No longer is Adam your example; now your example is Christ, that you should walk as He walked.[16]

But He is not a heartless and cold example, ready to destroy us if we fall. He is our help and encouragement. "Because he himself has suffered and been tempted, he is able to help those who are tempted" (Hebrews 2:18). He is not "a high priest who is unable to sympathize with our weaknesses, but one who in every respect has been tempted as we are, yet without sinning. Let us then with confidence draw near to the throne of grace, that we may receive mercy and find grace to help in time of need" (Hebrews 4:15-16).

Jesus *became* the Son of God by the resurrection; He *was eternally* the Son of God, but the great public declaration of the fact was accomplished by the resurrection.

[16] See I John 2:6; Ephesians 4:1; I Peter 2:21; Galatians 5:1; John 13:15—to which could be added many others.

CHAPTER V

Andrew the First Disciple

IN A SERIES on the Great Personalities of the New Testament, what shall we do about the twelve apostles? In one sense, all of them are great—great enough to have been chosen by Jesus. On the other hand, we know very little about several of them, and if we were to expand that in each case by what we know of the entire group, it would be repetitious. A few stand out with clear distinction: Peter, of course, and James and John. Is there one we can select to serve as a representative of the others? I think there is, and I have chosen Andrew for that place. Let me tell you why.

Andrew the disciple. How did Jesus begin His ministry? If you use the Gospel of Mark as a starting point (which is often used as a chronological basis for studying all the Gospels), you may get a mistaken idea that one day, when Jesus was walking along the Sea of Galilee, He saw two men fishing, and said, "Follow me and I will make you become fishers of men" (Mark 1:17), and that was it. Now tell me, would you give up your source of livelihood and follow a stranger? Neither would I. And I do not think Simon and Andrew did.

Most scholars today agree that it is impossible to harmonize the four Gospels (i.e. edit them so as to give one continuous and chronological account). Nevertheless I would like to try. You may not agree; but this is how I see it.

John the Baptist was baptizing, and the officials were sent to investigate his credentials. In the course of the conversation, John said, "Among you stands one whom you do not know, even he who comes after me" (John 1:26-27). The next day, he saw Jesus coming toward the group he was speaking to, and he said, "Behold, the Lamb of God, who takes away the sin of the world! This is he of whom I said, 'After me comes a man who ranks before me, for he was before me'" (John 1:29-30).

This was after the baptism of Jesus, as is clear from the verses that follow (31-34). And it was after the temptations; therefore at least forty days after the baptism. Meanwhile, John had continued his baptizing and preaching, and his disciples had continued to learn from him and to assist him. Hence it follows that they had had a chance to talk with John about this Figure who had come to be baptized, and on whom the dove descended.

The next day, John was talking with two of his disciples—I gather that the crowd was not present on this occasion—and seeing Jesus, John said, "'Behold, the Lamb of God!' The two disciples heard him say this, and they followed Jesus . . ." (John 1:35-37). One of the two was Andrew; the other is not named, but the best solution to the problem is to recognize him as John the son of Zebedee.[1] The two went with Jesus and spent the rest of the day in His presence. Andrew went and found his brother Simon and brought him to Jesus (cf. John 1:39-42).

The following day, Jesus found Philip, who may have been another of the disciples of John the Baptist; and Philip found Nathanael, much as Andrew had found Simon. It is not incredible that John found his brother James. So, within a few days Jesus had gathered about Himself five or six of His first disciples.

But I do not think He began His ministry at that time. It seems that He waited until John the Baptist had finished his. According to John's Gospel, and it is corroborated by incidental details in the others, Jesus remained in the vicinity of John the Baptist, that is in Judea or in the region of the Jordan, but took no place of leadership. He must have engaged in some preaching (John records that Jesus Himself did not baptize, John 4:2), and it would seem that His following became increasingly larger. But the main effort, the start of the Galilean ministry, did not begin until Jesus had heard that John had been thrown into prison (Mark 1:14). It was then that Jesus declared, "The time is fulfilled, and the kingdom of God is at hand" (Mark 1:15).

How long was the interval between the identification of Jesus by John and the beginning of Jesus' ministry in Galilee? We cannot be

[1] One of the strongest arguments, it seems to me, is the fact that James and John, who in the other three Gospels are part of the "inner circle" (Peter, James, and John), are not mentioned in the first twenty chapters of John. This can only be satisfactorily explained as modesty on the part of the author.

sure, but it was probably not long. The traditional date of the baptism of Jesus is January 6. The forty days of temptation would bring us to the middle of February. According to John, a Passover occurred not long after the wedding in Cana (John 2:13), which would fall between the middle of March and the middle of April. The Galilean ministry of Jesus occurred soon after that. These dates are to some extent speculative—but they offer a reasonable approximation.

It is at this point that I would put the call of Andrew and Simon and a few minutes later the call of James and John, recorded in Mark 1:16-20. What about the call as recorded in Luke 5:1-11? Though many will disagree, I believe that occurred still later. In other words, as I reconstruct those days, soon after Jesus received word of the imprisonment of John the Baptist, He called His first disciples together. He had already gotten to know them, and they Him, in Judea several months earlier. But now He wanted them to enter into full-time discipleship. I believe they misunderstood His purpose and continued with their ordinary occupations. This made necessary the second call, recorded in Luke—and this accounts for Peter's reaction (Luke 5:8).

We have been using the word "disciples." Let us define our term before we go further. A *disciple* is one who comes under the discipline of another. The pupil is the disciple of the teacher; although this term is not generally used today when a pupil has several or many teachers. Jesus wanted these men around Him continuously, so He could teach them, by word and by deed. Only thus would they become His disciples.

Jesus had many disciples. Some of them, such as Andrew and the other who was unnamed, had been disciples of John the Baptist, and then had become disciples of Jesus. Others were added during the days of His ministry. Some became strongly attached to their teacher and His teachings. Others became impatient with His program, and turned away from Him (cf. John 6:66). Some of His disciples were trained by the method of learning-through-doing, as were the seventy disciples who were sent out two by two (Luke 10:1-20). So it is possible for us to speak of the twelve disciples, the seventy disciples, or the great multitude of disciples; it is possible to speak of active disciples and passive disciples; it is possible to speak of true disciples and false disciples.

Andrew was a disciple: he was under the discipline and instruction of Jesus. It is accurate to say that he was the first disciple, or at very least one of the first two disciples. He had been a disciple of John the Baptist and was turned to Jesus by John. He had been called into discipleship by the sea in Galilee. He was in the closest circle of discipleship, and remained a faithful disciple throughout the ministry of Jesus.

Andrew the apostle. The public ministry of Jesus can be divided into three main parts which can be characterized as follows: the proclamation of the Kingdom resulting in a wide following and then opposition; the organization and training followed by the separation of true and false disciples; the disclosure of the person of Christ.[2] It is impossible to attach definite dates to these periods, but it seems to me that it must have been at least several months, perhaps as much as a year, before the strong opposition to Jesus developed. If the baptism of Jesus is dated in the early part of A.D. 28, it was probably late in 28 or early in 29 when Jesus planned to meet the opposition by definite organization. The death of John the Baptist made it clear that death was the only probable outcome of Jesus' work, and there must be not merely disciples to carry on the work, but men organized under a program with a specific objective.[3]

So one night Jesus went into the hills to pray, and He prayed through the entire night. A serious decision had to be made and, humanly speaking, the fate of the world for all generations to come hinged upon the proper choice. The next day He called to Him His disciples, and out of the group He chose twelve. These He called "apostles" (Luke 6:12-13). The Twelve are named four times in the New Testament,[4] and while the order is not the same in these lists, it is remarkable that the grouping is the same. The first group contains the names Simon Peter, Andrew, James the son of Zebedee, and John. The second group contains the names of Philip, Bartholomew (usually identified with Nathanael), Matthew (usually identified with

[2] These correspond approximately to what have been called the First, Second, and Third Periods of the Galilean Ministry, respectively.

[3] This kind of expression may be objectionable to some who keep the deity of Christ prominent (see the preceding chapter). We must remember, however, that the entire ministry of Jesus, including His choice of Judas, comes within the mystery of His twofold nature. He acts, usually, as one who is not omniscient, but who must gather knowledge from experience.

[4] Matthew 10:2-4; Mark 3:16-19; Luke 6:14-16; Acts 1:13. Seven of the names appear in John, but no list.

Levi), and Thomas (also called Didymus, or the twin). The third group contains the names of James the son of Alphaeus, Simon (Zelotes, or the Canaanean), Judas ("not Iscariot"; or Thaddeus, also called Lebbeus), and Judas Iscariot (this name, of course, is omitted from the list in Acts). Not only are these three groups always the same, but the first name in each group (i.e., Simon Peter, Philip, and James the son of Alphaeus) is always the same.

We should notice the words, "he called his disciples, and chose from them twelve, whom he named apostles" (Luke 6:13). Some disciples were chosen to be apostles, and some were not. This is an important distinction. It was possible to be a disciple of Jesus without being an apostle; but it was not possible to be apostle without being a disciple. A disciple, we have seen, is one who is taught by another. An apostle, as the word itself implies, is one who has been sent by another—but usually the word has a more specific meaning: one who is the officially delegated representative, one who has been sent on a specific mission in the name of the person or government who delegated him.

A few moments' reflection will show the logic and reason behind this move on the part of Jesus. He was sent into the world to represent the Kingdom of God; He was in turn sending into the world the Twelve who would represent the same Kingdom. They were to be the officially delegated representatives, the apostles, assigned to the task. They would receive their credentials in due time. But before they could even start on this work, they must be trained. And even before that, they must be carefully chosen. For that reason, Jesus gathered around Himself a large number of disciples. He trained them for several months. He observed them. He prayed about the matter. Then He chose twelve. The training would continue for at least another year.[5] They did not cease to be disciples, and indeed the expression, "the twelve disciples," is used in the Gospels. But once chosen, they were both disciples and apostles.

Mark makes clear the reason for the selection of the Twelve: "He appointed twelve, to be with him, and to be sent out to preach" (Mark 3:14). It seems that the Early Church understood this as a

[5] The length of the ministry of Jesus has been fully debated. I am convinced that at least two full years would have been necessary for the development of opposition, the training of the Twelve, and the other details recorded. This concurs with the view that finds three Passovers in the Gospel of John. I do not rule out the possibility of an additional year, but I do rule out the possibility of any less time.

principle for the apostolic office, for when they chose a successor to Judas, they first set forth the qualifications: "of the men who have accompanied us during all the time that the Lord Jesus went in and out among us, beginning from the baptism of John until the day when he was taken up from us" (Acts 1:21-22). Personal observation combined with discipleship was the first essential; to be based on this was the proclamation of what was seen and heard, or in the words of Acts, "one of these men must become with us a witness to his resurrection."

After appointing the Twelve, and ordaining them, Jesus delivered the "ordination sermon," which we know better as "The Sermon on the Mount" (Matthew, chapters 5 to 7).[6] As representatives of the Kingdom, they must know the ideals and principles of the Kingdom. John the Baptist came preaching, "The Kingdom of heaven is at hand." These men were to go out with this same proclamation, and men would certainly ask, "What is this Kingdom like? Is it like the other kingdoms of this world?" The Sermon on the Mount describes it.

Men say it will not work. Nor will it, while men believe that! Other men say they do not believe the rest of the Bible; they live by the Sermon on the Mount. Nonsense! They cannot live by the principles of the Kingdom and repudiate the King. When men truly accept the kingship of the Son of God, they will be able to live by His principles. If you say the Sermon on the Mount is idealistic and otherworldly, I thoroughly agree. Jesus Christ came into this world to bring ideals—heaven knows that this world needs ideals! And a Jesus Christ who is not other-worldly is not the Christ of the New Testament or the Christ of the historic Christian faith. He came into this world to bring heaven to earth, and ultimately to bring earth to heaven. The man who squirms under the teaching of the Sermon on the Mount sits in judgment on himself.

Jesus not only taught the Twelve;[7] He sent them out on a preaching mission (Matthew 10:5-33). That the details expressed in verses 9 and 10 were not intended to be applied literally throughout the age is clearly indicated in the words of Jesus Himself in Luke 22:35-36.

A beautiful summary of the apostolic office can be found woven

---

[6] Luke gives us the clue, in this case (cf. Luke 6:12-20); Matthew is obviously arranging his material logically and not chronologically.

[7] For a detailed study of this training, see A. B. Bruce, *The Training of the Twelve* (3d editon; New York: Richard R. Smith, Inc., 1930), 552 pp.

into the Lord's prayer in the seventeenth chapter of John: "I have manifested thy name to the men whom thou gavest me out of the world ... I have given them the words which thou gavest me, and they have received them. . . . I have given them thy word; and the world has hated them because they are not of the world, even as I am not of the world. I do not pray that thou shouldst take them out of the world, but that thou shouldst keep them from the evil one. . . . As thou didst send me into the world, so I have sent them into the world. . . . I do not pray for these only, but also for those who are to believe in me through their word . . ." (John 17:6, 8, 14-15, 18, 20).

The full apostolic mission, however, was not to be accomplished until the death and resurrection of Jesus Christ had become historic reality. The specific testimony of the apostolic band was to be centered in the death and resurrection of Jesus Christ—not the cross alone, as so many stress, but the cross and the resurrection. A careful study of apostolic preaching in the Acts and Epistles will justify this statement. It is the "yea, rather" of Romans 8:34 (unfortunately lost in RSV).

Moreover, this completed apostolic proclamation of the crucified and risen Lord needed in addition the power of the Holy Spirit. For this the apostles were commanded to wait: "Then he opened their minds to understand the scriptures, and said to them, 'Thus it is written, that the Christ should suffer and on the third day rise from the dead, and that repentance and forgiveness of sins should be preached in his name to all nations, beginning from Jerusalem. You are witnesses of these things. And behold, I send the promise of my Father upon you; but stay in the city, until you are clothed with power from on high'" (Luke 24:45-49). And again: "To them he presented himself alive after his passion by many proofs, appearing to them during forty days, and speaking of the kingdom of God. And while staying with them he charged them not to depart from Jerusalem, but to wait for the promise of the Father . . . 'you shall be baptized with the Holy Spirit'" (Acts 1:3-5).

Andrew the missionary. The distinction between "apostle" and "missionary" as used here is the difference between theory and practice. My choice of words is probably not good; but I have been unable to do better. We have seen Andrew, as a representative of the Twelve, called and trained as a disciple, appointed and given the principles of the office as an apostle. Now we want to see how Andrew carried out his mission.

Perhaps that is not the picture you get when you hear the word "missionary." Perhaps you think of a strange person, rather out of touch with the modern world, who comes home once in seven years wearing clothes that are seven years out of style. Or perhaps you think of some idealistic do-gooder, or a meddling busybody poking into the affairs of people who would rather be left alone. Or you may have gotten a notion from some novel that missionaries are hypocrites who can sin unafraid in lands where sin is not so clearly labelled. (The novelist sins, too; he loves to wallow in indecency in his mind and to infect other minds the same way!) But have you ever thought of a missionary as simply a man or woman who is carrying out a mission?

Andrew had a mission; it was to tell people about the Lord Jesus Christ. And one of the reasons I have chosen Andrew for this study is simply because he was always finding someone and bringing him to Jesus.

The first day Andrew met Jesus, he had to tell somebody about Him. And the first person he thought of was his own brother. "One of the two who heard John speak, and followed him, was Andrew, Simon Peter's brother. He first found his brother Simon, and said to him, 'We have found the Messiah' (which means Christ). He brought him to Jesus" (John 1:40-42). There are several possible attitudes that a man can have toward his own brother. He can despise him; he can ignore him; he can want to help, but because of his approach, he offends his brother; he can have great influence over him. I can think of illustrations of each kind among men I have known, and you can, too. The most difficult relationship is the last mentioned: the man who has true love and ability to express that love in such a way as to influence his brother. Andrew was such a man. He was interested in his brother Simon. He thought first of Simon. He wanted to share his new blessing with Simon. That was good. But what a revelation it is of the relationship to read, "He brought him to Jesus"! I think it shows that they had a prior common interest in the religious faith and hope of their nation, that they had talked about this very subject on previous occasions. It is not easy to bring your brother to Christ under any conditions, but when there is no common basis of religious faith to start with, it becomes almost impossible.

I have often asked myself, What would have happened to the

Christian Church if Andrew had not brought Simon Peter to Jesus? Such a question is, of course, an improper question, and involves God's foreknowledge, will, and many other subjects. But just speaking from our human point of view, we would have to say that Peter was the key figure for the start of the Church, and without him, it is hard to see how the Church could have gotten started. But we do not have to answer the question, for Andrew carried out his mission and brought his brother to Jesus.

I wonder if Andrew also brought Philip to Jesus? It is pure speculation, I admit, but they were both from the same town (Bethsaida: John 1:44); they both had Greek names, whereas the rest of the apostles had Hebrew names; their names are often joined in the New Testament; and on two occasions Philip came to Andrew to get his help or advice on some problem. If Andrew did get Philip, then he was also responsible for Nathanael (John 1:45)—but that, I repeat, is speculation.

One day, at the height of Jesus' popularity, He was teaching by the sea and a large crowd had gathered. The wonderful words continued to flow, perhaps urged on by the eager assemblage, until the day was almost gone. Now, there had been no indication that the meeting would last so long, and the people were not prepared for such an eventuality. There was nothing for them to eat. Jesus asked Philip, "How are we to buy bread, so that these people may eat?" The author adds, parenthetically, that this was to test Philip (John 6:5-6). Philip saw the financial difficulties in the problem. Andrew, who must have been near enough to overhear the conversation, had a different approach. "There is a lad here who has five barley loaves and two fish; but what are they among so many?" (John 6:9). Obviously, Andrew did not see any solution to the problem, but he did see a personal angle: he brought the boy to Jesus, and we all know the wonderful way Jesus multiplied the boy's gift to take care of the entire crowd.

Some months later, in the last week of Jesus' ministry before His atoning sacrifice, the Twelve were with Jesus in Jerusalem. And in the throngs that were there to take part in the coming feast of the Passover were some Greeks, proselytes to Judaism from the Gentile world. They wished to have an opportunity to talk with Jesus, and they found Philip, whose name probably indicates that he was a Greek-speaking Jew. Once again, Philip took the matter to Andrew, and Andrew took Philip and the request to Jesus (John 12:20-22).

The author of the Gospel does not tell us the outcome; he has used the story to move into discussion of the "hour" that had come. We suppose that Jesus acceded to the request; we know that Andrew was busy trying to bring men to the Saviour.

In the calendar of the Church of England, Saint Andrew's Day, November 30, is the day on which it is customary to have a sermon on missions. George Milligan regards Andrew as the first home missionary, for bringing Peter to Jesus, and the first foreign missionary, for bringing the Greeks to Jesus.[8] Whether we agree with this terminology or not, I am sure we agree that in principle Andrew represents all missionaries, even as he represents the lesser known but equally important members of the apostolic band.

[8] Cf. "Andrew," in Hastings' *Dictionary of Christ and the Gospels,* vol. 1, p. 53.

CHAPTER VI

Lazarus, Mary, and Martha

WHAT HAPPENS WHEN Jesus comes into a home? Does He release the Christ-spirit that enables you to meet every difficulty with poise? Does He guarantee health and happiness and joy unbroken? Does He unveil the truth that sickness and death are only illusions? I hear things like this on the radio and read such statements in newspaper columns. Now I would like to take you inside a home where Jesus often visited; I want you to meet some people who loved Jesus and whom He loved: the family of Martha and Mary and Lazarus.

Perhaps you are wondering what Lazarus did that he should be included in the great personalities of the New Testament. Some men enjoy reflected greatness. It is not so much what they do, as it is what happens to them, that makes them great. Because of what happened in the home of Lazarus, particularly because of what happened to him, crowds came to see him and crowds came to see Jesus. Because of what happened, crowds thronged the way into Jerusalem on the day that has come to be known as Palm Sunday. Because of the sudden surge of popularity—and so near Jerusalem, too!—the rulers decided to put Jesus to death at once. Because of the embarrassing evidence that Lazarus himself had suddenly become, the rulers decided to put him to death likewise. In the light of these momentous events, who can gainsay a place of prominence, even greatness, for Lazarus?

The home of Lazarus. There were two sisters and a brother, and the Scripture lists them in the order: Martha, Mary, and Lazarus (John 11:5). This in itself is remarkable in a world where women are usually named last, if, indeed, they are named at all. (We recall that the sisters of Jesus were not named.) The suggestion is reasonable that Lazarus was the younger brother, and Martha the oldest member of the family. According to tradition, for what it may be worth, Lazarus was thirty years old when the miracle took place, and lived thirty years more. If so, we could suppose that Martha was in her late thirties or early forties.

It is generally stated that the brother and the two sisters lived in Bethany. This village is located on the eastern side of the Mount of Olives, a little more than a mile and a half from Jerusalem, and was the starting-point for the Palm Sunday procession. However, Luke tells a story about Martha and Mary (Luke 10:38-42) that seems to be located in Galilee. Bible scholars explain this as a story put out of its geographical context by Luke in order to bring out the point he is making—and this is a valid explanation. There is another suggestion, however, that merits consideration. According to Chase, the sentence in John should have been represented in translation somewhat as follows, "Lazarus was from Bethany, [having come] from the village of Mary and Martha."[1] In other words, Lazarus had moved to Bethany at some previous time, from Galilee where his sisters still were living.

Well, in either case, Jesus was closely tied to this family in the bonds of love. We get the impression that Jesus not only visited the family, but that He felt free to drop in at any time. During the last week of His life, when He spent no night in Jerusalem, He may have made Bethany His home. His love for this family is specifically stated thrice (John 11:3, 5, 36) and implied throughout the story. Now let us see what happens in a home where Jesus is a frequent visitor and an intimate friend.

The home was a home of love, but it was not without its quarrels. Luke tells us about a dinner that was being prepared for Jesus, in the account of which Martha and Mary are the principal characters. The two women have the same characteristics in John's Gospel as are recorded by Luke. Martha was the fussy type; Mary was a bit carefree. When she entertained, Martha wanted everything to be just right. We all know women like her: the living room must be immaculate, the window drapes must be just so, the flowers on the table must not clash in color with the table setting; the best china and silver must be used, and everything arranged exactly right. The house is referred to as Martha's (cf. Luke 10:38). This probably refers to proprietary rights, but we get the feeling—and I imagine any visitor would have gotten the same impression—that Martha was running things in that house, no matter who owned it.

Mary, it seems, cared little about details. She liked a house to look "lived in," and toys on the floor or disarranged cushions on the

---

[1] F. H. Chase, article "Peter," in Hastings' *Dictionary of the Bible* (New York: Charles Scribner's Sons, 1899), vol. 3, p. 757. Chase discusses John's use of the prepositons *apó* and *ek*.

sofa never bothered her. When they had interesting company, she would rather sit and listen than stir the soup. We are not told whether these women had been married, but if not, perhaps it was because Martha was too efficient, and Mary was too easygoing.

I have known women like Martha. Their husbands prefer to spend the evening at the club, for they never feel comfortable at home. No, there is nothing wrong with Martha! She is a wonderful woman. You can depend on her. She will make a most efficient president of the Women's Society. She is clever. She has a fine sense of balance, she is artistic, she is devoted. You cannot find anything about her to criticize—unless it is that you cannot find anything to criticize! I have known women like Mary. One such wonderful woman used to attend church every time the doors were open. She went to every Bible conference in the area. She was active in all sorts of Christian service. And she used to tell me, "I can't get my husband interested in church!" Poor man, he hardly ever had a home-cooked meal! And I just did not have the courage to say to her, "Perhaps if you were more interested in your home, your husband would be more interested in church!"

Martha and Mary! What happened when Jesus came into the home? Did they suddenly resolve their tensions? Did they fall into loving embrace? Did Martha stop fussing, and did Mary start spending more time in the kitchen? We know better than that. Mary sat at Jesus' feet, and Martha said to Jesus, "Don't you care that my sister has left me to do all the work? Tell her to help me!" (cf. Luke 10:40). If we could only hear the tone of voice in Jesus' answer: "Martha, Martha, you are anxious and troubled about many things; one thing is needful. Mary has chosen the good portion, which shall not be taken away from her" (Luke 10:41,42). There is a minor textual problem here, as our Bible notes in the margin. Jesus may have said, "Few things are needful" rather than "one thing." It makes little difference. If we may paraphrase, He is saying something like this: "Now, Martha, let's stop and think about life. There are really not many necessary things. You are concerned with a lot of details, but you could live without them, if you had to. On the other hand, there are a few things that you just cannot live without, and Mary has found one of these. It shall not be taken from her." Jesus does not really condemn Martha, does He? And He does not praise Mary for her indifference in the home. I certainly would not want anyone to think that Jesus will criticize a woman for keeping a neat house, or that He will bless a woman who sits all day at His feet and does nothing else. This is not the point. The point that Jesus wants to get across is simply this: there ought to be a place in the busy-ness of life for meditation at Jesus' feet.

Matthew records a beautiful story which I believe refers to Mary the sister of Martha and Lazarus.[2] It happened in the house of Simon the Leper in Bethany—some think that was Martha's father or husband, who had died some time before this, the house still being called by his name—and Martha, as usual, was serving. Mary took a pound of costly ointment; Judas estimated its value at three hundred denarii (about sixty dollars; cf. John 12:5), and since a denarius was a day's wage for a laborer that would make it worth a year's pay. Pouring the nard on Jesus' feet, Mary wiped them with her hair. Some of the disciples were indignant, and Judas Iscariot was quite outspoken. What waste! Jesus said, "Why do you trouble the woman? For she has done a beautiful thing to me. . . . In pouring this ointment on my body, she has done it to prepare me for burial. Truly, I say to you, wherever this gospel is preached in the whole world, what she has done will be told in memory of her" (Matthew 26:10, 12-13). Men still object to waste in religion: expensive churches, beautiful windows, magnificent organs, representative salaries, money and lives sent to mission fields, etc. The Lord Jesus has little patience with ostentatious spending; but He honors the beautiful extravagance of love.

The sickness and death of Lazarus. One day Lazarus became seriously ill, and they sent word to Jesus, "He whom you love is ill" (John 11:3). Then follows a very strange statement: "Now Jesus loved Martha and her sister and Lazarus. So when he heard that he was ill, he stayed two days longer in the place where he was." That little

[2] The number of times that Jesus was anointed, and the identification of the women, is a problem on which there is wide difference of opinion. The accounts are found in Matthew 26:6-13 (clearly parallel with Mark 14:3-9), Luke 7:36-50, and John 12:1-8. Origen (A.D. c.185-254) said there were three different anointings; others combine the Johannine account with Matthew and Mark and reduce the number to two; still others combine all accounts into one. This last view, *ipso facto,* makes Mary of Bethany the sinful woman of the city, and Simon the Pharisee, Simon the Leper. J. B. Mayor gives a good summary of the views, lists six points at which the Lucan account differs from the others; see article "Mary," in Hastings' *Dictionary of the Bible,* vol. 3, p. 279.

word "so" relates the sentence that follows to the sentence ahead of it, and it means that when Jesus heard of Lazarus' illness, because of His love for the family He delayed for two days before responding to the message. That is a strange kind of love, is it not? If I were to send word to a very dear friend, "I need you; come at once," and he were to reply, "I love you dearly, am leaving in two days," I would feel that our friendship was wearing thin. But think a minute! Can it be that Jesus is deliberately delaying for a reason? The teaching that God always answers prayer immediately needs rethinking.

There is another strange statement in this story: "When Jesus heard it he said, 'This illness is not unto death; it is for the glory of God . . .'" (John 11:4). Be careful how you read! The illness did result in death (John 11:14). But the purpose of the illness was that the Son of God might be glorified by means of it—that is, by means of the illness and the death.

There is a teaching abroad in the world that sickness is not the will of God in this world. This is a false teaching. The present world is a world of sickness and death, and to confuse this world with the world to come, where there is no sickness and no more death, is to bring confusion into the revelation that God has given us. Sickness and death are not unreal. They belong to this world. They are very much with us, and Jesus, in the story we are studying, wants to make this perfectly clear. Listen to Him: "Lazarus is dead; and for your sake I am glad that I was not there" (John 11:14-15). Why? Was it because if Jesus had been there, Lazarus would not have died? Possibly so. That is what the sisters thought (John 11:21, 32). But the main point is that Jesus wanted all who witnessed this to know, first, that Lazarus was truly dead, and second, that Jesus the Son of God had power over death.

Jesus and the disciples were beyond the Jordan when they received the news about Lazarus. The trip from Bethany to Jericho can be made in a day (it is a little over twenty miles, downhill), and Jesus was probably not far on the other side of the Jordan. The return trip is much more difficult, for starting about 1,100 feet below sea level the road climbs to nearly 2,700 feet above sea level; and to make a trip of perhaps twenty-five miles altogether, and climb 3,700 feet at the same time is a gruelling day's journey. It took, then, a day for the news of Lazarus to reach Jesus; He delayed two days; and it took at least a day for the journey to Bethany. When Jesus reached Bethany,

Lazarus was already dead four days; in other words, Lazarus, as Jesus knew (John 11:14), was already dead when the news reached Jesus. We are forced to conclude that Jesus delayed His visit, not in order to let Lazarus die, but in order that the full impact of that death and the resurrection that was to follow might be felt by all who were present.

When Jesus was nearing Bethany, news of His coming preceded Him, and Martha (the active one!) went out to meet Him. Mary sat in the house. For four days, they had doubtless said to each other, "If Jesus had only been here!" When Jesus came, they said it to him, "If you had been here, my brother would not have died" (John 11:21, 32). There was no false appearance of peace and calm. Their hearts were broken. Death means heartbreaks, even when there is faith. To say, "If you know the truth, death will not touch you" is sheer nonsense. To say, "There is no death; it is only illusion" is utter folly. Death will break your heart. It broke the hearts of Martha and Mary. It even broke the heart of Jesus: "Jesus wept" (John 11:35).

Jesus was touched by all human infirmities. I cannot believe that He ever looked at anyone who was ill, deformed, or handicapped in any way, without feeling compassion. I cannot believe that He ever looked at a passing funeral without grieving. Yet we know as a fact beyond any contradiction that He did not cure all the sick or raise all the dead. He had it in His power. As a matter of fact, He had it in His power to abolish all sickness and death, just as much at that time as in the age to come. What we must realize is the simple truth that it is not God's will to banish disease and death in this present age! Until sin is removed from God's universe, disease and death must remain. Death is the last enemy to be destroyed. It would be no blessing to give eternal life to men who do not know how to use it! That would be eternal hell!

But Jesus did heal some diseases and He did raise some from the dead to convince men that He has the power which He claims and which He someday plans to use on a universal scale. Lazarus is perhaps the supreme example.

Jesus said to Martha, "Your brother will rise again" (John 11:23). Martha believed in the general resurrection, but she did not dare to hope that Jesus was speaking of a special resurrection for her beloved brother. "I am the resurrection and the life," said Jesus; "he who believes in me, though he die, yet shall he live, and whoever lives and

believes in me shall never die. Do you believe this?" (John 11:25-26).
Martha believed that Jesus was the Messiah, the Son of God, the One
who was to come into the world (John 11:27). That is splendid faith!
There is not much more that anyone could believe. But it still fell
short of believing what Jesus was planning to do for her. "Where have
you laid him?" asked Jesus. Then, when they had come to the tomb,
He said, "Take away the stone." That was too much for Martha, and
she protested, "Lord, by this time there will be an odor, for he has been
dead four days" (John 11:39).

Some tell us that there must be faith before there can be a miracle.
Some tell us that sickness, disease, and death are not real; that if
we have faith, these things disappear. Some tell us that if sickness is
not healed, it is because faith is not sufficient. Read this passage over
and over until you see that Martha did not have that kind of faith. If
faith by itself could heal, there would be many persons alive and well
today who died in faith. And if lack of faith prevented the work of
God, there would be many others in misery. God asks faith—but He
asks neither complete faith nor complete knowledge. He heals when
and where He pleases. Some, whose faith is weak, He encourages by
greater works than they would ever have believed possible. Others,
whose faith is strong, He allows to drink the cup of bitter sorrow. What
shall we say of the Lord Jesus Himself: was He lacking in faith? Yet
He suffered and died!

The resurrection of Lazarus. After thanking God for hearing Him,
Jesus cried with a loud voice, "Lazarus, come out" (John 11:43). And
Lazarus came out, bound hand and feet in the grave bindings, and his
face wrapped in a cloth. "Unbind him, and let him go," said Jesus—
and we are reminded that Jesus did for Lazarus only what his friends
could not do; He left the rest for them.

We call this "resurrection." But in a sense, it must be clearly differ-
entiated from the resurrection to come. Jesus brought Lazarus back
to this life: this life of sickness and death. There is an old tradition to
the effect that when Lazarus was unbound, the first thing he said was,
"Must I die again?" to which Jesus said "Yes." And from that time,
Lazarus never smiled again. The tradition may not be true; but it
contains a great truth. The resurrection of Lazarus was a mighty
demonstration of Jesus' power over death; but it was not the resur-

rection unto life eternal. Only Jesus' own resurrection could demonstrate that.

What is death like? Lazarus did not tell. There are many who would like to know. Is it darkness, or light? Is it painful, or blissful? Do you see the Lord at once? Do you see any of your loved ones who have gone on? Lazarus, who might have told us the answers to some of our questions, remained silent. There are two things, and perhaps only two, that can be said with certainty. We know, from the words of Paul, that to be "away from the body" is to be "at home with the Lord" (II Corinthians 5:8), and "that is far better" (Philippians 1:23). We know too, from specific teachings of Paul, and also from the implicit meaning of all Scripture, that death is not the perfection for which we hope; only the final resurrection can bring the age of glory (cf. Romans 8:18-23). Whatever Lazarus may have seen or experienced in death was not even to be compared with the glorious experience that awaits us in the resurrection.

There is therefore little profit in asking Lazarus, or anyone else, what is death like? Suppose you could get in touch with those in the "world beyond"; suppose you could talk with them and ask them what it is like—what would that tell you? Neither they nor anyone else, except the Lord Jesus Himself, can tell you what it will be like in the resurrection, for the resurrection has not yet taken place. And all that the Lord Jesus wants us to know about the resurrection life, He has already told us in His word.

The resurrection of Lazarus, however, was of great importance for the disciples. In just a few days, their Master would be seized, tried, and put to death. Their faith would be dealt a shattering blow. He had told them, not once but several times, that it was necessary for Him to suffer, to die, and to rise again; but they were so slow to believe! Even after the experience of seeing Lazarus come out of the grave, they would have difficulty holding on to faith in Jesus. But it would help. In the years to come, when they went out into the world with the message of redemption, they might be inclined to ask themselves, "Was it all real? Did it really happen?" Then the resurrection of Lazarus would be one very important event, among many events, to reassure them.

But how would that make any difference? Simply from the whole sequence of events that the resurrection of Lazarus set off. Shortly after that event, there was a supper in Bethany, and when the news got around that Lazarus was there, a large crowd came (remember that they were very close to Jerusalem, and it was just a week before the great feast), "not only on account of Jesus but also to see Lazarus, whom he had raised from the dead" (John 12:9). The rulers had already decided, several times,[3] that Jesus would have to be put to death. The resurrection of Lazarus, however, was the climax. It was the miracle that sent Jesus to the cross. "The chief priests and the Pharisees gathered the council, and said, 'What are we to do?' . . . So from that day on they took counsel how to put him to death" (John 11:47-53). Moreover, it would be necessary to put Lazarus to death (John 12:10-11)—at least that was their plan. The day after the supper was the day of the "Triumphal Entry" into Jerusalem. While it is probably not correct to say that the crowd was there just because of the resurrection of Lazarus, still John makes it clear that there was a close connection between the two facts (John 12:18). The sequence of events may not greatly impress modern scholarship; but it would certainly have impressed those who lived through it.

The resurrection of Lazarus is a source of comfort to us also. When we are called upon to lay our loved ones in the tomb, we are in need of comfort, and it is consoling to hear the words, "I am the resurrection and the life." We need to be reminded that the Lord Jesus has the power over the grave, power demonstrated when He called Lazarus forth from the tomb. We need to be reminded, also, that death is not something foreign to the present world. It is a very real enemy that is with us and will be with us until Christ has put all enemies beneath His feet. But that day of triumph shall certainly come, just as surely as the Lord Jesus by His own resurrection became the first fruits of those who have fallen asleep (cf. I Corinthians 15:20-26).

This, then, is a home that Jesus loved, a home He graced with His presence, a home He blessed with His greatest miracle. There was no escape from the trials and tragedies of life. There was no false optimism, no unreal love. There were the normal quarrels and jealousies of a normal home; there were the sicknesses and anxieties; there was death and grief. The presence of Jesus in the home did not exempt

[3] The decision is noted in John's Gospel in the seventh, eighth, tenth, and eleventh chapters.

that home from these things. There was faith, deep, self-committing faith, in Jesus. There was also a limit to faith, beyond which it found itself unable to go.

How much is your home like this home? The presence of Jesus in your home will not remove the realities of life, but He will help you to live through them and to triumph over them.

CHAPTER VII

Simon bar-Jonah

PETER'S RIGHT TO a place in the hall of fame will not be denied anyone. In all the lists of the apostles in the New Testament he stands first. As the ready spokesman for the Twelve he assumes and is granted a place of leadership. In the first stage of the history of the Early Church he is clearly the leader, and continues to be until Paul comes into prominence.

Unfortunately, because of certain anti-Romanist reactions, Peter has often been ignored by Protestants. Statements made about him by Jesus Christ have been stripped of much of their meaning. So far as some Protestants are concerned, the Church would have gotten along perfectly well if there had never been anyone called Peter. Just a side-light on this is reflected in the fact that whereas many Roman Catholic churches are named for Saint Peter, the name is uncommon among Protestant churches.

I believe we have made a mistake. There is a right of priority that belongs to Peter by Jesus' choice. He is the Rock with which Jesus began the building of His Church. He deserves careful study.

The great challenge. One day, passing along the shore of the Sea of Galilee, Jesus saw two men at their occupation of fishing. He said to them, "Follow me and I will make you become fishers of men" (Mark 1:17). One of the two was named Simon; the other was his brother Andrew. In another place, Simon is called "bar-Jonah," which is Aramaic for "son of John"; if he had been a Scandinavian, we would have called him Simon Johnson.

We have already devoted a study to Andrew,[1] and many of the things we have learned of Andrew are equally true of Simon. They should be reviewed in connection with the present study. When Andrew brought his brother Simon to Jesus, "Jesus looked at him, and said, 'So you are Simon the son of John? You shall be called Cephas'

[1] See Chapter V.

70

(which means Peter)" (John 1:42). We should add another parenthesis, "(which means Rock)." It would be clearer if we omitted the Greek and Aramaic words, and read it simply, "So your name is Simon? You shall be called Rock."

Now let us make sure that we do not misunderstand that statement. I do not think that Jesus intended simply to give a new name to Simon (although that is what it has amounted to); rather, I think Jesus was revealing a character. When Jesus called him "Rock," Simon was not very rock-like. Many times in his days of discipleship, he seemed more like shifting sand. But when we get to the end of his life, looking back over it, we are forced to admit that Jesus named him well. He was a Rock. But the development of that character took time; it took experience; it took trial. Most of all, it took a basic character that had to be there in the first place.

Perhaps an illustration will make clear what I am trying to say. It would be possible for a skillful worker to spend time and craft on a piece of wood, and for the finished object, because of the nature of the wood, to be of little value. The same worker could spend the same time on another piece of wood, and turn out a beautiful and valuable object. The difference is in the wood, for in one case it was soft, its grain was not suited to the purpose, it would not take the necessary finish, it would not stand the stresses and strains to which it would be subjected; in the other case the wood was hard, clear, straight-grained, strong and pliable, and just waiting for the artist to make something useful and beautiful out of it. Simon had the qualities in him that Jesus needed, and Jesus had the ability to fashion Simon into what was needed for the beginning of the Church. Therefore Jesus called him Peter—Rock.

Simon, like the others of the Twelve, was first a disciple, then an apostle. He, like them, heard the call and followed Jesus. He heard, observed, and talked with Jesus. But in addition, he had the opportunity of some special training.

The great confession. Jesus had been with His disciples for several months, possibly a year or more. The days of easy popularity and large following had turned gradually into days of stiffening opposition and hardening heart. Men who looked for a simple solution to the problems of the world were not sure that Jesus was offering the program they wanted. Ecclesiastical officials who cared more for political security than spiritual growth were afraid of the consequences of the words and works of the Galilean. Jesus had therefore chosen His Twelve, and started the intense training by which they would be ready to carry on the work when the time came. But they, too, needed sifting and testing.

One day Jesus took the Twelve away from Galilee into the region of Caesarea Philippi, located on the slopes of Mount Hermon. The Sea of Galilee is nearly seven hundred feet below sea level, and while it is beautiful to look at, because of the mountains and the prevailing winds it is usually sultry and enervating. On the slopes of Hermon, on the other hand, cool refreshing winds often roll down the mountain from snows that remain most of the year; many copious springs bubble forth from the mountain to form the rivers of Damascus or the tributaries of the Jordan. Moreover, the disciples were away from the milling crowds of Galilee and the suspicions of Judea.

Starting with a rather innocuous question, Jesus asked, "Who do men say that the Son of man is?" (Matthew 16:13).[2] That elicited interesting discussion which gives us some idea of the large and varied personality of Jesus who impressed men in so many different ways.

Jesus then asked, "But who do you say that I am?" Peter answered, "You are the Christ, the Son of the living God" (Matthew 16:15-16). Now, I cannot say certainly whether Peter was speaking for himself alone, or whether he was speaking for the Twelve. It is difficult to believe that the apostles had been with Jesus for so long, certainly having heard much discussion about Him and much speculation about His person, without discussing the matter among themselves. Personally, I believe they had talked it over any times, and had come to some sort of conclusion. I am sure that Peter would have participated in that discussion, and probably had a large part in reaching the conclusion. I cannot believe that it was a secret conclusion to which Peter had come independently—for Peter was not the kind of man to keep a secret. He was a talker. What happened at Caesarea Philippi, then, was probably what had happened earlier—only this time in the presence of Jesus. Peter had formulated the conclusions in his own words, having led the group in reaching those conclusions, and having the boldness to express in concrete terms what otherwise might have remained only in vague abstractions.

Jesus did not turn this statement aside; He accepted it. Those who

[2] Here again the expression probably conveyed little more than the force of a personal pronoun: "Who do men say I am?" See p. 42, above.

deny the Messianic consciousness and claims of Jesus seem to ignore
Jesus' willing acceptance of this confession of faith. "Blessed are you,
Simon Bar-Jona! For flesh and blood has not revealed this to you,
but my Father who is in heaven" (Matthew 16:17).[3]

Then Jesus added the words that have been discussed almost without end: "I tell you, you are Peter, and on this rock I will build my
church, and the powers of death [Hades] shall not prevail against it.
I will give you the keys of the kingdom of heaven, and whatever you
bind on earth shall be bound in heaven, and whatever you loose on
earth shall be loosed in heaven" (Matthew 16:18-19).

There is a distinct play on words in the expression, "You are Peter
[=Rock], and on this rock." Some have obscured it by pointing out
that *Petros* (*Peter*) is masculine and *petra* (rock) is feminine. Some
have tried to show that these two Greek words have different meanings, perhaps like "stone" and "rock." But Jesus doubtless spoke
Aramaic—and Aramaic does not have masculine and feminine forms
of this word. The distinction was a necessary one in Greek, because the
man's name (*Petros*) had to have the masculine form. To the best of
my knowledge and understanding, we are forced to admit that Jesus
was designating Peter as the Rock on which He was beginning the
building of His Church.[4] The subsequent work of Peter in Acts will
substantiate this statement.

The words that follow, "I will give you the keys of the kingdom of
heaven, and whatever you bind on earth shall be bound in heaven, and
whatever you loose on earth shall be loosed in heaven" (Matthew 16:
19), have to be interpreted in the light of Peter's activities in the book
of Acts.

The great revelation. "From that time Jesus began to show his disciples that he must go to Jerusalem and suffer many things from the
elders and chief priests and scribes, and be killed, and on the third
day be raised" (Matthew 16:21). Once the issue was settled, once the
apostles were committed to faith in Jesus Christ as the Son of God,
Jesus undertook to prepare them for the coming Passion. According

---

[3] That the Father had revealed it does not mean that a process of consideration
and discussion had not taken place, such as I have tried to describe. God's
revelations are often, perhaps most often, through historic situations; dreams
and visions are, I believe, less common means of revelation.

[4] Some think "rock" refers to Peter's confession of faith; but according to

to the Gospel of John, both His messianic revelation and the prediction of His death were given in the earlier part of Jesus' ministry (the "Early Judean Ministry"). I see no necessary contradiction. The ideas may have been expressed, even with considerable clarity, and still not understood. That certainly was the history of the disciples' comprehension as portrayed in the Synoptic Gospels (Matthew, Mark, Luke). The full implication of the declared sacrificial ministry, however, would not be felt until there had been sufficient background of the revelation of the person of the Master, and this took time.

Even after the great confession at Caesarea Philippi, however, Peter was not ready to accept the necessity of the ministry of suffering, and had to be strongly rebuked by Jesus (cf. Matthew 16:22-23).

Something more was needed, and in order to reveal this to His disciples, Jesus selected the three who had made the greatest progress in comprehending His revelation. We usually refer to Peter, James, and John as the "inner circle." This term is only correct if we understand that it was not a clique, it was not a steering committee or a lobby, it was not even a favored few. There was nothing of the sort in Jesus' fellowship, and when two of the three misunderstood the purpose of the special training they had been receiving, and sought for places of honor in the Kingdom, Jesus promptly set them straight.[5] Any teacher who is truly interested in his calling will devote special teaching to his more serious students. So it was that Jesus took Peter, James and John up a high mountain,[6] where He was transfigured before them (cf. Matthew 17:1-8).

The transfiguration revealed Jesus in His heavenly glory. This was Peter's evaluation, after years of considered judgment: "We were eyewitnesses of his majesty. For when he received honor and glory from God the Father and the voice was borne to him by the Majestic Glory, 'This is my beloved Son, with whom I am well pleased,' we heard this voice borne from heaven, for we were with him on the holy mountain" (II Peter 1:16-18). Possibly this is what John referred

Acts, the confession by Peter at Caesarea Philippi was not a sufficient confession. After all, the devil himself could have subscribed to the truth of Peter's confession; there is no commitment involved.

[5] See Mark 10:35-45. In Matthew 20:20-28, it was the mother of James and John who actually made the request. The lesson is the same in either case.

[6] Traditionally, Mount Tabor. The setting of the story, however, makes this unlikely; I believe it was Mount Hermon.

to when he said, "We have beheld his glory, glory as of the only Son[7] from the Father" (John 1:14).

The transfiguration also set the prophecy of the coming death and resurrection against the background of the Old Testament revelation. Moses and Elijah, who appeared with the glorified Jesus on the mountain, were the representatives of the Law and the Prophets. Luke records for us the fact that Moses and Elijah "spoke of his departure, which he was to acccomplish at Jerusalem" (Luke 9:31). After the resurrection, Jesus likewise emphasized the truth, that the Law and the Prophets contained all the essential elements of the passion ministry (cf. Luke 24:27, 44-47).

It was as though Jesus were anticipating questions that would be asked and objections that would be raised—and I think He was. One question would certainly be, "How can You be the Son of God and talk about suffering and dying?" This is a major stumbling block to many: it was to Peter, when he said, "This shall never happen to you" (Matthew 16:22); it was to many Jews, as Paul realized (see I Corinthians 1:23). So, in order that the apostles would have a clear understanding of both His mission and His person, Jesus was revealed in the effulgent glory of deity, while at the same time His death and resurrection were declared. A second question, or perhaps an objection, would be that such a ministry of suffering is not part of the Old Testament revelation of the Messiah. The presence of Moses and Elijah, and their knowledge about and interest in the sacrificial work to be accomplished at Jerusalem, anticipated that objection.[8]

The great denial. It takes human beings so long to learn! As a teacher, I am constantly on the horns of a dilemma, whether to move more rapidly to cover the subjects that need to be taught, or to move more slowly to teach the students who need to be taught. And woe to the teacher who says, "I answered that question yesterday!" or "We covered that subject last week!" Peter was slow to learn, but sometimes those who learn slowly learn best. Perhaps that is why Peter is

---

[7] Some versions, through confusion of two similar Greek words, read "the only begotten of the Father." The word translated "only" means "unique, only one of its kind," and certainly does not weaken the doctrine of the deity of Christ.

[8] On the transfiguration, see G. C. Morgan, *The Crises of the Christ*, pp. 213-267, and A. M. Ramsey, *The Glory of God and the Transfiguration of Christ* (London: Longmans, Green & Co., Ltd., 1949), pp. 104-147.

such a helpful person to the rest of us. He learned well, when at last he grasped the lesson.

When Jesus asked, "Who do you say that I am?" Peter had the answer: "The Christ, the Son of the living God." Jesus said, "I must go to Jerusalem and be killed." Peter said, "Never!" But that is the Son of God you are talking to, Peter—you yourself just said so! When they went up to the mountain, and Jesus was transfigured before them, and Moses and Elijah were talking with Jesus about Jerusalem, Peter said, "It's nicer here; let's build three tabernacles [the word really means something like huts, lean-tos] and stay here." No wonder God spoke from heaven and said, "This is my beloved Son . . . listen to him!" (Matthew 17:5).

There was still time for Peter to learn, and in the weeks that followed Caesarea Philippi, Jesus returned to the subject of His death and resurrection more than once. Finally, the hour was at hand, and Jesus met with His Twelve for the Passover. The closing part of the ritual, which had to do with the messianic expectation, He directed toward Himself, thereby establishing the Lord's Supper. During the meal, probably before the institution of the bread and the wine, Jesus took a basin of water, after He had laid aside His clothing and put on a towel, and He began to wash the disciples' feet. It was a needed lesson in humility and service, for the disciples had gotten so far away from the heart of the Master that they were quarrelling over greatness (see Luke 22:24-27). Peter completely missed the point of the lesson, first by protesting, "You shall never wash my feet" (John 13:8), and then by asking that he be completely washed.

Patiently, Jesus explained the meaning of His action, and said, "If I then, your Lord and Teacher, have washed your feet, you also ought to wash one another's feet" (John 13:14). Then He declared that there was a traitor in their midst—a statement that seems to have truly hit each one of the Twelve at the depths of his conscience (see Matthew 26:22). Finally, Jesus was ready to turn to the closing teaching, and He said, "Where I am going you cannot follow me now; but you shall follow afterward." Peter had a ready answer for that, "I will lay down my life for you." Then it was that Jesus told him that before the crowing of the cock at the next dawn, he would deny Him three times (see John 13:37-38).

In the garden of Gethsemane, when Jesus asked the three to watch with Him as He entered into that last great agony, they promptly fell asleep—three times! Peter was one of them (see Matthew 26:36-46).

When the soldiers came to take Jesus for trial, Peter seized his sword and slashed away, hacking off the ear of the high priest's servant—as if the Son of God needed Peter, or any other human being, to defend Him! (see Matthew 26:51-54). What was Peter trying to do? Was he trying to prevent the death of Jesus, after Jesus had tried in so many ways to show that it was necessary?

The climax came while Peter was sitting by a fire in the courtyard of the house of Caiaphas the high priest. One of the maids saw him and thought she recognized him. "You also were with the Nazarene, Jesus." Peter denied it, and moved away. At the gateway, the maid said, "This man is one of them." Again Peter denied it. But one of the bystanders was impressed by the girl's accusation, and he noticed Peter's Galilean accent: "Certainly you are one of them for you are a Galilean." This was too much, and Peter collapsed under the strain. He not only denied knowing Jesus, but the record tells us quite clearly that He cursed and blasphemed.[9] At that moment the cock crowed, and Peter remembered the words of Jesus and broke down and wept (see Mark 14:66-72).

The great restoration. After Judas Iscariot betrayed Jesus, when he realized what he had done, he went out and hanged himself (see Matthew 27:3-10). Peter could have done the same thing. If there is any difference between Peter and Judas, it is not in the heinousness of their crime. Only our own attempts at self-justification lead us to judge Judas more harshly. To deny that you ever knew your best friend is utterly reprehensible. To deny the Lord Jesus, when you have been chosen for the express purpose of telling men about Him, is even worse. But whereas Judas went out and hanged himself, therefore denying with finality that God is willing to forgive, Peter held on to some slender thread of faith.

Three days later, when women brought the incredible report that the tomb of Jesus was empty, Peter and John ran to the garden, and saw the empty grave cloths in the place where Jesus had been laid (see John 20:2-10). It seems that Peter failed to comprehend the meaning of what he saw. According to an early tradition[10] preserved by the Apostle Paul (see I Corinthians 15:5), the risen Christ appeared

[9] Why so many expositors have tried to tone this down I fail to understand. The words in the Scripture are the strongest possible.

[10] The use of this word does not imply that it was not true; it had been handed down, probably by word-of-mouth, until Paul was led by the Spirit to record it; see I Corinthians 15:3.

to Peter first of the apostles. When this happened we are not told, but it must have been in the morning or early afternoon of resurrection day (cf. Luke 24:34), and it doubtless served to strengthen Peter's feeble faith. Likewise, the word of the young man to the women at the tomb, when it was reported to Peter, must have been a source of strength: "Go, tell his disciples and Peter" (Mark 16:7).

The great restoration of Peter, however, took place by the Sea of Galilee, some days later. Simon had returned to his occupation of fishing, and Thomas, Nathanael, James, John, and two others were with him. Jesus appeared on the shore and asked whether they had any fish. They had caught nothing. So Jesus said, "Cast your net on the right side of the boat, and you will find some" (John 21:6). When that resulted in a huge haul, John recognized Jesus (was it because of what had happened, rather than by sight?), and told Peter. Peter jumped into the sea, seemingly anxious to hurry to shore.

After they had eaten breakfast, Jesus turned to Peter and said, "Simon, son of John, do you love me more than these?" There was a time when Peter would have promptly said "Yes." "Though they all fall away because of you, I will never fall away" (Matthew 26:33). But now Peter will not compare himself with the others. He says simply, "Yes, Lord; you know that I love you." Jesus asked the question a second time, and a third time. Each time Peter replied in the affirmative, and each time Jesus gave him the commission to take care of His sheep.[11]

It has often been pointed out that, as Peter denied His Lord three times, Jesus gave him the chance to declare his love three times. This may well be the reason behind Jesus' threefold question. Certainly there can be no doubt that Jesus was stressing the fact that Peter was henceforth to be a shepherd of the flock of God.

How well Peter learned that lesson is reflected, I think, in his letter to the elders of the church of the dispersion: "Tend the flock of God that is your charge, not by constraint but willingly, not for shameful gain but eagerly, not as domineering over those in your charge but being examples to the flock. And when the chief Shepherd is manifested you will obtain the unfading crown of glory" (I Peter 5:2-4).

[11] Two different Greek words for "love" are used in the passage, and many scholars believe that there is a difference in the meanings of these words. I fail to find the difference, but have no strong conviction on the matter.

CHAPTER VIII

Peter the Rock

THE PRIMACY GIVEN to Peter by Jesus—using the word "primacy" in its fullest meaning, and not in the ecclesiastical sense used by the Roman Catholic Church—was accepted by Peter and the rest of the believers immediately after the ascension of Jesus. According to the record in the first paragraphs of the book of Acts, the risen Jesus met with His followers from time to time during a period of forty days, teaching them about the Kingdom of God, and impressing upon them that they must wait in Jerusalem until they were baptized with the Holy Spirit (Acts 1:3-5). At the end of the forty-day period, Jesus gathered His disciples to Bethany, and, with a parting word of instruction, ascended to heaven in their sight. The disciples thereupon returned to Jerusalem, to wait in prayer for the promised Spirit (Acts 1:6-14). It was there that Peter asserted his leadership, suggesting that a successor to Judas should be chosen and setting forth the qualifications for the office (Acts 1:15-22). Matthias was chosen by lot from the two who were qualified.[1] Peter did not make the selection and Peter did not ratify it. He presided, and the disciples acted.

Peter and Jerusalem. The disciples had waited for about ten days, when suddenly on the day of Pentecost there was a sound from heaven, tongues of flame appeared on each one, and they were filled with the Holy Spirit (Acts 2:1-4). The noise must have been heard not only in the house but throughout the city, for it brought a crowd

---

[1] Some believe that Peter erred in this suggestion, not having received the Holy Spirit as yet, and that Paul should have been the twelfth apostle. But Paul could not meet the basic requirement, which was set forth not only by Peter but by the Lord Jesus as well (if I correctly understand Mark 3:14), namely, that these men were to be eyewitnesses not only of the risen Lord, but of His previous ministry as well. If the Christian faith was to be rooted in the historical, it had to have witnesses to all that had happened historically. Moreover, the choice was not really a *successor* to Judas (no successor to James was chosen when he was killed), but rather the selection of an *alternate* who had been in exactly the same relationship to Jesus and the eleven as Judas had been.

to see what was happening. When they had gathered, they were amazed by the fact that the followers of Jesus were speaking "in other tongues," and each one heard them speaking "in his own language" (Acts 2:4, 6).[2] Jerusalem was filled with pilgrims from many lands for the feast of First-fruits or Weeks—the name Pentecost had come in with Greek influence, signifying that the feast occurred fifty days after Passover—and the speaking in tongues served a twofold purpose: to startle the crowd into recognizing that a miraculous act was occurring, and to present the message in a form that would be intelligible at once to all. The miracle, incidentally, was not confined to the Twelve, but involved the entire group of disciples, about one hundred and twenty (Acts 1:15; 2:4).

After the first reaction to the miracle, the crowd became more critical, and some said mockingly, "They're drunk!" Now, much as I dislike the heckler, I am forced to admit that it is a good thing to have him around. He often speaks out the doubts that lie unspoken in the minds of others, and he keeps the speaker or doer on his toes.

Peter, standing with the other apostles, accepted the challenge and spoke to the point. They were not drunk, but this was the fulfillment of the prophecy which God had given through Joel, the outpouring of the Spirit on all flesh, to the end that whoever would call on the name of the Lord should be saved (Acts 2:17-21; cf. Joel 2:28-32). That salvation, Peter hastened to point out, was made possible by the crucifixion of Jesus Christ (Acts 2:23). It took Peter a long time to learn that lesson: from Caesarea Philippi to Calvary! But he had learned it well, and never forgot it. This crucified Jesus God raised up; this crucified and risen Jesus had poured forth the Spirit (Acts 2:22-36).

Peter's sermon applied the sword to the consciences of his hearers. If Jesus was indeed God's Anointed, and they had been responsible for His crucifixion, what should they do? Peter replied in clear terms, "Repent, and be baptized every one of you in the name of Jesus Christ for the forgiveness of your sins; and you shall receive the gift of the Holy Spirit. For the promise is to you and to your children and to all

---

[2] The phenomenon has been called, from the Greek term used, "Glossolalia," and has come into prominence in modern times by the emphasis of the Pentecostal movement. More recently, some of the "staid old denominations," including the Episcopalians, have received publicity through the experiments of certain ministers with Glossolalia. In the absence of any Scriptural proof that the miracle has ceased, the Church should not deny the possibility that it continues, but rather try to bring it under the sound principles of I Corinthians 14:1-19.

that are far off, every one whom the Lord our God calls to him" (Acts 2:38-39). This is not all that Peter said—he used "many other words"—but this is quite sufficient. It opens the door wide for all who repent to come back to God through Jesus Christ. Some say that Peter and Paul, in their theology, were poles apart. Cullmann not only rejects this notion, but says, "Indeed, I should go even further and definitely assert that within the circle of the Twelve he [Peter] is the one who in this respect *stands closest to Paul.*"[3]

One day, Peter and John were going to the temple to pray—we should take note of the fact that the Christian community did not break with Judaism. At the gate of the temple was a lame beggar more than forty years old: how many years his friends had been bringing him there we are not told, but it was a daily occurrence and he was well known by sight to the people. Peter was led by the spirit to heal the man (Acts 3:6), and the beggar's excitement over his new ability to walk quickly drew a crowd. Peter seized the opportunity to disclaim any power in himself and to declare that the miracle had been performed by the power of the crucified and risen Jesus. Once again Peter called on his hearers for repentance and faith in Jesus.

The crowd and the excitement at the gate of the temple brought the priests and the Sadducees, and these were annoyed because Peter and John were speaking about Jesus and the resurrection. Therefore, they took the apostles into custody for the night. Luke, who has recorded that three thousand were converted at Pentecost, adds that the number had now reached five thousand.

The following day the religious leaders assembled to question the apostles: "By what power or by what name did you do this?" (Acts 4:7). How could Peter help following up a lead like that? He proceeded to preach Jesus the crucified and risen Saviour (see Acts 4:10, 12). Peter never preached anything else except this message. It is important that we note how he weaves the crucifixion and the resurrection into every message, and comes to some kind of presentation of a call to repentance. This was too much for the officials; but they could not deny the miracle (Acts 4:16), so they settled for a stern admonition to the apostles to cease speaking and teaching in the name of Jesus. Peter and John rejected this as a violation of their conscience;

[3] Oscar Cullmann, *Peter: Disciple—Apostle—Martyr* (trans. by F. V. Filson; London: SCM Press, 1953), p. 65 (italics his).

they returned to their friends, and all joined in prayer, asking for boldness to meet the new threat (Acts 4:24-30).

Peter's disciplinary leadership, as well as his prominence in preaching, is indicated by the incident of Ananias and Sapphira (Acts 5:1-11). We should be thankful that God does not so deal with every hypocrite in the church!

Peter in Judea and Samaria. The death of Stephen was the signal for the start of violent persecution and the Church was scattered throughout the region surrounding Jerusalem, that is, Judea (principally to the south and west) and Samaria (principally to the north and northwest). The apostles, however, remained in Jerusalem (see Acts 8:1-3). The scattering could be likened to scattering fire in dry brush: instead of stamping out the new faith, the persecutors only caused it to spread farther afield. The Church had become large, and organization had become desirable. Seven men had been chosen to handle administrative details in order that the apostles could devote their entire time to preaching the gospel. One of the seven was named Philip, and following the outbreak of persecution he[4] became active in preaching the gospel in Samaria. When word of this reached the apostles at Jerusalem, they sent Peter and John to pray for the new converts that they might receive the Holy Spirit.

It is possible to read too much into this event, and likewise possible to read too little. There can be no doubt that the Early Church felt a sense of unity and a sense of responsibility that is lacking in many Christian denominations today. The apostles and, later, James the brother of Jesus, held a position of oversight at Jerusalem that has been likened to an episcopacy; James has in fact been called the Bishop of Jerusalem. The accuracy of the title and the extent of the authority are points on which there will be varying opinions, and this is not the place to discuss the matter. In my opinion, the extremes of independency and hierarchy are both dangerous and to be rejected.

Peter's work (his apostolic supervision of new churches?) led him to Lydda. At nearby Joppa there was a disciple named Tabitha, the Aramaic word for "gazelle." We know her best by the Greek form of her name, Dorcas. Dorcas was one of those wonderful Christian women who express their love and devotion to the Lord Jesus by good

---

[4] Some identify this Philip with the apostle of the same name; I think Philip the apostle remained in Jerusalem.

deeds. We sometimes forget, when we are discussing the gifts of the Spirit, that these powers are not limited to preaching and teaching and speaking with tongues. Paul lists service, liberality, giving aid, and doing acts of mercy also as gifts of the Spirit (Romans 12:8), and when speaking of the offices that God has appointed in the Church, he mentions helpers and administrators along with prophets, healers, and speakers in tongues (I Corinthians 12:28). Dorcas was a Spirit-filled woman, doing the work that God had appointed for her by the gift of the Spirit in her.

Dorcas became sick and died, and since the church in Joppa knew that Peter was in Lydda, they sent for him. When he arrived, they took him to the room where the body of Dorcas was lying, and the heartbroken members of the Christian fellowship could not help but show Peter some of the coats and garments that Dorcas had made for them. Peter was led to put the mourners out of the room and raise Tabitha from the dead (Acts 9:40)—and then he called the members of the Christian community and restored her to them.

Why is this story told in Acts? Was it part of an effort by Luke to reconcile the Peter–Paul tension in the Church? I do not think so. That is largely the product of modern critical imagination. Was it the Early Church constructing legends about its heroes? Then why was there not more of this kind of material? For myself, I believe it happened as told by Luke in Acts. Perhaps if the Church today were to spend more time in fellowship with the risen Lord and less in discussing human doubts, we too would have such power! But another question deserves to be asked: why was it that on some occasions—not many, but some—such deeds of power occurred? I can only give my conviction. This was the Lord's way of demonstrating to the young and tender Church the truth of His word, "I am with you always, even to the end of this age."

While Peter was in Joppa, a man in Caesarea, about thirty-two miles to the north, had a vision. The man, whose name was Cornelius, was a Gentile, a centurion in the Roman army; he was moreover one of those Gentiles who had despaired of the religion of paganism, and who had found spiritual help in the religion of Israel: Cornelius was a worshiper of God. In the vision, God told him to send to Joppa, to the home of Simon the tanner, and to get Simon Peter to come to Caesarea (see Acts 10:1-8).

The next day, Peter had a vision during a noonday prayer on the roof-top. In his vision, he was being commanded to kill and eat unclean, or non-kosher food. When he refused, the voice said, "What God has cleansed, you must not call common." The vision was seen by Peter three times (Acts 10:9-16). While he was puzzling over the meaning of the vision, the emissaries of Cornelius arrived, and the Spirit told Peter, "Go down, and accompany them without hesitation; for I have sent them" (Acts 10:20).

After giving them hospitality and a night's lodging, Peter went with them to the home of Cornelius, where he told what had happened to him, and Cornelius recounted his experience. Peter began to preach the gospel of Jesus Christ, including the crucifixion and resurrection (Acts 10:39-40), but before he had finished, the Holy Spirit came on the assembled group as He had on the day of Pentecost, and the Gentiles began to speak in tongues (Acts 10:46). Peter was convinced by this miracle that God had included Gentiles in the redemptive work, and therefore he baptized those who were present (Acts 10:47-48).

News of this reached the apostles and other members of the Church in Judea, and when Peter returned to Jerusalem an inquiry was held. The principal spokesmen are referred to as "the circumcision party" —a name which came to be used of them at a later time, and was used here proleptically (much as I have been using the term "Christian," although that name was not conferred until later). These men were sincerely convinced that Jews should abide by all the laws of *kashrût* (ceremonial cleanness), and that Peter had violated this principle when he went into a Gentile home and ate non-kosher food (Acts 11:2-3). Peter told the story of his vision and his experience in the home of Cornelius. His closing words summarized the argument: "If then God gave the same gift to them as he gave to us when we believed in the Lord Jesus Christ, who was I that I could withstand God?" (Acts 11:17).

This event is one of the most important in the history of the Early Church. It marked the opening of the discussion of a subject that was to ocupy the Church for perhaps twenty or twenty-five years, and which was to result in the establishment of a principle that the Church has not yet fully learned. The problem began with the simple question, was the Christian Church to continue as a sect within Judaism? In other words, was the Church required to observe the ceremonial laws of the Jews? The question, however, became larger:

Was the Church to consist of two groups, Jewish-Christians and Gentile-Christians? Ultimately, this has to lead to the discussion of the principle, are there second-class citizens in the Kingdom of God? We shall return to a fuller discussion of this subject in a later study. But it must be obvious, however, that the Church cannot settle for anything less than God's will, and in the case of Cornelius and his household, at least, God had willed that they should receive the gift of the Spirit.

This incident has often been referred to in such terms as "the Gentile Pentecost," "Peter's second use of the keys," etc. In the light of Acts 15:7 it is probably correct to say that Peter used the keys of the Kingdom to open heaven's gates to Gentiles as well as to Jews. We shall safeguard our ideas against extremes if we recall that Peter did not act unilaterally: he did only what God instructed him to do, and he had to account to the apostles and the brethren for his actions.

Peter unto the ends of the earth. Herod Agrippa I had gradually acquired control of Palestine, his most recent additions being Judea and Samaria. As a Jew (which Herod the Great was not), Agrippa soon became involved in the anti-Christian hostilities, and put to death James the brother of John (Acts 12:2), and when he saw that this pleased the Jews,[5] he proceeded to arrest Peter. The apostle escaped death only by a miraculous intervention of the Lord in answer to the prayers of the Christian community, and after reporting his deliverance to the Church, he "departed and went to another place" (Acts 12:5-17).

Some few scholars have taken this to mean that Peter died in prison, and his spirit visited the Church. This clearly is not what Luke intended, for Peter appears again in the account of the Jerusalem conference (Acts 15:7 ff.), and if we ignore this portion of Acts, we may as well ignore the twelfth chapter.

A more serious problem is, Where did Peter go after he departed from Jerusalem? The death of Herod Agrippa I occurred in A.D. 44. According to some Roman Catholic scholars who follow the tradition preserved by the church historian Eusebius, Peter went to Rome at

[5] I dislike to use the term, for it is misleading. At that point in the history of the Christian Church, it was almost 100 per cent Jewish. As Luke uses the term in Acts 12:3 it refers to that segment of Judaism that was hostile to the new movement.

this time; others hold that he went to Antioch, as indicated in Galatians 2:11, and at a later date went to Rome.[6] Protestant scholars are divided on the question of whether Peter was ever in Rome, probably the majority taking the negative position.[7] The problem is certainly not an item of essential faith.

Leaving tradition out of the consideration for the moment, we know from Scripture that Peter was in Antioch (almost certainly Antioch-on-the-Orontes, or Syrian Antioch) prior to the writing of Galatians. Whether that was written before or after the Jerusalem conference of Acts 15 is a problem in itself, which cannot be discussed here.[8] We also know that Peter was in Jerusalem for the conference. At some date between the founding of the Church in Corinth (probably A.D. 51) and the writing of First Corinthians (probably from Ephesus c. A.D. 56), Peter and his wife visited Corinth—at least this seems to be the implication of Paul's reference in I Corinthians 9:5; the statement in I Corinthians 3:6, on the other hand, makes it clear that Peter did not found the Corinthian Church. If we are not persuaded that Paul's statement implies that Peter visited Corinth, we must at least admit that it testifies to missionary activity on the part of Peter, and probably an itinerant activity rather than one that was settled in any particular place.

Scholars are not unanimous concerning the authorship of First Peter, but all would admit that it preserves an early tradition that Peter was an apostle "to the exiles of the dispersion in Pontus, Galatia, Cappadocia, Asia, and Bithynia" (I Peter 1:1). This area approximates the central, northern, and western portions of modern Turkey, extending from Kayseri to Efes (Ephesus) and north to the Black Sea, a sizeable and difficult territory that would occupy an apostle's time even if he limited his activities to the Jewish communities. At the end of the same epistle we read, "She who is at Babylon, who is likewise chosen, sends you greetings; and so does my son Mark" (I Peter 5:13). It is an early tradition of the Church that Mark was Peter's interpreter. The identification of "Babylon" is more of a problem. Some take it

[6] Both suggestions are noted in *A Catholic Commentary on Holy Scripture,* § 833g.

[7] For a good survey of the discussion of the question, see O. Cullmann, *Peter: Disciple—Apostle—Martyr,* pp. 71-77.

[8] For a full discussion and bibliography, see F. F. Bruce, *Commentary on the Book of Acts* (The New International Commentary on the New Testament; Grand Rapids, Mich.: Wm. B. Eerdmans Publishing Co., 1956), pp. 298-302.

literally: Babylon on the Euphrates. This seems highly questionable, for Babylon had been thoroughly ruined, scarcely repaired, and the capital had moved to Seleucia in 275 B.C. According to Strabo (first century B.C.), Babylon was almost entirely deserted.[9] The usual interpretation is to take Babylon as a figurative expression for Rome. If we accept the canonicity of First Peter, as I do, it seems that only a perverse anti-Romanism can refuse to interpret Babylon here, as in Revelation 18, to mean Rome.

Does accepting the primacy of Peter and his final location in Rome mean accepting the Roman Catholic view of Peter with reference to the papacy? I do not think so. To say that Peter was first of the apostles is one thing; to say that this primacy was passed on by apostolic succession is another. To say that Peter reached Rome toward the end of his life and was martyred there is one thing; to say that he was the first pope is something entirely different.[10] Protestants have done some muddy thinking at this point. There is no Scriptural support for the election of a successor to Peter; this is admitted by Catholic scholars who base their argument on tradition plus the question, Why would Jesus have instituted the office if He had not intended to continue it?—which is a misunderstanding, as I have tried to show, of the apostolic office. As for the primacy of the Roman See, both Jerusalem and Antioch have prior and more convincing claims. But above all, Peter drops out of Luke's story in Acts. Now Luke had one clear-cut objective in Acts: to tell the story of how the gospel got to Rome. Luke drops Peter, after keeping him in the center for many chapters, not because of any attempt to resolve a Peter–Paul feud, and certainly not because Paul was his personal friend (Luke was too honest a historian for that!), but because Peter was not the one who took the gospel to Rome. The conquest of the Gentile world for Christ was Paul's appointed task; Peter was responsible for reaching the Jews. The Petrine epistles support this view of his ministry.

According to an old tradition, when fierce persecution of Christians broke out in Rome, the Church there convinced Peter that he should flee. As he was leaving the city, he met the Lord Jesus who was walking toward Rome. *"Quo vadis, Domine—where are You going, Lord?"*

[9] Strabo, *Geography,* 16.1.5.
[10] After struggling with the problem for years and coming to this conclusion (not at all popular with many Protestants!), I was pleased to find that Cullmann comes to a similar position in his *Peter: Disciple—Apostle—Martyr.*

he asked. "I am going to Rome," answered Jesus, "to be crucified again for you." At those words, Peter returned to Rome where he was crucified, head downward, because he felt he was unworthy to die in the same fashion that His Lord died.[11] This tradition may have nothing more behind it than an early attempt to explain the words of John 21:18-19. But it seems so much like Peter that many of us are willing to accept it. Traditions can sometimes be right, you know.

[11] For the full story, cf. "Acts of the Holy Apostles Peter and Paul," *The Ante-Nicene Fathers,* vol. 8, pp. 844-845.

CHAPTER IX

Stephen the Protomartyr

ACCORDING TO A widely held modern heresy, preachers are responsible for preaching, and deacons are responsible for financial matters in the church. I used the word "heresy"; perhaps I should defend that. Heresies develop from ignorance or denial of the Word of God. Sects, on the other hand, develop from overemphasis of some part of the Word and de-emphasis of some other part. The modern attitude toward preachers and deacons is a heresy, and to correct it we must study the Word of God, not just in part, but in full. We must search out the entire body of Scripture until we have been corrected in our thinking and instructed in what the Word of God teaches. Obviously, that is too large a task for this chapter,[1] but we hope at least to make a beginning, and we shall do this by studying Stephen, the first deacon and the first martyr of the Christian Church.

First steps in Church organization. In the sixth chapter of Acts we have the account of the first steps in organization made by the Early Church. The occasion is given: "Now in these days when the disciples were increasing in number, the Hellenists murmured against the Hebrews because their widows were neglected in the daily distribution" (Acts 6:1). Two words need to be explained, "Hellenist," and "Hebrew." "Hellenist" is a technical term used in the book of Acts meaning Greek-speaking Jews. That is not the usual meaning of the word, and if you check it in an English dictionary you will get an entirely different impression; but the word is used enough times in Acts that we can control the specialized sense in which Luke uses it. Jews of the Dispersion who had given up the use of the Hebrew language and had become Greek-speaking Jews are "Hellenists," whereas those

[1] A very fine approach to the problem is G. W. Bromiley, *Christian Ministry* (Pathway Books; Grand Rapids, Mich.: Wm. B. Eerdmans Publishing Co., 1960), 118 pp.

who had remained in the Land and continued to speak Hebrew or Aramaic[2] are called "Hebrews."

There were tensions between the two groups of Jews. The Hebrews had a pride of place and language. They were not subject to the uncleanness of the Gentile world. They were living in the land that God had given their Fathers. They were speaking the Holy Language. They were fulfilling obligations of the Law that could only be fulfilled by men living within easy traveling distance of Jerusalem. The Hellenists, on the other hand, were not without their own feelings of pride. Many of them had lived in the Gentile world long enough that now, having returned to Palestine to live, they had greater appreciation of the blessings of the Land. They were also more sensitive of the finer values of Judaism, the spiritual realities that were developed when ritual was impossible.

Conversions to Christianity had introduced serious difficulties that can be seen by reading between the lines. Pilgrims to Jerusalem who had heard the gospel and had accepted Jesus as their Messiah were reluctant to leave. This may have been largely due to the teaching that He was going to return from heaven and that this return would be localized at the Mount of Olives—and of course they would want to be nearby when that happened! Perhaps many of them were without employment; some may not even have sought employment, for why work when the Lord is coming back soon?[3] Others found it impossible to get work, for Judea was not an industrial area. The Early Church sought to meet some of the difficulties by a "daily distribution" —a bread line, soup kitchen, or something of the sort.

The Hellenists began to murmur because the Hebrews were getting fed and clothed and they were being neglected. That may or may not have been true. When men are in an unfavorable economic condition, minority groups feel that they are the victims of unfair discrimination. Usually they are; but sometimes the feeling is unjustified. However—and this is what modern politicians have too often forgotten—you cannot allow such discontent to continue to grow, whether it is justified or not. This is even more true in a group such as the

---

[2] Formerly it was generally accepted that Aramaic was the language commonly used, and that it was called in popular speech "Hebrew." Since the discovery of the Dead Sea Scrolls, however, it is recognized that Hebrew was much more widely used than had been believed, and it is possible that the word "Hebrew" in the New Testament means Hebrew as well as Aramaic.

[3] This heresy crops up even today; it is fully answered in the New Testament.

Early Church. The apostles therefore called together the disciples and made a suggestion.

Underlying the suggestion was an important principle: "It is not right that we should give up preaching the word of God to serve tables. Therefore, brethren, pick out from among you seven men of good repute, full of the Spirit and of wisdom, whom we may appoint to this duty. But we will devote ourselves to prayer and to the ministry of the word" (Acts 6:2-4). This is clearly a sensible distribution of responsibility, based not on privilege or rank, but on qualification. The men who had been with Jesus were the men who should proclaim the message. Since this task is of primary importance, and since it is of extremely large proportions (there is a world waiting to be evangelized), no time should be taken from the apostles to do the jobs that others could do equally well. The suggestion pleased the multitude, and they accepted it.

The qualifications for the office are sketched briefly in verse 3. The men were to be chosen from the fellowship of the Early Church ("from among you"). They were to be men of good reputation. They were to be Spirit-filled men. They were to be men of common sense.[4] No church should settle for less in its officers!

It is interesting to read the list of names of the men chosen for the task: Stephen, Philip, Prochorus, Nicanor, Timon, Parmenas, and Nicolaus a Proselyte (Acts 6:5). They are all Greek names; six of them are Hellenists, and one is a Proselyte (a Gentile converted to Judaism). That sounds as though they had been chosen from the group doing the complaining, therefore men in a position to know the situation at first hand. As a result—at least I think that is why Luke added the statement at this point—"the word of God increased; and the number of the disciples multiplied greatly in Jerusalem" (Acts 6:7).

From time to time we hear objections to church organization. Some say, "Oh, if we could only get back to the Church of the first century!" Men have even attempted to establish churches conforming to their ideas of first-century Christianity. But a careful study of the Early Church will clearly reveal an organization—not for the sake of

---

[4] The word *sophia*, "wisdom," has a wide range of meaning, from knowledge and skill in the common things of daily life to specialized learning. In the light of the kind of men whom Jesus chose to be apostles, I doubt that the word here means specialized or philosophical wisdom.

organization, however, but to meet the complex and growing needs of the Church. Our greater problem is that we fail to adjust organization to need, we impose American organization on missionary churches in Borneo and elsewhere, and we think of organization as an end in itself.

Stephen and his work. Stephen was chosen to take care of the temporal problems of the Church in Palestine. Nothing is said of how he fulfilled his office; I suppose he did a fine job, but it is taken for granted. We are told, however, quite a lot about other work that he did, "over and beyond his call to duty." Perhaps that is not the way we should say it. These are the things that he did as a Christian, and in addition to these things he fulfilled the office of deacon. He was a "witness." All Christians have been called to be witnesses. "You shall be my witnesses," said Jesus, and the book of Acts tells the story of some of the witnesses. The duty of a witness is to tell what he knows, "the truth, the whole truth, and nothing but the truth."

Stephen was not only a witness, he was also an advocate. He was not content merely to tell what he knew, but he got into active discussion with those who did not agree with him. "Some of those who belong to the synagogue of the Freedmen (as it was called), and of the Cyrenians, and of the Alexandrians, and of those from Cilicia and Asia, arose and disputed with Stephen" (Acts 6:9). The "Freedmen"[5] were those who had been taken captive (perhaps by Pompey) and later they or their children had been set free. Cyrenians and Alexandrians came from Africa; Cilicia and (proconsular) Asia were in Asia Minor. All of them were Hellenists.

What was it Stephen said that stirred them so deeply? Stephen was a Hellenist; how had he irritated these other Hellenists? We are not told in so many words, but I think we can reconstruct it from the story. They charged Stephen, for example, with speaking "blasphemous words against Moses and God," and "against this holy place and the law" (Acts 6:11,13). It seems obvious that Stephen had attacked the Temple (God) and the Law (Moses).[6] How? Where did

[5] King James Version reads "Libertines," a translation which should be rejected, since the word has come to have an immoral connotation.

[6] The identification of the Temple with God may seem farfetched, but as a matter of fact, the words became so closely identified that God is still called *ha-Maqôm* ("the Place") by Jews who seek to avoid using the word for God.

he get such an idea? Some tell us that it was his Hellenistic background which had given him ideas foreign to Judaism. But a study of Hellenistic Judaism will quickly prove that this is fallacious. The supreme example of Hellenistic Judaism is Philo of Alexandria (c.20 B.C.—c. A.D. 50), and he is extremely positive in his attitude toward the Law, arguing that the laws of Scripture are like the laws of nature: they do not change. Moreover, Stephen was having his difficulties with Hellenistic Jews. Certainly it was not Hellenism that had led him to his position!

But if we study the teachings of Jesus, we soon discover where Stephen got his peculiar notions. Jesus denied the hereditary view of religion that said, Because our Father is Abraham, we are God's children. Jesus said, In order to be Abraham's children, you must have the vital faith that Abraham had (cf. John 8:39). Jesus denied the legalistic view of the Law. The Pharisees asked, "Why don't your disciples wash their hands before eating?" (cf. Mark 7:1-5). They were referring, of course, to ritual washing, and not to sanitation. The disciples might have just washed their hands; but if it had not been done according to the correct ritual, they would still be "unclean." Jesus went on to point out that "there is nothing outside a man which by going into him can defile him; but the things which come out of a man are what defile him" (Mark 7:15). Jesus challenged the righteousness of the Pharisees (see Matthew 5:20). Jesus particularly and pointedly challenged their attitude toward the Sabbath, stating as a principle that "the sabbath was made for man, not man for the sabbath" (Mark 2:27). To illustrate this principle, Jesus on several occasions deliberately broke the Sabbath (as interpreted by the traditions of the elders).[7] For example, one day in the home of a ruler of the Pharisees there was a man who had dropsy. Jesus had been invited there to dine, and it was the Sabbath. Jesus asked, "Is it lawful to heal on the sabbath, or not?" (Luke 14:3). According to their tradition, healing was work, and work was forbidden by the Sabbath commandment. Jesus deliberately forced the problem into the open, and then proceeded to heal the man.

Further, Jesus denied the view that worship was either limited to a particular place, or more advantageous if performed at a certain place. When the woman of Samaria raised the question by saying, "Our

[7] For a forceful study of the way Jesus dealt with the Sabbath, see A. G. Hebert, *The Throne of David* (London: Faber and Faber, 1951), pp. 143-163.

fathers worshiped on this mountain; and you say that in Jerusalem is the place where men ought to worship," Jesus replied, "The hour is coming when neither on this mountain nor in Jerusalem will you worship the Father . . . the true worshipers will worship the Father in spirit and truth . . ." (John 4:20-24).

According to tradition, Stephen had been one of the Seventy. If we prefer not to accept that tradition, we must still admit that Stephen had been taught by men who had been with Jesus. Stephen had begun to think, and the more he thought the more he realized the implications of Jesus' teachings. Law was a matter of the spirit and intent of the heart, and not mere ritual. Worship was a matter of spirit and truth, not geography. If we carry these principles to their logical conclusion, the Law can be replaced by the Spirit of God in the heart, and the Temple can be replaced by spiritual fellowship between redeemed man and his Saviour God.

To the Jew, brought up as he had been to think of the Law and the Temple as essential elements in his religion, this was a hard teaching. The Jewish Church in Acts had much difficulty at this point, and for many years the Church seemed about to be torn into two churches. Peter got into the struggle; so did James the Lord's brother, and Paul. We shall have to return to it again. For the present we simply wish to point out that Stephen was the first man to step out in faith into the deeper significance of the teachings of Jesus. And just as Jesus had run into serious difficulty and opposition, so did Stephen.

Stephen's defense. The accusation of blasphemy was serious enough to warrant a formal trial. Witnesses—false witnesses—were brought in (cf. Acts 6:13), as had been done in the trial of Jesus. When they had finished, Stephen was given the opportunity of speaking on his own behalf. The seventh chapter of Acts is usually referred to as "Stephen's defense."

It is strictly speaking not a defense of Stephen so much as it is a defense of his teaching. He is defending Christianity. He is defending the larger view presented by Jesus. It might better be termed an "apology," using the word in the original meaning, the defense of a cause or doctrine.[8] Stephen does not mention himself. He does not

---

[8] It is an interesting illustration of the way words change in meaning, that "apology," which formerly meant, "these are the reasons why I am right," now means, "I am sorry that I made a mistake."

mention the charges made against him. He stays with the central issue, which could be paraphrased, The prophetic view of Scripture versus the legalistic.

Let me make clear what I mean by the terms. The prophetic view of Scripture tries to get the truth out of Scripture; the legalistic view tries to force Scripture into a mold. The prophetic view says, God has spoken, now let us try to get the fullest and clearest possible meaning of what He said. The legalistic view says, God has spoken, and this is the way our fathers understood Him; this is therefore what God meant, and we shall resist any attempt to make it mean anything else.

There are many sincere people teaching the Bible today who follow in the tradition of legalism. If you were to suggest to them that they walk in the steps of the Pharisees, they would doubtless feel insulted. Yet it is quite obvious that they are not trying to let the Scripture lead them into all truth; rather, they are trying to jam the truth into the little molds which they received from those who taught them. "It was good enough for Mother, and it's good enough for me." They do not think that way of their washboard, their horse-and-buggy, or their medical doctor, but they do think it about their religion. Now it certainly must be obvious, in the light of what I have already said, that I am not challenging the fundamental doctrines of the Scriptures; I am speaking about interpretation of the Scriptures, about the application of the truth of God to the life of man.

Stephen undertook to meet the legalistic attitude by a long, involved argument. Some scholars think he missed the point; that it is not an argument at all, but simply a rambling, pointless speech. It seems to me that he has a very clear-cut argument. Let me sketch first the points I think he is making; then check them, if you will, in Acts.

He started by pointing out that the original covenant was made by God long before the time of Moses, long before the time of Solomon; it was made with Abraham, when there was no Law and no Temple. Yet Abraham could worship God acceptably. This covenant was not made in the land of Canaan; it was made in Mesopotamia. The law was not given in Jerusalem; it was given in Sinai. God's activity therefore had not been limited to Palestine. It had been operative on behalf of Joseph in Egypt, and again in Egypt for all of Israel. Now, if worship was acceptable to God and God's redemptive activity was available to men, before there was a Law and before there was a Temple, these things were not essential elements, certainly not essential forms. Moreover, God's revelation has been progressive. God has been dealing with the race as a parent deals with a child: a little at a time, increasing as the child increases in understanding. God's revelation increased as we pass from Abraham to Moses, and continued to increase as we pass from Moses to Solomon, and then to the prophets. Why, then, could it not continue to increase still more as we come down to the time of Jesus? If God's promise originally made to Abraham had included the blessing of the Gentiles, certainly it was not intended to stop with the Jewish people.

Now, I grant that Stephen did not say these things as I have said them. But check over his speech, and see whether I have misrepresented his train of thought. When he came to the matter of progressive revelation, he introduced the other side: human inertia. The great problem has not been that men have moved ahead of the prophets; the great problem has been that men have refused to move with the prophets. "Which of the prophets did not your fathers persecute?" (Acts 7:52). These prophets, who had announced the coming of the Righteous One, Stephen ties in with Jesus, and the Righteous One, the Messiah of Israel, he identifies with Jesus.

This was too much! A speech like this may make its point with thoughtful men, as they have time to sit down and ponder its subsurface truth. But the mention of the murder of Jesus was inflammatory, and men of inflamed passions do not take time to sit down and think. Stephen's defense is one of the great prophetic messages of the Early Church. It is a pioneer speech that moves out into unexplored territory of thought. But its immediate result was the death of Stephen.

The stoning of Stephen.   Stephen was stoned for blasphemy. According to the Law, "He who blasphemes the name of the Lord shall be put to death; all the congregation shall stone him" (Leviticus 24:16). Stephen was stoned outside the city, in accordance with the Law, "Bring out of the camp him who cursed" (Leviticus 24:14). The witnesses stoned him first, for the Law said, "The hand of the witnesses shall be first against him to put him to death, and afterward the hand of all the people" (Deuteronomy 17:7).

Not only was the Law specific on the matter, but the tradition of the Fathers was clear and detailed. The Talmud says that after the witnesses have been heard, and sentence is pronounced, the condemned man "is led forth, while some one precedes him announcing: Such a one, son of so and so, is led forth to be stoned for such an offense; so and so are the witnesses; whoever has anything to produce in his favor, let him produce it." When they are about six feet from the place of execution, the condemned man is stripped, and "one of the witnesses casts a stone, and if this does not kill the man, then another, and then, if death has not ensued, the people take up the task" (*Sanhedrin,* 6).

"One of the witnesses casts a stone, and if this does not kill the man . . ."—think of that a moment! That stone was thrown so as to kill! I have seen an angry mob take up stones. I have seen stones fly. Once I thought we were going to get stoned, but we were able to get to a waiting car. Those stones come in with the force and accuracy of big-league pitching! In such a manner Stephen was stoned to death, and like his Lord, he died uttering the words, "Lord Jesus, receive my spirit. Lord, do not hold this sin against them" (Acts 7:59, 60; cf. Luke 23:46,34).

"And the witnesses laid down their garments at the feet of a young man named Saul" (Acts 7:58). "And Saul was consenting to his death" (Acts 8:1). Augustine observed, *Si Stephanus non orasset, ecclesia Paulum non habuisset,* "If Stephen had not prayed, the Church would not have had Paul."

So Stephen, whose name means "crown," received the crown of the martyr. And so the language received another word, for the Greek word *martys* (genitive, *martyros*) originally meant simply "witness," but because of the great crowd of witnesses who paid for their testimony with their blood, came to mean what our English word "martyr" means. Stephen is the protomartyr, the first Christian martyr.

> The martyr first, whose eagle eye
>   Could pierce beyond the grave,
> Who saw his Master in the sky,
>   And called on Him to save;
> Like Him, with pardon on his tongue,
>   In midst of mortal pain,
> He prayed for them that did the wrong:
>   Who follows in his train?

I like to think of Stephen, too, as the first great apologist for the Christian faith, the first to follow in the train of his Master in stepping from narrow Judaism into the prophetic message and ministry of world-wide Christianity. And he was only a deacon!

What kind of church officer are you? Are you content to leave the Christian witness for the minister? Or will you join the ranks of those who look to Stephen as their example of a true Christian layman?

CHAPTER X

Saul of Tarsus

IN THE New Testament there are two men; the one is the persecutor of the Church, the other is the apostle of Christ. The former, if he had not been crucified with Christ, would have done his best to destroy utterly the infant Church. The other, if he had not been born from above, would not only have failed to see the Kingdom of Heaven himself—you and I probably would not have seen it either. And yet, as any student of the New Testament knows, these two men are one. The first is Saul of Tarsus; the second is Paul the apostle.

These two are one; yet they are different men and we must study each separately. Saul of Tarsus is the man of the flesh; Paul the apostle, by the grace of God, is in his own words, ". . . the least of all the saints," but in the words of the historian John Lord, "After Jesus, the most colossal figure of the ages." We plan to spend two studies on this great figure, and we shall develop these studies about cities prominent in the record of his life and ministry.

Tarsus.[1] Tarsus had a long and rich history. Excavations have uncovered successive civilizations from c.4000 B.C. Situated in a rich plain, protected from the cold winter winds by the lofty Taurus mountains to the north, the region was an ideal place for a young civilization to get started. The Cydnus River, navigable as far as Tarsus for small boats, formerly emptied into the Rhegma a few miles south of the city, the Rhegma being a lake or harbor that served as a seaport for the Mediterranean. Two great trade routes passed through Tarsus, one from the Euphrates valley and the other from Egypt via Palestine and Syria; from Tarsus they proceeded first northward, to pass through the Cilician Gates (a natural pass, widened c.1000 B.C., through the Taurus range) thence to central Anatolia and the west. It is therefore no mere figure of speech to say that Tarsus was a meeting

[1] For a detailed study, see W. M. Ramsay, *The Cities of St. Paul* (London: Hodder and Stoughton, 1907; reprinted, Grand Rapids, Mich.: Baker Book House, 1960), pp. 85-244.

place of East and West, for commercial and military expeditions of scores of centuries passed through that city.

Antiochus IV (Epiphanes) visited Tarsus in 170 B.C. and made it an autonomous Greek city, probably planting a Jewish colony there at that time. It was made a free city by Mark Antony, and the privileges of a free city were confirmed by Augustus. To be able to claim to be a citizen of Tarsus was to claim proudly to be a citizen of "no mean city" (Acts 21:39).

Tarsus was a university city. Ramsay said it was one of the three great university cities of the Mediterranean world, but later modified that statement.[2] The two outstanding universities, it would seem from Strabo, were at Athens and Alexandria, but what Tarsus lacked in greatness, however, it made up for in zeal for knowledge.[3] The term "university" as used here does not mean what it probably implies to us today. It was not an institution with a faculty, curriculum, and student body. Rather, it was a place where lecturers who were passing through could give their lectures, where teachers could establish themselves, gathering around them townspeople and receiving from them fees by which they supported themselves. When we are discussing Saul's education, however, it is necessary for us to be reminded that there is no means of measuring the effect of this intellectual environment on Saul during his formative years.[4] He spoke Greek, the language of the city, and as Deissmann has pointed out,[5] it was the vernacular rather than the classical language of the rhetoricians. Saul was certainly acquainted with either the teachers or the writings of the Stoic school of philosophy.[6] His few quotations from the Greek poets, however, are very slender grounds on which to build a supposition of vast formal learning.[7] Tarsus was a prominent Roman

[2] The original statement was published in his article, "Tarsus," in Hastings' *Dictionary of the Bible,* vol. 4, p. 687, and corrected in *The Cities of St. Paul* (London: Hodder and Stoughton, 1907), p. 233.

[3] Strabo, *Geography,* 14.5.13.

[4] Cf. J. Strahan, "Tarsus," Hastings' *Dictionary of the Apostolic Church* (New York: Charles Scribner's Sons, 1915), vol. 2, p. 549.

[5] Cf. A. Deissmann, *Light from the Ancient East* (trans. by L. R. M. Strachan; New York: George H. Doran Co., 1927), pp. 238 ff. A careful critical reading is necessary to distinguish this great scholar's a priori judgments from objective scholarship.

[6] Cf. J. B. Lightfoot, *Saint Paul's Epistle to the Philippians* (4th ed.; London: Macmillan and Co., 1878), pp. 304 ff.

[7] Cf. J. B. Lightfoot, *Biblical Essays* (London: Macmillan and Co., 1893), p. 206. The entire essay, "St. Paul's Preparation for the Ministry," pp. 201-211, is worth reading. For a defense of Paul's classical background, see Evelyn Howell,

city,[8] and since Saul had been born to a Roman citizen, he could claim that he was a freeborn Roman citizen (Acts 22:28). The pride and the responsibility of his citizenship became, after his conversion, an ideal worthy of the gospel, and we find it expressed several times in his writings and speeches (cf. Philippians 1:27 and Acts 23:1; see also Ephesians 2:12; and Philippians 3:20).

Far more important, however, than the Greek or Roman heritage which was Saul's in Tarsus was the heritage which was his through his parents. Both father and mother were Hebrews (Philippians 3:5), hence Saul grew up to know the God and the Scriptures of the Jewish people, even though it was in the Hellenistic world.[9] Since his father was of the tribe of Benjamin, the young boy had been named after the first king of Israel, the Benjamite Saul. His upbringing had been according to the strictest sect of the Pharisees, doubtless antedating his formal training in Jerusalem, in a home where the Law was rigidly observed. The origin of Saul's second name (Paul) is disputed; some hold that it was probably derived from the well-known Pauli family in Rome, his father having been a manumitted slave who received his name and citizenship for some great service; others hold that it was taken by Saul in honor of Sergius Paulus, the proconsul whom he converted at Paphos (Acts 13:7).

So we see that Saul obtained from Tarsus the three elements so prominent in his life, and so important in the world of his day: Roman citizenship, the language and culture of Hellenism, and the religion of the Jews.

Jerusalem. Saul had a sister, and from the fact that her son lived in Jerusalem and had access to the barracks (see Acts 23:16), it is usually assumed that she lived in Jerusalem. It is further assumed that Saul went to live with this sister, probably not long after his twelfth year, becoming subsequently a disciple of the famous rabbi Gamaliel (see Acts 22:3).

"St. Paul and the Greek World," *Expository Times* 71 (August 1960), pp. 328-332.

[8] Shakespeare has reminded succeeding generations that it was here that Antony and Cleopatra met, the Egyptian beauty's bark navigating the river into the very city. *Antony and Cleopatra,* Act II, Scene ii, lines 192 ff.

[9] I have not seen the fact noted that, although Saul might accurately have been classified as a "Hellenist," he refers to himself as a "Hebrew." This implies that his Hebrew characteristics were deliberately emphasized above his Hellenistic characteristics.

This Gamaliel, known as "the elder" to distinguish him from two others of the same name, was the son of Simon and the grandson of Hillel. So highly was Gamaliel the elder regarded by the Jews that it is recorded in the Mishnah that "with the death of Gamaliel, the reverence for the law ceased and purity and abstinence died away."[10] He was the first of seven rabbis to be called by the highest title "rabban." He was of the school of Hillel, as opposed to that of Shammai, and therefore represented a broader and more liberal view among the Pharisees (cf. Acts 5:38-39). He was interested in Greek literature, and encouraged the reading of it. He also held a more spiritual view of the Law, and encouraged Jews to have friendships and social relationships with foreigners. At the same time, there can be no doubt that he was a strict Pharisee, and that the young Saul was given training in the tenets of this sect at the feet of the great rabbi (cf. Acts 22:3).

Saul was born about the beginning of the Christian era and probably came under the influence of Gamaliel sometime in the second decade of the first century. The conversion of Saul is usually dated between A.D. 33 and 36, and since Gamaliel did not die until c.57 or 58, it is a reasonable assumption that Saul was under the influence of Gamaliel for several years at a time when the young disciple was at a very impressionable age, and the master in the ascendancy of a very brilliant career.

It would be interesting to be able to trace in detail the development of young Saul for the next ten or fifteen years. From several references in his speeches or letters we can gather that he developed into an ardent Pharisee, extremely zealous for the Law. If Acts 26:10 means what it is generally interpreted to mean, Saul became a member of the Sanhedrin.[11] The statement is sometimes found that members of the Sanhedrin had to be married men, therefore Saul was married. This reasoning is unfortunately based on two uncertainties: first, it is not certain that Saul was a member of the Sanhedrin; and second, it is not clearly established that members of the Sanhedrin had to be married. It is certain from I Corinthians 7:7 and 9:5 that the Apostle was not married when he wrote this epistle, and the inference of the former reference seems to be that Paul had not been a married man. On the other hand, there is a tradition preserved in Eusebius,[12]

[10] Mishnah *Sota* 9.15.

[11] The ruling council of the Jews, consisting of 23 (the small Sanhedrin) or 71 (the great Sanhedrin) members. Cf. *Sanhedrin* 1, 6 .

[12] *Ecclesiastical History,* 3.30. Eusebius lived from A.D. 260-264 to c.340.

that the Apostle married Lydia at Philippi and refers to her later as "true yokefellow" (Philippians 4:3). The tradition does not commend itself.

If Saul was in Jerusalem between the years A.D. 26 and 30 the question naturally comes up, had he seen or heard Jesus? Scholars can be found on both sides of the question, and quotations of Scripture can be found to support either side. Speaking for myself, I get the general impression from reading Paul's letters that he had not known Jesus prior to the resurrection.

Saul became extremely active in his zealous endeavor to keep the Law of Moses, and gained sufficient reputation that he could refer to this as proof of his earnest devotion to Judaism (Acts 22:3; 26:5).

It is not clear that Saul had engaged in the persecution of the Church prior to the stoning of Stephen. Saul was present at that event, and consented to it (cf. Acts 7:58; 8:1). This is not quite the same, however, as what he says concerning his active persecution of the Church, "I cast my vote against them" (Acts 26:10). We might be justified in concluding that Saul was merely consenting inwardly to what was being done in the case of Stephen, and that at some later date he became a member of the Sanhedrin that took part in voting to persecute Christians unto death.[13]

The very fact that Luke has chosen the stoning of Stephen as an introduction to Saul seems to imply a logical connection. As I understand the story, it was the stoning of Stephen, or more accurately, the trial that preceded the stoning together with Stephen's strong words, that stirred in the heart of Saul an unholy zeal and led him to participate in the great persecution that broke out that day against the Church in Jerusalem (Acts 8:1-3).

The difference between the moderating view of Gamaliel and the zeal of his disciple which amounted almost to rage, has drawn comment from several writers. It would seem to me that two forces were struggling within Saul, even from boyhood. On the one hand, there was the Hellenistic ideal that must have influenced anyone born in the Dispersion; on the other hand there was the strong Judaism that enabled him to say later, "I am a Hebrew of Hebrews." On the one hand, there was the broad liberalizing tendency of his master, Gamaliel the elder; on the other hand, there was the rigid narrowness us-

[13] We have already seen that membership in the Sanhedrin is not definitely implied in Acts 26:10.

ually associated with those who were zealous for the Law. If these forces were struggling within Saul, the trial of Stephen made it clear what the logical implications must be. If Jesus had said and done the things which His followers attributed to Him, then indeed He was a blasphemer. If His followers attributed to Him the place of glory and honor which belonged to God alone, as Stephen had done in the closing part of his defense, then certainly these believers deserved to be put to death as blasphemers. And if the breadth and tolerance of Hellenism made it possible for a man like Stephen to accept the transiency of the Law and the Temple, then it was time for Saul to make up his mind! This was the logical position from which Saul seems to have been fleeing until this moment. But once it became clear, he knew what road he must take. He could no longer remain quiescent or passive; he had to become active in his zeal for the Law: he had to persecute the Church. There was no middle course.

Something of Saul's struggle with the demands of the Law seems to be preserved for us in the seventh chapter of his epistle to the Romans.[14] He was not finding in the Law the peace of heart that he sought, and, like Martin Luther, he had a deep struggle of soul for something which the Law could never provide. It is the nature of Law not to provide, but to demand. Law requires rigid obedience and it can neither tolerate short measures and partial fulfillment, nor provide satisfaction or forgiveness. The Law was driving Saul more and more in a relentless pursuit of something that would satisfy the deep yearnings of the heart, but it was not providing satisfaction for those yearnings. Saul's outburst of fanatical zeal against the Christian Church may be looked upon as one of the means by which he sought to satisfy the Law's demands.

This has been the experience of others who have been seeking truth, but who have begun by rejecting the basic claims of Jesus Christ. Having rejected those claims and being driven by a relentless zeal to do whatever it is that God wants men to do, they find outlet for their zeal, not in persecution of the Church, but in an effort to undermine the basis for Christian faith. They attack the credibility of the Gospel record and seek to prove that Jesus was a fraud or, at best, a deluded

---

[14] The debate whether this chapter refers to his preconversion experience or his soul-struggles after conversion can be studied in almost any commentary on Romans. Certain portions seem to me to reflect an earlier struggle, even though the chapter seems to refer to experiences after the conversion.

young visionary. In their own unbelief they seek to destroy the belief of others, and if this cannot be done by reason, they seek to do it by ridicule. Books that are the products of such mentality range all the way from little blue books to learned discourses in many languages by some of the world's greatest minds.

In Jerusalem, "Saul laid waste the church" (Acts 8:3). The persecution was thorough and the results are reflected in Acts at several points. Saul was not satisfied, but "still breathing threats and murder against the disciples of the Lord, went to the high priest and asked him for letters to the synagogues at Damascus, so that if he found any belonging to the Way, men or women, he might bring them bound to Jerusalem" (Acts 9:1-2).

It was on the road to Damascus, for the purpose of carrying out this project, that Saul had his great experience. Luke, who has demonstrated in many ways that he is a careful author and historian, felt it necessary to record this story at three different points in the Book of Acts (Acts 9:3-18; 22:6-16; 26:12-18). The accounts are sufficiently different that anyone looking for difficulties can find them; the accounts agree, however, in reporting the essential event. It was about the noon hour in the full strength of the sun, not far from Damascus, that Saul saw a brilliant light from heaven and fell to the ground blinded by it. He heard a voice saying to him, "Saul, Saul, why do you persecute me?" He replied, "Who are you, Lord?" The voice from heaven said, "I am Jesus, whom you are persecuting; but rise and enter the city, and you will be told what you are to do" (cf. Acts 9:4-6).

Damascus. At Damascus there was a disciple named Ananias, and the Lord said to him in a vision, "Rise and go to the street called Straight, and inquire in the house of Judas for a man of Tarsus named Saul; for behold, he is praying, and he has seen a man named Ananias come in and lay his hands on him so that he might regain his sight" (Acts 9:11-12). If you were Ananias, what would you do? Nothing has been said to indicate that Saul has been converted. Ananias knew, probably by the grapevine,[15] that Saul had come to Damascus to do to the Church there what he had done in Jerusalem. So Ananias began

[15] This amazingly rapid spread of rumors and news will astound the Westerner. I have experienced it in the Near East and the Far East, and have been in situations where we were traveling (by horse) thirty miles a day, with no means of

to make excuses. The Lord said, "Go, for he is a chosen instrument of mine to carry my name before the Gentiles and kings and the sons of Israel . . ." (Acts 9:15). Ananias went. As a result, Saul received his sight and was baptized (Acts 9:18). In the synagogues, Saul declared his faith, saying of Jesus, "He is the Son of God" (Acts 9:20).

Saul's hatred of Christ and the Church, if we have analyzed it correctly, was due to Saul's conviction that Jesus was blaspheming in making the claims He made, while the Christians were guilty first of failing to repudiate His blasphemy, and then of making equally blasphemous statements. This, then, is the key to Saul's new message. Jesus was either a blasphemer or He was the Son of God. Formerly, Saul had taken the view that Jesus was a blasphemer; after his conversion experience, Saul declared that Jesus was the Son of God. It is either the one or the other; there is no third position.

What made the difference? Saul makes it clear: he saw the risen Christ. If Jesus was alive, then God had raised Him from the dead. Certainly God would not raise up a blasphemer. By raising Jesus from the dead, God had declared Him to be the Son of God. It was as simple as that!

Men have written many books or parts of books about the conversion of Saul. They have tried to discover reasons for his conversion in all sorts of experiences: in psychological and emotional factors, the stoning of Stephen, sunstroke, a fall from a horse, epileptic fits, and other suggestions. To Saul it was a simple matter, and he never attempted to make it more complex: he had seen the risen Lord. That explanation can only be set aside on two grounds: it is insufficient to account for the change; or it is incredible because it is impossible. It is my personal conviction that it is sufficient to account for the change. A sunstroke or an epileptic fit would not be sufficient; many men have suffered such things, but where is a second Saul of Tarsus? But if Jesus actually appeared to Saul, if the credentials offered to Saul were unmistakable, as they had been when offered to Thomas and the other apostles, if Saul (who certainly must have been as hard to convince as Thomas) was convinced that he had seen the risen Lord, so that this appearance could be listed with the others (see I Corinthians 15:8),

---

communication except word-of-mouth; yet when we arrived at our destinations, word of our coming had preceded us. Our only explanation is that someone was always traveling, bearing the news, while we were halting for food, rest, and other incidents of the route. This is the "grapevine."

then we have a sufficient explanation of Saul's conversion. It does not need amplification, and any attempt to augment it only weakens it.

As for the other objection, that it is impossible, what man is so wise that he dares to say that it is impossible for God to raise His own Son from the dead? That man belongs in the category of those who said it was impossible to reach the East by sailing west, or those who said it was impossible to convert mass into energy. Arguments from human non-experience are no stronger than arguments from silence. It takes only one experience to overthrow them; and Saul had such an experience.

At some point, Saul made a journey to "Arabia," according to his own testimony (see Galatians 1:17). Personally, I am inclined to put this journey between Acts 9:21 and 22. In other words, before Saul was able to present compelling proof that Jesus was the Christ, he had to think over the implications of his new experience. Saul had come to his convictions concerning Jesus and the new Christian religion as a result of his careful study of Judaism. This could not be overthrown quickly. And while it is true that the simple experience on the Damascus road is sufficient to account for his conversion, it is also true that this experience had to be reconciled with all that he had been taught previously—or to put it the other way, his previous learning had to be rethought in the light of the data provided by this new experience.

We forget to take this factor into consideration, oftentimes, when we are seeking the conversion of a well-educated person. The "simple gospel" is sufficient for conversion (although we may in some cases refuse to admit that it is conversion), but many rational obstacles remain. For Saul, the Old Testament and the teachings of the rabbis were as authoritative as are the teachings of science to a young college graduate today. And to harmonize these things with the claims of Jesus Christ is not easy. How long it took, we do not know; the upper time limit, from Galatians 1:18, is three years, but it could have been, and probably was, less. Where Saul went we do not know. Some think he went to Sinai; it is far more likely that he went to some secluded place not far from Damascus. When he had finished, he had thought through his faith and was ready to offer it to the world. Saul's statements concerning the origin of his faith leave no doubt that it did not come from the apostles; it came from his training in the

Old Testament Scriptures and his personal experience of the risen Christ.[16]

After being driven from Damascus, Saul began preaching in the synagogues of the Hellenists in Jerusalem (Acts 9:29)—taking up the work, it would seem, that had been left by Stephen. Saul, of course, encountered the same opposition that Stephen had; the opposition turned to murderous hatred, and they sought to kill him. He was saved by the activity of the Christians in Jerusalem—what complete reversal of poetic justice!—and went to Caesarea, thence to Tarsus. But no longer was he the old Saul of Tarsus; now he was a new creation in Christ Jesus.

[16] For a fully detailed, scholarly and thoroughly documented study, see J. G. Machen, *The Origin of Paul's Religion* (London: Hodder and Stoughton, 1921), 329 pp.

CHAPTER XI

Paul the Apostle

YEARS OF STUDY in the Book of Acts and the epistles of Paul have impressed me with the excellency of Paul's strategy and method. There is a lesson here that has too often been overlooked by the Church in its mission, a lesson that is being learned again by some mission boards. The strategy of missions in recent centuries has been to try to get enough missionaries (preferably American or British, and certainly white) to spread all over the world in order to "preach the gospel to every creature." That method is doomed to fail, for at least two reasons: it exalts the white Westerner; and the population of the world increases far more rapidly than missionaries can be supplied. The Apostle Paul, on the other hand, did not try to do the work alone, and he did not try to cover the whole population of any region. He located in important strategic centers on the great trade routes, established schools where he trained the native men and women, encouraged them to develop their own leadership and to evangelize their own people, and once the local church was established, moved on to the next center.

The advantages of such strategy are obvious at once. Workers are multiplied. Instead of one Paul there are scores of fellow workers. These workers know the people, the language, the customs, etc., far better than any foreigner coming into the area can ever come to know them. The developed sense of responsibility helps strengthen the local church. Perhaps most important of all, there is no inference, stated or implied, that "we can do the job better than you can." But I am stating my conclusions before presenting my evidence. As we study Paul the Apostle, keep your eyes open, and watch him mastermind his program of evangelization.

The cities of Galatia. Paul's "first missionary journey" covered the island of Cyprus and the southern portion of the Anatolian plateau. The cities of Antolia, after leaving the coastal region of Perga, were

Antioch in Pisidia, Iconium, Lystra, and Derbe. To study these places on a map, or even to read about them in a modern guide, may leave you puzzled, for only Iconium (modern Konya) is of any importance. But a visit to Antioch (just outside modern Yalvach) will quickly convince you that this was an important and large city in the Roman period. Lystra was reasonably large. In fact, of all the cities of Paul that I have visited, Derbe is the only place that was not of sizeable importance.[1]

Antioch, Lystra, and Iconium were located in the area of Galatia, and Derbe was on its southern border.[2] Paul's letter to the Galatians was written to the churches in these cities, probably to the Church at Antioch in particular, and his first recorded sermon was delivered in Antioch. The apostle had first visited Galatia as the result of some sickness, perhaps malaria contracted in the Pamphylian plain.[3] The Galatians had received him with undue kindness—they would have plucked out their eyes for him (cf. Galatians 4:15)—and Paul was bound by a strong bond of affection to them. Their later defection from the faith disturbed him emotionally, as is evident from the language of his letter to them, and this again gives us some idea of the relationship between the missionary and the people he was serving.

His sermon in Pisidian Antioch gives us several indications of his method and approach. The area was, of course, Gentile, but Paul had gone to the Jewish community and had taken his place as a worshiper in the synagogue. I suppose that Paul wore the robe of a rabbi or some indication that he was a qualified teacher in Israel—although it is possible that this information had been given upon his arrival in the city. At any rate, after the reading of selections from the Law and the Prophets, the visitors were invited to speak a word of exhortation, and Paul accepted. He began with a historic survey of Israel which

[1] The site of Derbe as established by Ramsay is now questioned by the discovery of Michael Ballance. Unfortunately, although I covered the region thoroughly, I could find neither Ballance nor anyone who knew where he was exploring. See M. Ballance, "The Site of Derbe: A New Inscription," in *Anatolian Studies* 7 (1957), pp. 147-151.

[2] I accept the "south Galatian" theory as fully established, and suggest that travel in Galatia will convince all but the most stubborn. For discussion, see W. M. Ramsay, *A Historical Commentary on St. Paul's Epistle to the Galatians* (New York: G. P. Putnam's Sons, 1900), pp. 103-234; *The Church in the Roman Empire Before* A.D. *170* (London: Hodder and Stoughton, 1893), pp. 16-89; and "Galatia," in Hastings' *Dictionary of the Bible*, vol. 2, pp. 81-89.

[3] Cf. Ramsay, *Galatians*, pp. 417-428.

led through the Davidic kingship to Jesus the promised Saviour. He told of the death of Jesus at the hands of the Jewish rulers. He proclaimed the resurrection and the post-resurrection appearances of Jesus, and declared that this was the fulfillment of God's promises to the Fathers. "Let it be known to you therefore, brethren, that through this man forgiveness of sins is proclaimed to you, and by him every one that believes is freed from everything from which you could not be freed by the law of Moses" (see Acts 13:14-41).

As in the case of Peter's preaching we notice the insistence on the historical. The apostles preached no vague message of personal encounter in a suprahistorical realm; they declared that the events of divine redemption took place in time and space. The crucifixion of Jesus, the resurrection, and the personal witness of these events, is intimately tied to the forgiveness of sin. In Paul, however, we find a note that is not found in Peter's first sermons (it is, however, in Peter's speech before the Jerusalem council, Acts 15:10), namely, that the Law of Moses cannot give deliverance. Was Paul speaking out of his own experience of the frustrating demands of the Law?

There were present in the synagogue when Paul spoke a number of Gentile Proselytes ("you that fear God" in 13:6). To me one of the most discouraging features of Judaism for a Proselyte would be the legalistic obligations; and some Jews would agree with me. Some have expressed themselves as not in favor of seeking to convert Gentiles in words like these, "Why make him exchange the seven commandments of Noah for the 613 commandments of Moses?" Jesus suggested that the Pharisees made it onerous for Proselytes (Matthew 23:15). Imagine the reaction, then, when Paul stated that Jesus had freed all that believe in Him from the Law (Acts 13:39)! "The next sabbath almost the whole city gathered together to hear the word of God" (Acts 13:44).

In the multitude that gathered were many Gentiles, and the sight of Gentiles (not Gentile Proselytes, who were acceptable) stirred up deep resentment among the Jews (Acts 13:45). This led to the great decision on the part of Paul: "It was necessary that the word of God should be spoken first to you. Since you thrust it from you, and judge yourselves unworthy of eternal life, behold, we turn to the Gentiles" (Acts 13:46).

If I understand Acts correctly, Luke has introduced this statement because it signals the beginning of a deliberate program to win Gentiles. Prior to this, if God wanted a Cornelius in the Church, there was no objection (there was a mild protest, but it was satisfactorily answered). If a few Gentiles here and there heard the message and were converted, there would be problems, but there was no overt objection. But there was no definite program to bring Gentiles into the Church. In other words, it was a Jewish-Christian Church. Paul is now launching out on a program that may make it a Gentile-Christian Church. Up to this point, the members of the Church, except for a small Gentile minority, continued to perform the ritual of Judaism. With the admission of large numbers of Gentiles, it will be only the small Jewish minority that will continue the practices of Judaism. The Gentiles "were glad" (Acts 13:48), but not the Jews.

Obviously this introduced a new problem in the young Church. When Paul and Barnabas returned to Syrian Antioch from their first journey, and told of their successes in this new Gentile campaign (Acts 14:27), they soon began to encounter opposition. Men from Judea had come and were saying, "Unless you are circumcised according to the custom of Moses, you cannot be saved" (Acts 15:1). Paul and Barnabas stubbornly rejected this doctrine, and the result was the appointing of a commission to go to Jerusalem to lay the problem before the apostles and presbyters (Acts 15:2).

This opens what is known as the Judaizer controversy, which continued in the Church for years, and its subcurrents are felt even down to the present time. The issue, bluntly stated, is simply this: *Must a Gentile become a Jew in order to become a Christian?*

We are amused by the question today. That is because we are a Gentile Church. But turn the question around: Must a Jew become a Gentile in order to become a Christian? Must an Oriental become a Westerner in order to become a Christian? Must a Negro become a white man in order to become a Christian? Basically, the question is one of second-class citizens in the Kingdom of God. Shall there be in the Church of Christ two groups: those who are saved and in addition they also keep the Law; and those inferior ones who are merely saved? Shall we erect a partition down the middle of the Church and put signs over the doors, admitting the special-class members to the one side and relegating the second-class members to the other?

It makes no difference what the "plus" is, the result will be the same. The church that establishes as a rule of membership, "In order to belong to this church, you must believe in the Lord Jesus Christ and——," regardless of what is written in the blank, comes under the Judaizer problem.

At the Jerusalem conference, the Judaizers, in reply to the report of Paul and Barnabas, stated their principle: "It is necessary to circumcise them, and to charge them to keep the law of Moses" (Acts 15:5). This was debated. Peter spoke, telling of the experience he had in the case of Cornelius, and asserting his principle, "We believe that we [Jews] shall be saved through the grace of the Lord Jesus, just as they [Gentiles] will" (Acts 15:11). Barnabas and Paul were given a chance to speak. Then James the brother of Jesus, sometimes known as the Bishop of Jerusalem, summarized the problem, and gave his judgment (Acts 15:19-20). The Church gave its answer, and appointed representatives to take that answer back to the Gentiles in Antioch of Syria. The answer: Gentiles are not to be forced to become Jews in order to become Christians! (see Acts 15:28-29).

There shall be no second-class citizens in the Kingdom of God.

The cities of Greece. Paul's new program carried him farther and farther into the Gentile world on his "second missionary journey," until he had crossed over into Europe and journeyed through Greece (Macedonia and Achaia) to Athens and Corinth. These two cities symbolize the best and the worst of the pagan world. We have seen Paul as the champion of the liberty of the gospel. Now let us see how he measures up to the problems of paganism.

Athens was in many respects the glory of Greece. Architecture, sculpture, philosophy: to say these words is to think of Athens. Standing in the Agora, proclaiming Jesus and the resurrection, Paul was looking up at the Acropolis crowned by the Parthenon. Around him were the magnificent temples and statues that today, except for the Hephaesteion, are only foundations and broken bits of marble. That is where Plato had his academy, Aristotle the lyceum, and Zeno his stoa or porch. Paul mentioned none of the wonders of the city or its history; he preached Jesus and the resurrection.[4] The council of learned men, the Areopagus, wanted to know more about this doctrine, and Paul made his address.[5]

---

[4] The word for "resurrection" in Greek is feminine and perhaps was misunderstood as a female deity (cf. the name Anastasia), which would explain the curious statement, "He seems to be a preacher of foreign divinities" (Acts 17:18).

[5] Whether the address was made before the large council or the smaller one

The two dominating philosophies at that time were Epicureanism and Stoicism. Epicureanism is atheistic and materialistic. There is no creation, no soul. Life has no higher moral purpose than self-gratification. From the Greek word for pleasure it is sometimes called hedonism, and in popular thought it is looked upon as a morally low system of thought and behavior. Actually, it can be either high or low. A person can find his highest pleasure in some of the fine things of life: nature, art, the theatre, music, literature, and the like; or he can find his highest pleasure in the base and sensual experiences. To be an Epicurean does not mean that you have to be immoral; it means that you find your greatest purpose in self-gratification. There is no God, no tomorrow, so live it up today.

Stoicism is pantheistic: everything is God. Matter is inseparable from Deity. Reason, not pleasure, should be man's guiding principle. The moral system is accordingly much higher, and scholars have found numerous points of contact between Stoicism and Christian ethics.[6] Since man is God (all is God), man is self-sufficient (to call on God for help is to call on yourself), which of course leads to pride and rugged individualism.

Paul faced these two philosophies in his address to the Areopagus. Some writers feel that Paul completely missed the mark; it seems to me that he subtly undercut the basic premises of both philosophies. He started well, by referring to "an unknown God," and proceeded to tell of the God who made the world and everything in it (certainly not the atheism of Epicureanism and not the pantheism of Stoicism!), who requires of men that they should seek Him (certainly not the self-gratification of Epicurus nor the reason or pride of Zeno's Stoicism), and who has appointed a day of judgment when the world will be judged (where is there room for a day of judgment in the no-tomorrow view of Epicureanism?). At this point, Paul moved into the presentation of Jesus (unnamed) and the resurrection (Acts 17:31).

Some mocked. Some wanted to hear more—but "later." But "some

---

of twelve men, whether it was made in the council chamber or on the hill facing the Acropolis (Mars Hill), I leave for classical scholars to debate. Except for those who demand to see "the exact spot" it makes little difference.

[6] S. V. McCasland, art. cit., Interpreter's Bible, vol. 7, p. 84, points out that the concept of universal brotherhood is not Pauline or New Testament, but Stoic, later becoming absorbed by Christian theology. J. G. Machen had already made the same observation, The Origin of Paul's Religion, p. 226.

men joined him and believed" (Acts 17:34). We are told that Paul failed; nothing happened, no church was founded, no epistles were written to Athens. But since when is the success of a preacher to be measured by the number of converts? If Paul had had only one convert in Athens, that one being Dionysius the Areopagite—which is the equivalent of invading a great university center and converting one of the intellectual leaders—his mission could not be called a failure. Far more important than numbers are key persons. If the Christian Church would stop measuring growth by numbers and set its sights on the political and intellectual leadership of the world, the influence of the gospel would be far greater—and the numbers would also increase.

If Athens was the glory of Greece, Corinth was its cesspool. Located on the trade routes, where ships from the west docked to transfer cargo to ships for the east (or, for smaller boats, to be rolled across the isthmus), Corinth was a typical liberty port. No, not quite typical, for on Acrocorinth, the hill behind the city, there was a temple of love with free prostitutes in great numbers for all who would worship the goddess of love. Look up the word "Corinthianize" in your English dictionary, and you will get a good idea of what Corinth was like. In Greek, the word is even more expressive of its sin.

The Church at Corinth was made up of men and women who had for the large part been rescued from sin. Read the letters of Paul to the Corinthians, and you will quickly learn that while the Corinthians had been taken from sin, not all sin had been taken from the Corinthians. No other church in the New Testament had the problems of immorality that we find in the Church of Corinth.

Would the Gospel of Jesus Christ meet the needs of the people in Corinth? Paul went there "in weakness and in much fear and trembling" (I Corinthians 2:3), but the Lord told him that He had many people there and Paul stayed a year and a half (Acts 18:9-11). I am sure that Paul soon lost his fear and trembling as he saw the power of the gospel at work in the lives of men and women redeemed from sin. The epistle to the Romans was written from Corinth on Paul's second (or third?) visit to that wicked city, and it is almost certain that Paul's picture of the sin of the Gentile world (Romans 1:18-32) was drawn from experiences such as he had in Corinth, as was his firm conviction that the gospel is the power of God for salvation to everyone that believes (Romans 1:16).

The churches in Asia. On his "second missionary journey," Paul had wanted to go into Asia, but was forbidden by the Spirit (Acts 16:6). "Asia" is used in Acts of the Roman province, and denotes a portion of southeastern Asia Minor. The principal city was Ephesus, an important seaport (although its importance in that respect was diminishing, due to the fact that the harbor was silting up), capital of the province, and terminus of the road that stretched across Asia Minor to the east, connecting with Syria, Palestine, and Egypt, with Mesopotamia, and with Persia and India. Paul not only visited Ephesus on his "third missionary journey," but even located there for an extended period, possibly as much as three years (Acts 19:8,10,22).

In some respects Ephesus is Paul. I am inclined to believe that Luke reserved his discussion of Paul's method until the story of Ephesus was to be told because Ephesus pictures Paul most fully.

As was customary, Paul began his work in the synagogue. Even though he had turned to the Gentiles years before (Pisidian Antioch was visited first c. A.D. 47; the Ephesian ministry began c.54), he never turned from the Jews. They were his brethren, his kinsmen, for whose conversion he could wish himself "accursed and cut off from Christ" (Romans 9:3). His invariable plan was to go to the synagogue and preach there as long as possible; at Ephesus this was about three months (Acts 19:8). Then, when that door was closed to him, he opened a school near by (at Corinth it was next door to the synagogue, Acts 18:7), taking his disciples with him.

His daily program was to teach his disciples for some period of the day, and to visit from house to house. At Ephesus he taught in the hall of Tyrannus, according to some ancient manuscripts of Acts between the hours of 11 A.M. and 4 P.M. (Acts 19:9). Some have pointed out that this is the least likely time of the day for a school; on the other hand, as visitors to the Near East know, shops are shut during these hours, the people eating their noonday meal (the main meal of the day) and taking their rest. It is precisely the time of the day that there would be no interference with the daily obligations. The house-to-house instruction is mentioned only incidentally (Acts 20:20).

At the end of two years, "all the residents of Asia heard the word of the Lord, both Jews and Greeks" (Acts 19:10). Strong churches were established at Colossae, Hierapolis, and Laodicea in the Lycus Valley almost a hundred miles to the east, and probably at Magnesia, Tralles, and Nyssa along the intervening route; it is almost certain that the other churches of Asia mentioned in Revelation were also founded at this time: Smyrna, Pergamum, Thyatira, Sardis, and Philadelphia; and there are several other places where strong churches were located early in the next century that can probably be traced to the same origin. Since Paul stayed in Ephesus to conduct his program of training, we can only conclude that Paul's disciples were busy in evangelizing the surrounding territory.

Ephesus was an important religious center, the location of the splendid temple of Artemis. This was one of the seven wonders of the ancient world, and attracted pilgrims from far and wide. The religion was a type of nature-worship,[7] honoring Cybele the mother goddess, and far removed from the Greek and Roman idea of the goddess Artemis or Diana who was the symbol of chastity. The religious concept at Ephesus had come from the east, and was spreading into the west, carrying with it grossly immoral sexual practices. The Apostle Paul, as a matter of principle, had to strike at the roots of this religious system. The way he did it is of considerable interest and importance.

The goddess Artemis was represented as a many-breasted woman, symbol of fertility. Small statues and shrines of the goddess were used in the home and probably carried on the person, perhaps as amulets, much as the more superstitious among us have small figurines of the Madonna on the dashboard of their cars. At Ephesus there was an important industry, involving a number of silversmiths, which thrived on the manufacture of silver shines of Artemis.

One day "there arose no little stir"[8] over the Christian opposition to Artemis. Demetrius, perhaps the leader of the silversmiths' union, agitated his fellow craftsmen with the words, "not only at Ephesus but almost throughout all Asia this Paul has persuaded and turned away a considerable company of people, saying that gods made with hands are not gods. And there is danger not only that this trade of ours may come into disrepute, but also that the temple of the great goddess

[7] It is hardly a mere coincidence that the concept of the "mother of God" (*theotókos*) entered the Christian Church at Ephesus via the Council of A.D. 431. For some stimulating ideas, see W. M. Ramsay, *Pauline and Other Studies* (London: Hodder and Stoughton, 1906), pp. 125-159.

[8] The careful reader of Acts will be aware of the fact that Luke often employs litotes, the figure of speech in which an affirmative is expressed by the negative of its contrary. Thus "no little stir" and "no small dissension" actually mean a large commotion and a heated argument.

Artemis may count for nothing, and that she may even be deposed from her magnificence" (Acts 19:26-27). Even allowing for understandable exaggeration such as is common in inflammatory speeches, we must understand that Paul had hurt the business of making Artemis shrines!

The riot got out of hand for a couple of hours, but finally the town clerk restored sufficient quiet to reason with the crowd. What he said should be carefully noted: After pointing out the place of honor that belonged to Ephesus because of the temple of Artemis, he went on to say, "You have brought these men here who are neither sacrilegious nor blasphemers of our goddess" (Acts 19:37).

Think of it! For two years Paul had been preaching in Ephesus. By driving home the principle that "gods made with hands are not gods," he had brought the silversmiths' business to a serious crisis. Yet in public assembly it could be said that he had never blasphemed their goddess!

That is preaching! It avoids name-calling, but gets down to the basic issues. It cuts clean with a sharp edge—but it cuts principles and not persons. Let every preacher and every missionary learn from the Apostle Paul!

CHAPTER XII

Barnabas and Mark

WE HAVE ALREADY learned that there were disciples and apostles among the followers of Jesus, and that before a man could become an apostle he had to be a disciple. We have learned that Jesus chose twelve of His disciples and commissioned them as apostles; they are the Twelve Apostles, or simply the Twelve.

There are other apostles in the New Testament. Matthias was chosen to fill the place vacated by Judas; Paul is called an apostle, likewise James the brother of Jesus, and Barnabas whom we shall study in this chapter. In Romans 16:7, Adronicus and Junias are mentioned in such a way that they may be called apostles,[1] and in I Thessalonians 2:6, it is probable that Silas (Silvanus) is included as an apostle. That seems to complete the list. Timothy is definitely excluded by the opening words of Second Corinthians and Colossians. Apollos is not named as an apostle in Scripture, and he seems to be ruled out by the words of Clement, who probably knew him, and who certainly knew the Corinthian Church.[2]

A clear understanding of the New Testament usage of the term "apostle" will help us better to understand the idea of "apostolic succession." If the first prerequisite of the office was that a man should have been an eyewitness to the resurrection, that establishes a clear dividing line. Timothy, who was converted in Lystra (or possibly

[1] The expression, "They are men of note among the apostles," according to James Denney, is as vague in Greek as in English, and may or may not mean that they were apostles; see *The Expositor's Greek Testament* (reprint; Grand Rapids, Mich.: Wm. B. Eerdmans Publishing Co., n.d.), vol. 2, p. 719. The Church Fathers understood it to mean that they were apostles; cf. W. Sanday and A. C. Headlam, *A Critical and Exegetical Commentary on the Epistle to the Romans* (International Critical Commentary; 5th edition; Edinburgh: T. & T. Clark, 1902), p. 423.

[2] The First Epistle of Clement to the Corinthians, *The Ante-Nicene Fathers,* vol. 1, p. 18 (chap. 47); as the passage is constructed, "towards apostles . . . and towards a man" can only refer to the apostles Paul and Cephas and the man Apollos.

Derbe), and Apollos, who came from Alexandria and was given fuller instruction in Ephesus, obviously could not meet that qualification. Andronicus and Junias, on the other hand, who were Christians before Paul's conversion (cf. Romans 16:7), could have had the opportunity of witnessing the risen Lord in Palestine. Most emphatic is Paul's argument, "Am I not an apostle? Have I not seen Jesus our Lord?" (I Corinthians 9:1). On this basis, the only apostolic succession can be a succession in the work, and not a succession in the qualifications: in other words, a much looser usage of the term.[3]

Barnabas was, beyond all doubt, an apostle (Acts 14:14). He had seen the Lord, and he had been commissioned by the Church at Antioch for the work. There is no doubt that he was commissioned as an apostle to the Gentiles (Acts 13:2; 15:12). Barnabas manifested the signs of an apostle (II Corinthians 12:12). We might devote an entire study to the apostolic office; but I prefer to look at a different side of Barnabas: I would like to study him as a man who had faith in people.

Barnabas and the Early Church... We first meet Barnabas in the fourth chapter of Acts. His name was Joseph, and the apostles had called him "bar-Nabas," an Aramaic expression meaning "son of encouragement (or exhortation)" (Acts 4:36). He was a native of Cyprus, a Levite, and he owned a field or possibly several fields (Acts 4:36-37)—which was contrary to the Law, for the tribe of Levi was not supposed to have a land inheritance; but this law was not always observed. Barnabas was considered as a prophet and teacher by the Church (Acts 13:1), and "a good man, full of the Holy Spirit and of faith" (Acts 11:24). It is possible that he, like Paul, was not married— but the reference is not clear (I Corinthians 9:5-6).[4]

Barnabas was probably robust and attractive. When he and Paul were in Lystra, after Paul had healed a cripple, the people wanted to honor the visitors, saying, "The gods have come down to us in the likeness of men!" They thought Barnabas was Zeus and Paul was Hermes (Acts 14:11-12). Statues of Zeus that have been preserved

[3] For an important discussion, see J. B. Lightfoot, *St. Paul's Epistle to the Galatians* (7th edition; London: Macmillan and Co., 1881), pp. 92-101.

[4] In the fifth verse Paul is discussing the apostle's right to be married, and in the sixth verse, the apostle's right to work with his hands. Barnabas is mentioned in verse 6, hence it would seem that he is also included in the "we" of verse 5.

from ancient times always present him as a big, husky, handsome man, the chief of the gods. Hermes was his messenger.[5]

Barnabas is introduced to us in an account telling that he sold a field and gave the proceeds to the apostles, to meet the needs of members of the Early Church. The Church's efforts in this difficult situation are sometimes called "communism," but this is a misnomer. In the first place, the practice was not applied to the State but only to the Church, and there is never any indication that the apostles intended either to extend it to other areas beyond the Jerusalem Church or to present it as an ideal for the State. In the second place, it was purely voluntary and in no sense compulsory, as the subsequent story of Ananias and Sapphira clearly states (Acts 5:4). The Church was attempting to solve a serious problem in a commendable way: those who had more than they needed sold their goods and gave the money to the apostles; those who had less than they needed received from the apostles to meet their needs (Acts 4:34).[6] Barnabas felt the sense of community, the oneness of the Church, and entered into this demonstration of Christian love.

That was an indication of his faith in the Church, and his faith in the people that make up the Church. In order to enter into a movement of this kind, you have to believe that men will not take advantage of the situation. Christian charity and all welfare efforts break down, or at least stagger, under the burden of freeloaders. I am perfectly willing to help the man who cannot help himself, but I am unwilling to make my productive abilities available to someone who is just as able to take care of his wife and family as I am. For the same reason I resent the intrusion of the State at this point.

Now I suppose the Early Church was more ideal in some ways than the Church of the modern day—at least this is what we are told sometimes. And yet as I study the Book of Acts, I think I can honestly conclude that even the Early Church was not without its share of men and women who wanted to take advantage of others.

But when we have expressed our negative feelings, and agreed that in this sinful society, even in the Church of the redeemed (which

[5] An early tradition of Paul, incidentally, describes him as short, bowlegged, bald-headed, with meeting eyebrows and a long nose. Cf. The Acts of Paul and Thecla, *The Ante-Nicene Fathers,* vol. 8, p. 487.

[6] The Marxist ideal is sometimes quoted, "From each according to his ability, to each according to his need." We have no objection to the ideal; it is the method of enforcing it that is significant: in communism it is the State; in the Church it is love.

is not without sin in this world), the idealism of the Early Church is not practical, we still rejoice to find someone like Barnabas. Whether or not his faith in people was always justified, he had something that we would like to have. The Church will be poor indeed when it has no men like Barnabas, men with great faith in their fellow man.

Barnabas and Saul.   After Saul was converted, he went to Jerusalem and attempted to join the disciples (Acts 9:26). Saul had been in Jerusalem before, and the disciples knew all about him: he was the key figure in the persecution that had broken out following the stoning of Stephen (Acts 8:1, 3). Saul had become so personally involved in the anti-Christian movement that he had gone to Damascus to persecute the disciples in that city. As a result, the Christians in Jerusalem wanted nothing to do with him. We know, of course, that in the meantime Saul had been converted and had returned to Jerusalem to try to make amends for his former hatred and persecution. They did not know that, or if they had heard it, they did not believe it.

But Barnabas did believe it. He took Saul to the apostles (according to Paul's account, he saw only Peter and James the brother of Jesus; Galatians 1:18-19), and "declared to them how on the road he had seen the Lord, who spoke to him, and how at Damascus he had preached boldly in the name of Jesus" (Acts 9:27). The intercession of Barnabas on Saul's behalf was successful, and Saul was able to initiate a ministry that only had its beginnings in Jerusalem. I think we agree that it was a good thing there was somebody like Barnabas in the church at Jerusalem. Speaking from the human viewpoint, we would have to admit that if Saul had been unsuccessful in meeting the apostles in Jerusalem (even though, as he asserted, he received nothing to add to his gospel from them), he would have had an extremely difficult if not impossible task. For whether or not he received his gospel from the apostles, he still had to have their credential; his letter to the Galatians, as a matter of fact, depends in a large part for the force of its argument on the fact that his apostleship had been accepted by the apostles (Galatians 2:9).[7]

Again at Antioch, Barnabas demonstrated his faith in Saul of

---

[7] This side of the argument is often played down in the effort to stress the independency of Paul's gospel. But Paul's whole ministry, his periodic return to Jerusalem and to Antioch to report on his work, and particularly his part in the great discussion at the Jerusalem conference, deny any notion of independency. To him the Church was a body, and no part could say of any other, "I have no need of you" (I Corinthians 12:12-26).

Tarsus. After telling the story of the scattering of the Church by describing Peter's work in Samaria (Acts 9:32—11:18), Luke picks up another thread of the story: "Now those who were scattered because of the persecution that arose over Stephen traveled as far as Phoenicia and Cyprus and Antioch, speaking the word to none except Jews. But there were some of them, men of Cyprus and Cyrene, who on coming to Antioch spoke to the Greeks also, preaching the Lord Jesus. And the hand of the Lord was with them, and a great number that believed turned to the Lord" (Acts 11:19-21). News of this work reached Jerusalem, and the Church in Jerusalem sent Barnabas to Antioch to find out what was going on—at least I can only conclude that the mission was a kind of investigation, for as yet the Church felt no sense of call to a ministry of this type.

The word "Greek" needs to be defined.[8] We have previously seen that Luke uses "Hellenist" in a special sense, meaning a Jew who spoke Greek. He likewise uses "Greek" in a special sense, meaning Gentile. The classical use of the word "Greek" set it over against "barbarian" but this is found only once in the New Testament (Romans 1:14). In Luke the term "Greek" seems to include even barbarians (cf. Acts 14:1 and perhaps 16:1). This is another step outward, then, in the progress of the preaching of the Early Church. It is an emphasis, made by some, designed to reach Gentiles. We cannot yet describe it as a deliberate plan or program of the Church; that did not occur, as we have seen, until the first missionary journey a year or more later. Those who initiated the work among Gentiles were men from Cyprus and Cyrene, doubtless Jews of the Dispersion who were sufficiently Hellenized that they had a sense of mission to Gentiles and freedom to put it into practice. They had been converted to Christianity in Jerusalem (note that "some of them" refers back to "those who were scattered"), but their eyes were on the world. They had listened to the words of Jesus carefully, whether from His lips or from those of His faithful disciples, and they knew that the gospel was to be preached to all the world.

Barnabas saw the work in Antioch as a demonstration of the grace of God and he rejoiced. He not only rejoiced; he encouraged the work, and as a result, "a large company was added to the Lord" (cf. Acts 11:22-24). More than that, he saw the possibility of expanding the

---

[8] Some manuscripts read "Hellenists" in Acts 11:20. Internal evidence, however, requires "Greeks."

work still further if he could get the right man to help him—and
Barnabas knew the right man, and he thought he knew where to find
him. So he went to Tarsus to look for Saul (Acts 11:25). It took time,
but it resulted in a wonderful year of Christian activity in Antioch,
and more than that—but let us not run ahead of the story.

I wonder why Barnabas thought of Saul? We have a ready answer:
"Saul was the apostle to the Gentiles." But is that the right answer?
Did Barnabas know that at that time? Was Barnabas even thinking
in terms of a Gentile ministry at that time? Antioch-on-the-Orontes
was a huge city, perhaps one of the most beautiful ever built, and,
as third largest city of the empire, capital of the East. There was a
large Jewish population there. There were probably many Proselytes.
Even without thinking of a Gentile ministry, Barnabas saw a great
opportunity.[9] But why Saul? What had he been doing? Some tell
us that after leaving Jerusalem (Acts 9:30), Saul went to Tarsus and
spent about ten years making goat-hair cloth. I doubt it! Barnabas
did not want a weaver, he wanted a preacher. The letter from the
Jerusalem conference was addressed "to the brethren who are of the
Gentiles in Antioch and Syria and Cilicia" (Acts 15:23). Syria-and-
Cilicia was the name of the Roman province around Antioch, including Tarsus. At the start of his second missionary journey, Paul
visited the Churches of Syria and Cilicia to strengthen them (Acts
15:41). Where did these Churches come from? Paul told the Galatians that after he left Jerusalem he went into "the regions of Syria
and Cilicia" (Galatians 1:21). It is my belief that Saul had spent ten
years or so preaching in the province around his home town.[10] I think
Barnabas knew something of that work. I think it took Barnabas some
little time to find Saul because he was out preaching; if he had been
weaving, Barnabas could have found him quickly. Barnabas wanted a
man with experience for the work that was opening up. Saul was the
man.

The Church in Antioch was led by the Spirit to commission

[9] The fact that believers were first called "Christians" in Antioch is too well
known to need repetition, Acts 11:26. I should point out, however, that the
author of Acts is much more careful than I have been in the use of the term, and
where I have spoken of "Christians" before this point in the history of the
Church, Luke would have used one of several synonyms, "disciples," "believers,"
"those of the way," etc.

[10] R. C. H. Lenski, on the other hand, takes a strongly opposite view in *The
Interpretation of the Acts of the Apostles* (Columbus, Ohio: Lutheran Book
Concern, 1934), pp. 372-373, 615.

Barnabas and Saul for the work to which He had called them (Acts 13:2). This was the beginning of organized missionary activity by the Early Church. Their first journey took them to Cyprus and to the south-central portion of Asia Minor.

Why did they go to Cyprus? I think it is obvious: Barnabas came from there. He had friends, and probably relatives, who lived in Cyprus, and he wanted them to hear the gospel. It is a sound missionary principle to start where you have the most in common with your hearers. Failure to apply this principle is perhaps the greatest single reason for the vast number of missionaries (estimated at between 50 and 80 per cent) who do not return to the field after their first term of service. Before Barnabas and Saul set out on their first missionary journey, they had had at least twelve or thirteen years of Christian service. Even then, they went into an area that one of them knew, and among people with whom they had something in common.

Barnabas and Mark. Barnabas and Saul took with them on their missionary journey a young man named John (Acts 13:5) who was also named Mark (Acts 12:12). The expression, "And they had John to assist [or, minister to] them," is not clear; some think that Mark performed personal services, others think that he helped to catechize the converts.

John Mark was a cousin of Barnabas (Colossians 4:10). Mark's mother Mary (Acts 12:12) was a prominent woman in the Church in Jerusalem, and it was in her house that the disciples were praying for Peter when he had been seized by Herod. From this the inference has been drawn that Mary had a large house and the double inference that she was wealthy. Some have supposed that the Last Supper was held in an upper room in her house, and that the disciples waited in prayer for the Holy Spirit in that same Upper Room.[11] Mary the mother of Mark cannot be identified with any other Mary in the New Testament.

John Mark was called "my son Mark" by Peter (I Peter 5:13). On the strength of the parallel whereby Paul calls Timothy his son, many

[11] This guessing game goes even further. The young man who wore only a linen cloth and who lost it in the Garden of Gethsemane (Mark 14:51-52) was Mark. He knew where Jesus would be, because he overheard the discussion in his mother's house. He knew the soldiers had come for Jesus, for they came first to Mary's house. He wore only a sheet because he had not taken time to dress, but ran to warn Jesus. All guesses!

conclude that Mark was converted by Peter's preaching—and this is possible. We must point out, however, that it is not certain that Paul converted Timothy, for Timothy's mother and grandmother were believers (II Timothy 1:5); it is possible that "son" in the case of both Timothy and Mark refers to association and training in Christian service.

We first meet Mark in the year A.D. 44, when he is already a Christian and a respected member of the Church in Jerusalem. When Barnabas and Saul returned to Antioch, after their famine-visit to Jerusalem (cf. Acts 11:27-30), they took Mark with them (Acts 12:25). As we have seen, they subsequently took Mark on the first missionary journey.

Later, Mark was associated with Peter, and still later, he wrote the Gospel called by his name. According to an early tradition of the Church, Mark served as interpreter on Peter's missionary journeys, and after Peter's death Mark wrote down the words of Peter.[12] This would account for the graphic style of the Gospel of Mark. If the early Christian preachers used catechetical methods of instruction, as seems likely, and if Mark assisted the apostles in this instruction, this would account for formal elements of the Second Gospel, which in turn would account for some of the verbal agreements between Mark and other Gospel sources.[13]

When the apostolic mission reached Perga, John Mark turned back. We are not told why, but we know that it caused a serious breach between Paul and Barnabas (Acts 15:39). Various suggestions have been given concerning the cause of Mark's defection. Some think he had experienced a great deal of sickness; it is entirely possible in that part of the world. Some think he was worrying about his mother; that too is possible, and many men have had to give up work they would like to do for the sake of the parents they love. Some think he was afraid; I am inclined to doubt that reason. It seems to me that the "sharp contention" between Paul and Barnabas, however, requires a much more significant reason than any of these expressed. The only

[12] For a summary of the numerous sources of this tradition, see H. B. Swete, *The Gospel According to St. Mark* (3d edition; London: Macmillan and Co., 1927), pp. xxiii-xxiv.

[13] This is certainly not the place to get into a discussion of Source- and Form-Criticism. For a helpful introduction to the subject, see F. F. Bruce, *The New Testament Documents*, pp. 29-46. On the catechetical motives, see Vincent Taylor, *The Gospel According to St. Mark* (London: Macmillan and Co., 1952), p. 133.

reason that would have sufficient magnitude would be one arising from the Judaizer problem. Paul seemed to be able to tolerate almost anything else; but when anyone suggested that anything should be added to the gospel of grace, Paul could find no point of compromise. On this issue he was willing to censure Peter, yes, even Barnabas (Galatians 2:11-14). As I reconstruct the situation, Mark had found Paul's work with Gentiles contrary to his own view of the Law. When it became obvious that they were going to move into territory where Gentiles would predominate, Mark drew the line. He went home.

Barnabas still had faith in Mark. When the Jerusalem conference was over, and Paul said, "Come, let us return and visit the brethren in every city where we proclaimed the word of the Lord" (Acts 15:36), Barnabas said, "Fine; let's take Mark with us." When Paul stubbornly refused, "Barnabas took Mark with him and sailed away to Cyprus, but Paul chose Silas . . ." (Acts 15:39-40). That Mark justified the faith Barnabas put in him, even Paul would admit. Years later, when Paul was in prison waiting for the executioner's sword, he wrote to Timothy, "Get Mark and bring him with you; for he is very useful in serving me" (II Timothy 4:11). What would have happened if Barnabas had not had faith in Mark? Humanly speaking, it is possible that Mark would have dropped out of Christian work altogether. If we had not had his Gospel, we would not have had either Matthew's or Luke's Gospels, for they draw large portions from Mark. But God would not let a man like John Mark get away—that was one of the reasons why He had Barnabas!

Barnabas was not perfect; no one is. The Bible presents its characters without make-up; we see them as they really were—and that is encouragement for the rest of us. Barnabas lost sight of the need of preserving the pure gospel and Christian unity. Under the pressure of Peter and others, he "was carried away by their insincerity," and had to be sternly rebuked by Paul (Galatians 2:13). I am not trying to excuse Barnabas; I am convinced that Paul was absolutely right in his intransigence at this point. The purity of the gospel must be preserved at all cost. The unity of the Church cannot be denied by the erection of a special class of Christians. But I wonder if even at this point it was not Barnabas's faith in people that got him into difficulty. I wonder if he was not trusting the brothers who had come from Jerusalem, if he was not trusting Peter's hasty action, rather than pursuing cold logic.

Well, it did not destroy Paul's respect for him. Paul speaks of Barnabas only in terms of appreciation. Even in the situation described in Galatians, Paul mentions Barnabas, but he puts the burden of his argument on Peter. After all, you can't help loving a man like Barnabas!

CHAPTER XIII

Luke the Beloved Physician

THERE IS ONLY one Gentile author included in the Bible: Luke, who wrote the Third Gospel and Acts. That Luke was a Gentile is clearly indicated in Colossians, where Aristarchus, Mark, and Jesus Justus are distinguished from Epaphras, Luke, and Demas, the first three being "the only men of the circumcision among my fellow workers" (Colossians 4:11), and therefore the only Jews.[1] The writings of this lone Gentile, which comprise the largest part of the New Testament by any single writer, are magnificent literature. Even a man who is not interested in the spiritual values of the writings will appreciate the literary qualities, the composition, style, and other elements, of Luke's works. Luke's appreciation of beauty is evident often, but perhaps especially in the fact that he alone of the New Testament writers recorded the hymns, *Benedictus, Magnificat,* and *Nunc Dimittis,* hymns which have become part of the liturgy of the Church.

Luke the physician. Luke was a scientific man and a doctor. I used to love to make that statement to the college students in my course at Lafayette College. Naturally, it would raise an immediate objection. "Doctor? Witch doctor, maybe! How would you like to have Luke operate on you?" Well, now let us stop a minute and think.

The science of medicine has a great history, and it is worth our while to review some of the facts. When Galen of Pergamum (A.D. 130-200) wrote his medical treatises, medical science had reached a high point which it did not exceed for thirteen hundred years. In fact, no further advances were made in medical science until the nineteenth century. But medical science did not begin with Galen;

---

[1] In spite of the clear statement in Scripture, an occasional author, trying to defend the theory that Romans 3:2 requires that all Scripture writers be Jews, insists that Luke was a Jew. Romans 3:2 refers to the Old Testament. Moreover, if God was breaking down the wall that separated Jews and Gentiles, why would this not also apply to the writers of Scripture?

as a matter of fact, it ended with him in antiquity. Medicine achieved greater advances between the sixth century B.C. and the second century A.D. than at any other time in history until the last century and a half. But even that is not the beginning of medicine.

The origins of medicine are lost in antiquity. The Egyptians looked upon Imhotep (c.2700 B.C.) as a sort of patron saint of medicine. Egyptian medical texts go back to c.1700 B.C., but it is questionable, in my opinion, whether these deserve the term "scientific," for they are "a hodge-podge of home remedies based on a lore of herbs and of sympathetic magic, outright witch-doctoring in the forms of charms and incantations, and shrewd observation on the functions of the body."[2] It seems there was some knowledge of broken bones, and possibly the setting of them; and certainly the knowledge of the abdominal cavity and its organs had been learned from the process of mummification, but no scientific knowledge is recorded. In Mesopotamia medical skill was more nearly a science. A Sumerian text from c.2200 B.C. contains a collection of prescriptions which has been called "the oldest medical 'handbook' known to man";[3] it is notably lacking in magic spells and incantations. In the Code of Hammurabi (c.1700 B.C.), laws regulated the amount physicians could charge for operations and for bone-setting (§§ 215-225). One operation, the meaning of which is not entirely clear, seems to be for an ulcer or abscess of the eye, and some scholars think it means a cataract.[4] The penalty for destroying the eye, we should add, was the loss of the surgeon's hand—which certainly limited the number of failures the doctor could make! Grave excavations at Mycenae (dated 1650-1550 B.C.) have uncovered skulls that give clear evidence of skillful trepanation (brain surgery performed by removing a piece of the skull),[5] and in one instance, at least, the patient recovered, for the bone had partially grown back over the saw-cuts.

Strictly speaking, however, these were skills rather than science. The rise of science can be dated to the sixth century B.C., and was

[2] J.A. Wilson, *The Culture of Ancient Egypt* (Chicago: University of Chicago Press, 1956), p. 56. This work was published in 1951 under the title, *The Burden of Egypt*.

[3] Samuel Noah Kramer, *From the Tablets of Sumer* (Indian Hills, Colo.: Falcon's Wing Press, 1956), pp. 56-60.

[4] Cf. G. R. Driver and John C. Miles, *The Babylonian Laws* (Oxford: Clarendon Press, 1955), vol. 2, pp. 78-81 and 251-253.

[5] Cf. George E. Mylonas, *Ancient Mycenae* (Princeton: Princeton University Press, 1957), p. 138.

largely due to the Greek ability to abstract principles from empirical data.[6] In medicine, the name of Hippocrates (460?-377? B.C.) is significant, and the *Collection of Hippocrates,* dealing with wounds of the head, is a model of what succinct clinical records ought to be. Herophilus of Chalcedon is regarded as the father of anatomy, and Erasistratus of Chios as the father of physiology. The body had been dissected, and the brain, nervous system and circulatory system had been explored (although some of the theories make us smile today). The center of medical science was along the Ionian coast of the Aegean Sea—which is where Luke seems to have spent much of his life.

Luke was a scientist. Science is the process of observation, comparison, control, and deduction, or the abstracting of principles. That method was already well known in the Greek world and particularly in the medical world, and Luke was heir to a science of medicine that could compare favorably with any medical practice up to the early part of the last century.

According to some scholars, Luke was born in Syrian Antioch. He certainly shows great familiarity with Antioch and with the Church there. Others think that Luke came from Philippi in Macedonia. We first cross his trail in Troas (Acts 16:10; his use of "we" will be discussed shortly), and he is personally involved in the apostolic mission to Philippi. Luke was apparently a Christian before he met Paul, but we have no knowledge of his conversion. There is some rather convincing evidence that Luke was familiar with the sea and with ships; and the suggestion that he was at one time a ship's doctor would fit in with this evidence. We know that Paul had some kind of affliction that he refers to, and the suggestion has been made that Luke was called in to treat Paul. All these suggestions are attractive—but we must bear in mind that they are only suggestions, not established facts.

Some years ago one scholar made a detailed study of the medical language of Luke,[7] and was convinced (and convinced others) that

[6] For an illuminating treatment, see Benjamin Farrington, *Greek Science* (Pelican Book A142; Baltimore, Md.: Penguin Books, 1953), 320 pp. It is not generally known that, working from philosophy, mathematics, and observations, the Greeks had computed the circumference of the earth to within about two hundred miles and had conceived of its sphericity three centuries before Christ. See Strabo, *Geography*, 2.5.7 and 34 on size, and 2.5.2 and 10 on shape.

[7] William K. Hobart, *The Medical Language of St. Luke* (Dublin: Hodges, Figgis & Co., 1882; reprinted, Grand Rapids, Mich.: Baker Book House, 1954), 305 pp.

the evidence demonstrated that Luke was a physician. He proved too much, and modern scholars have reacted perhaps too far in the other direction; but at any rate it is safe to say that Luke's medical profession, if established by other evidence, would account for his use of technical terminology. There is other evidence. Luke shows great interest in healing. Of the four Gospel writers, he is the only one to tell of the Good Samaritan (Luke 10:25-37), the casting out of the demons (Luke 11:14-36), the healing of the man with dropsy (Luke 14:1-6), the healing of the woman with the unclean spirit (Luke 13: 10-17), and the cleansing of the ten lepers (Luke 17:11-19). Likewise in Acts, he tells of the healing of the lame man at the Temple gate (Acts 3:1-8), the healing of Aeneas (Acts 9:33-34), the healing of the cripple at Lystra (Acts 14:8-10), the resuscitation of Eutychus at Troas (Acts 20:9-12), and the curing of Publius' father on Malta (Acts 28:7-10).

Luke shows a deep interest in women and children, which would also be true of a medical doctor. Of the Gospel writers, Luke alone records the details of the birth stories and the childhood details (Luke 1:5—2:52). He alone tells of the raising of the widow's son (Luke 7:11-17), of the anointing of Jesus by the sinful woman (Luke 7:36-50);[8] he alone tells the story of Martha and Mary (Luke 10:38-42), and the parable of the importunate widow (Luke 18:1-14). Likewise in Acts, women are included at numerous points in the story of the Early Church.

In the account of Paul's healing ministry on Malta there is an indication that Luke may have added his medical skill to Paul's miraculous healing. Two different Greek words are used: the first in the statement "and Paul visited him and prayed, and putting his hands on him healed him" (Acts 28:8), where the word conveys the idea of healing brought to its completion; the second word is used in the next verse, "the rest of the people on the island who had diseases also came and were cured" (Acts 28:9), where the word conveys the idea of the healing process from its beginning.[9] We might paraphrase by saying that Paul healed the first, Paul and Luke treated and cured the others. Is this why Luke records, "They presented many gifts to us"?

[8] See my note, p. 63, above.
[9] The first word is from *iáomai* "to heal," the second from *therapeúō* "to treat medically, to cure."

Luke the historian. In the providence of God this man with scientifically trained powers of observation became the historian of the Early Church. The opening of his Gospel gives an idea of his method and purpose: "Inasmuch as many have undertaken to compile a narrative of the things which have been accomplished among us, just as they were delivered to us by those who from the beginning were eyewitnesses and ministers of the word, it seemed good to me also, having followed all things closely for some time past, to write an orderly account for you . . ." (Luke 1:1-3).

Luke states at once in the Gospel that he was not an eyewitness; he used available sources. There are some believers who hold such a narrow view of inspiration that they feel we dishonor the Holy Spirit when we speak of sources. The historic view of inspiration teaches that the Holy Spirit inspired men in their use of materials, including sources.

In the case of Acts, on the other hand, Luke was an eyewitness of some of the things he had recorded. In Acts 16:10, the first person pronoun "we" slips unobtrusively into the record, and continues to verse 17; the account then is told in the third person ("he" or "they"). In Acts 20:5 another "we" section occurs, continuing to Acts 21:25; and a third "we" section is found from Acts 27:2 to 28:16. Now the name of Luke does not occur in the Book of Acts. The question therefore naturally arises, How do we know that "we" is intended to include Luke; is there any way to check on this? There is. The periods covered by the "we" passages are the following: from Troas to Philippi on the second missionary journey, from Philippi to Caesarea on the third journey, and from Caesarea to Rome on the first journey to Rome. We can find in the writings of Paul indications of these periods and references to his associates. Luke is mentioned in the New Testament only three times: two of these references are from the Roman imprisonment (Colossians 4:14; Philemon 23), which agrees with the third "we" section.

Have you ever heard of Aristarchus? He was not a very important person, so far as the record goes; he is mentioned only five times in the New Testament. Paul mentions him twice: each time in connection with Luke (Colossians 4:10; Philemon 24). The other three references are in Acts (19:29; 20:4; and 27:2)—in each instance in a "we" passage. It is clear, then, that when Aristarchus was present Luke was also present. Speaking for myself, I am convinced that this is no mere coincidence, and that Luke was Paul's companion for the parts of Acts indicated.[10]

For the balance of the material in Acts, Luke used sources. From the itinerary sketched by the "we" sections, we can tell with reasonable certainty what some of these sources may have been. There was Paul, of course, who could have told Luke all about the stoning of Stephen, his own conversion, the first missionary journey, the Jerusalem conference, and all the other details that involved Paul when Luke was not present personally. There was Silas, who certainly knew important details of the Jerusalem Church, for he was one of the leaders there (Acts 15:22). At Caesarea there was Philip the evangelist (Acts 21:8), who surely knew the details of the choosing of the Seven (the deacons) and the conversion of the Ethiopian, as well as the story of Simon Magus and other incidents in Samaria (Acts 6 and 8). Since Luke was present in Caesarea both at the end of the third journey and at the beginning of the journey to Rome, it is a reasonable supposition that he remained in the general area for the intervening two years, and it is also reasonable to suppose that he used some of this time to collect material for the Third Gospel. The sources for this material would be able to furnish information for the remainder of the early chapters of Acts.

Luke has gathered together in Acts an amazing mass of detail. According to one scholar, one hundred and ten persons are named in Acts.[11] Place names, geographical details, official names and titles, with other factual data, are found on every page. In 1880, William M. Ramsay made his first visit to Asia Minor, the beginning of research that was to occupy him for the next thirty-four years. He was a classics scholar, with a critical view of the Scriptures. As he became acquainted with detail after detail, fact after fact, he came to realize that Luke was the master historian. In 1911 Ramsay stated: "Every person is found just where he ought to be: proconsuls in senatorial provinces, asiarchs in Ephesus, strategoi in Philippi, politarchs in Thessalonica, magicians and soothsayers everywhere."[12] Ramsay's

---

[10] For a recent and full discussion, see A. H. McNeile, *An Introduction to the Study of the New Testament* (2d edition, revised by C. S. C. Williams; Oxford: Clarendon Press, 1953), pp. 103-110.

[11] Lenski, *Interpretation of the Acts of the Apostles*, p. 5.

[12] W. M. Ramsay, *The Bearing of Recent Discovery on the Trustworthiness of*

many volumes have had considerable effect on many scholars, and have convinced not a few of the general correctness of his conclusions.

Luke has preserved the color, the character, the verisimilitude of widely different persons and situations. The speeches he has preserved retain the personal characteristics of the speakers. The local customs are accurately reflected. Life is filled with endless variety; Luke has observed that variety, and recorded the details with unerring eye and ear. Peter is Peter and Paul is Paul; Antioch is Antioch and Athens is Athens. Try to record the details of your travels sometime (I have tried, often!), and you will appreciate Luke as never before. Try to portray an imaginary journey, and you will realize how empty is the argument that Luke wrote fiction. Hollywood hired technical advisors for the production of a Biblical film and when they were finished, scholars in the audience laughed at the errors in detail. Luke had no staff of technical advisors, no research library, no electronic equipment. And Sir William Ramsay, who had few peers in classical studies and none in the historical geography of Asia Minor, could find no flaw in Luke's production! Luke was a scientifically trained historian.

Luke the evangelist. Luke wrote his books not just to write, but to save a soul. Scholars are generally convinced that he had in mind a larger circle of readers—and possibly he did. But the undeniable fact is that he addressed both works to Theophilus for the express purpose of setting the truth before Theophilus. He wanted to present the story of Jesus Christ in the most convincing form, which was to tell the truth with beauty and clarity; likewise he wanted to present the story of the origin of the Christian faith. There are some who believe that Theophilus was a dignitary in a place of authority, and that Luke was using this means of writing Paul's defense. This may be so. I feel, however, that as a defense of Paul the works are too subtle to accomplish the purpose. That Theophilus was a person entitled to be addressed with honor and respect is evident from the words of Luke, "most excellent Theophilus."

Luke is called "the Evangelist" because he wrote the Gospel that

---

the New Testament (2d edition; London: Hodder and Stoughton, 1915; reprinted Grand Rapids, Mich.: Baker Book House, 1953), pp. 96-97. The lecture was delivered in 1911.

bears his name. I am using the term here, however, in the broader sense: Luke was at heart an evangelist. He wanted to proclaim the Evangel, the Good News. When Luke first met Paul, Silas, and Timothy, they were at Troas. That is the last place in Asia: before you lies the narrow water that separates Asia from Europe, and Europe can be seen very clearly. We read that Paul saw a vision in the night, a man of Macedonia, urging Paul, "Come over to Macedonia and help us" (Acts 16:9). Some think this vision was caused by the plea which Luke had been making on behalf of Macedonia. It is an interesting suggestion. We know that the subconscious often works at night on problems that we have tried to thrust aside during the day.

Philippi was "the leading city of the district of Macedonia" (Acts 16:12). Named for Philip II of Macedon, the city overlooked the Plain of Drama, where in 168 b.c. the Roman general Aemilius Paulus had overcome the last of the Macedonian kings, and where in 42 b.c. Brutus and Cassius were slain and the hopes of the Roman Republic died before a rising Empire. But most important, it was from Philippi that Alexander the Great went forth to conquer the world. Luke was proud of Philippi; that is one reason why he is often identified with the city. Perhaps he looked upon it as the place to defeat the empires of the world and to start a kingdom not of the world. Perhaps he thought that a Greater than Alexander had come. But we are only speculating. One thing we do know: Paul and his party went into Europe, to Philippi, and Luke was with them.

There, by the river outside the city, for there was no synagogue (which means that there were not ten male Jewish property-owners in the city), a woman from Thyatira in Asia Minor, a business woman, a Gentile woman who had come to worship the God of the Jews, heard the gospel and was converted. She was Lydia. Her house became the meeting place of the Church in Philippi (Acts 16:11-40). At Philippi a slave girl was delivered from a spirit of divination (Acts 16:16-19). The Church there grew and came to be known as one of the most generous of the Pauline churches (Philippians 4:14-18). Every morning the Jew blesses the Lord who has not created him a Gentile, a slave, or a woman (*Talmud Berakoth* 60b).[13] Paul may have had

---

[13] The reference is taken from Philip Birnbaum, *Daily Prayer Book* (New York: Hebrew Publishing Company, 1949), pp. 16, 18. The prayer runs, "Blessed art thou, Lord our God, King of the universe, who hast not made me

such a prayer in mind when he wrote, "There is neither Jew nor Greek, there is neither slave nor free, there is neither male nor female; for you are all one in Christ Jesus" (Galatians 3:28). At Philippi, the conversion of the Gentile woman Lydia and the healing of the Gentile slave girl testify strongly to this principle of oneness in Christ.

Luke remained at Philippi when Paul and the others moved west to Thessalonica. He rejoined Paul perhaps four or five years later when Paul was enroute to Jerusalem. In the meantime it is possible that Luke had been sent to Corinth. In II Corinthians 8:18 there is a curious verse that has puzzled Biblical scholars for centuries. Paul was planning to send Titus to Corinth, and he adds, "With him we are sending the brother who is famous among all the churches for his preaching of the gospel." Who is this brother? As early as the time of Origen (A.D. 185?-254?), he was identified as Luke. (This would explain, in my opinion, the absence of the name Titus from Acts, if he were Luke's brother.) In a colophon at the end of II Corinthians, found in some manuscripts of the eighth and ninth centuries and in some English editions, are the words, "Written from Philippi by Titus and Luke." This would support the view that the brother sent with Titus was Luke. Once again, it is interesting speculation, and may indeed be true.

Luke's interest in the gospel of salvation, however, is not speculation. It is firmly established. His Gospel alone records the parables of the lost coin, the lost sheep, and the prodigal son and his lost brother (Luke 15). His Gospel alone tells the story of Zacchaeus, who climbed a tree to see Jesus, and whose house Jesus graced with the words: "Today salvation has come to this house. . . . For the Son of man came to seek and to save the lost" (Luke 19:1-10). The Book of Acts is the message of salvation from beginning to end. The disciples waited until they had received the Holy Spirit; then they began the preaching of the gospel. Stephen was chosen to serve tables, but he preached the gospel. Saul was the persecutor of the Church, but when the risen Lord appeared to him he began at once to preach the gospel. To see this truth is to know Luke the Evangelist.

In my ministry I have known three physicians who were fine Bible teachers with important Bible classes. I have known several others who

---

a heathen . . . who hast not made me a slave . . . who hast not made me a woman."

were active witnesses to the power of the gospel both in their churches and in their medical practices. They are following in the footsteps of Doctor Luke. Luke should be an inspiration and a challenge to any medical doctor, in fact, to any man of a scientific mind, for he combines the rare gifts of scientific training and evangelical passion, the care of the body and the care of the soul.

CHAPTER XIV

Priscilla and Aquila

PREVIOUSLY WE VISITED the home of a brother and two sisters where Jesus was often present, and we learned a little about that home. Now let me take you to a home which was often visited by Paul. In fact, he lived with this man and wife for months, probably for years, and a friendship developed between them that stretched across sixteen or seventeen years. I refer, as I am sure you have guessed, to Priscilla and Aquila.[1]

Priscilla and Aquila. We first meet this couple in Corinth at the time of Paul's second missionary journey: "After this he [Paul] left Athens and went to Corinth. And he found a Jew named Aquila, a native of Pontus, lately come from Italy with his wife Priscilla, because Claudius had commanded all the Jews to leave Rome. And he went to see them; and because he was of the same trade he stayed with them . . ." (Acts 18:1-3).

Aquila, then, was a Jew, born in Pontus, which is in the north-central part of Turkey, toward the eastern end of the Black Sea. We do not know the age at which he moved to Rome, or the reason. He could have been taken as a slave while still a boy. Priscilla and Aquila are mentioned six times in Scripture and Priscilla's name stands first four of the six times. Perhaps this is not significant; some scholars, however, feel that it indicates that Priscilla was of a higher social standing than her husband. The name Aquila is found among Roman slaves of the period (it is also found among the freemen, so we cannot make too much of the point). Therefore, it is possible that Aquila had been a slave in a Roman household and had married one of the daughters of that family. We know that manumitted Roman slaves had come to be regarded as equals.[2] The name Priscilla[3] is purely a

[1] This name is frequently mispronounced; it is accented on the first syllable: ăk'wĭ-luh.

[2] See Jérôme Carcopino, *Daily Life in Ancient Rome* (New Haven: Yale University Press, 1960), chapters III-IV.

[3] The name means "little old lady"—how this came to be given to babies

Roman name, hence Aquila's wife was not a Jewess. Again we may surmise that Priscilla had become attracted to Aquila's God, and perhaps had even become a proselyte to Judaism before she married Aquila.

We are not told when this married couple first became Christian. Paul makes no mention of the fact and gives no indication that he was instrumental in their conversion, so it is safe to suppose that they were already Christians when he first met them. If so, they were already Christians when they came from Rome.

Priscilla and Aquila had been forced to leave Rome by the edict of the emperor Claudius. Suetonius, the Roman historian of the second century A. D., records that "since the Jews constantly made disturbances at the instigation of Chrestus, he [Claudius] expelled them from Rome."[4] According to Ramsay, the edict is to be dated in the end of A.D. 50, and the arrival of Priscilla and Aquila in the early months of A.D. 51.[5] The name "Chrestus" has been discussed many times, and while no compelling conclusion has been reached, it seems reasonable to suppose that this word is to be linked with "Christ" or "Christian," and that the disturbances in Rome were due to disputes between Christian Jews and non-Christian Jews, such as occurred at Jerusalem and elsewhere. The Claudian edict was not rigidly enforced for very long, and soon the Jews began to return to Rome.

Paul was in Corinth when Gallio was proconsul (Acts 18:12), and Gallio became proconsul in July, A.D. 51. Priscilla and Aquila had come to Corinth early that same year, hence Paul's arrival must have been at approximately the same time. According to Acts 18:11, Paul stayed in Corinth for eighteen months, and if Acts 18:18 is to be added to that, the period was a bit longer. Nothing is said of Priscilla and Aquila during that time, but when Paul left for Syria, he took with him Priscilla and Aquila, and left them at Ephesus (Acts 18:18-19). That would have been early in A.D. 53, probably as soon as the sea lanes opened. Whether Paul returned to Ephesus that fall or early the

---

(the masculine form also occurs), we can only guess. Probably someone said, "Why, she looks just like a little old lady!" hence the name.

[4] Suetonius, *Claudius,* 25.

[5] Cf. W. M. Ramsay, *St. Paul the Traveller and the Roman Citizen* (10th edition, London: Hodder and Stoughton, 1908; reprinted Grand Rapids: Baker Book House, 1951), p. 254.

following year cannot be determined. By the time he reached Ephesus, Apollos had already been instructed by Priscilla and Aquila and had gone on to Corinth (Acts 18:26—19:1). Luke does not tell us anything else about the couple, but we can add a few details from incidental references in Paul's writings.

Paul wrote his first letter to the church in Corinth toward the end of his stay in Ephesus. The length of this Ephesian ministry is not exactly determined, but the following time references are given by Luke: three months in the synagogue (Acts 19:8), two years in the hall of Tyrannus (Acts 19:10), plus an additional period (Acts 19:22). His arrival in Ephesus was dated late in A. D. 53 or early 54; hence the close of the Ephesian ministry must be dated in A.D. 56 or perhaps even 57.[6] First Corinthians, then, was written perhaps in A.D. 56, and according to the closing chapter, Prisca (the more formal name, invariably used by Paul) and Aquila joined in sending greetings, "together with the church in their house" (I Corinthians 16:19). It is therefore possible to conclude that this Christian couple had spent three years or more in Ephesus, had opened their home to the young Church there, had devoted themselves to Christian instruction, and had been generally useful in assisting Paul.

Toward the end of Paul's third missionary journey, when it was obvious that he could not go on to Rome at that time, he wrote the epistle to the Romans. The letter was written from Corinth, and almost certainly was sent to Rome by the hand of Phoebe, "a deaconess of the church at Cenchreae" (Romans 16:1). At that time, Priscilla and Aquila were back in Rome and a Church was meeting in their house (Romans 16:3-5).[7] When they had returned to Rome we are not told, but it had to be between the time Paul left Ephesus (A.D. 56/57) and the time he was ready to leave Corinth (A.D. 57/58).

Only one other reference remains; that is in Paul's last letter. At that time, when he was awaiting his execution, writing his last words to Timothy who was then at Ephesus, he added, "Greet Prisca and Aquila" (II Timothy 4:19).

Putting these details together, we can reconstruct the outline of the

[6] F. F. Bruce comes to a slightly earlier date; cf. *The Book of Acts*, p. 405.

[7] I accept the conclusion of Romans as an original part of the epistle. Many modern scholars think it was originally part of the letter to Ephesus; but the preponderance of Roman names rather supports the Roman destination. For discussion see James Denney in *The Expositor's Greek Testament*, vol. 2, pp. 580-582, and, conversely, T. W. Manson, "St. Paul's Letter to the Romans—and Others," *Bulletin of the John Rylands Library* 31 (November, 1948), pp. 1-19.

life of Priscilla and Aquila rather completely from beginning to end. For the period from our first meeting with them, about the year A.D. 51, to the time of Paul's last letter, perhaps A.D. 67, they traveled from Rome to Corinth to Ephesus, thence to Rome, and a second time to Ephesus. They spent about two years in Corinth, about three years in Ephesus, and from five to ten years in Rome before returning to Ephesus again. In each case they were active in Christian work and their home was open to the local Church for its meetings. Church buildings, of course, had not yet come into existence. Aquila was a weaver of goat's hair tent cloth. It is hardly likely that this provided sufficient income for travel; we can suppose that Priscilla had some personal wealth that made their journeys possible.

Priscilla and Aquila and Paul. Paul first met this Christian man and wife in Corinth. What brought them together was their trade of weaving goat's hair cloth. This material, also known as *cilicium* from the fact that it originated or became prominently known at Cilicia, is usually made on long looms set up along the street in a certain part of the town; sometimes the looms are fifty feet or more in length. It is difficult for the average American, unless he has traveled through the Near or Far East, to think of areas of commercial concentration, such as a street of basketweavers or silversmiths, an area where each shop will sell identical items and where nothing else is sold. To our way of thinking, this is unnecessary and useless competition, but to the Oriental there is a splendid camaraderie, and the coppersmith who does not have an item to please you will cheerfully direct you to one of his fellow craftsmen in a nearby shop. I suppose Paul found his way to the street of the tent-cloth weavers, as Aquila had done a few weeks or months earlier, and there he began to work at his trade. There he doubtless met Aquila. They probably soon found that they were believers in the same Saviour, and the next thing, Paul was invited to stay at the home of Aquila and his wife (cf. Acts 18:3).

Since Luke does not say much about Priscilla and Aquila, we have to read between the lines; but we have little difficulty doing this, for we know Paul's interest, and we soon get to know the interests of his friends. Aquila had recently come from Rome. Not long after the account of the meeting of Aquila and Paul, Luke records Paul's decision, "I must also see Rome" (Acts 19:21). This suggests only one thing to me: Aquila and Priscilla had told Paul about the Christian community in Rome.

We know little or nothing about the origin of Christianity in Rome. According to the view held by some, Peter founded the Roman Church c. A.D. 44. This seems unlikely.[8] But if we are correct in surmising that Priscilla and Aquila were Christians before leaving Rome, and if we are correct in identifying "Chrestus" with Christ and the Christian movement, then the gospel had reached Rome prior to the Claudian edict of A.D. 50. This is borne out, to some extent, by Paul's strong statement in his epistle to the Romans, "your faith is proclaimed in all the world" (Romans 1:8)—a statement which certainly requires some prior period of development.

I suppose that Priscilla and Aquila told Paul of the developments in Roman society. Slavery was passing through a strange process of democratization, and so many slaves had been set free that two things had become necessary: first, more and more slaves had to be sought in the outlying regions of the Empire, and second, the laws of manumission were made more rigid by Augustus.[9] Men were shocked by the free rein that was being given to youth, and by the cheapness of human life.[10] Things had reached such a state that many were ready for something like the gospel. Moreover, Rome was the center of the empire. The future belonged to the West. And certainly Paul was enough of a strategist that he could visualize the importance of locating a strong Christian training center in Rome.

Paul also had his heart on Ephesus. Early in his second journey, he had seen it as a strategic place to locate the gospel but he had been prevented from going there by the Spirit's direction (cf. Acts 16:6). It became clear to him that Ephesus had to precede Rome in his itinerary and so he hit upon a clever plan. It was his custom, as a good Jew, to return to Jerusalem as often as possible to participate in the religious festivals. He had been away long enough, so he planned to make his pilgrimage from Corinth, before taking up the work in Ephesus. But meanwhile, he could get the work there started; and this he did by the simple expedient of taking Priscilla and Aquila to Ephesus and leaving them there while he went on to Jerusalem (Acts 18:18-19).

It is quite clear to me that Paul acted out of his experience. For a period of about two years Paul had worked and lived with Priscilla and Aquila in Corinth. He knew the kind of work they could do. He knew their zeal and devotion, their knowledge of the Scriptures, their

[8] See p. 86, above.
[9] Suetonius, *Augustus*, 40.
[10] Cf. Carcopino, *Daily Life in Ancient Rome*, pp. 58, 79f.

knowledge of the basic facts of the Christian faith. If Aquila was a manumitted slave, he had Roman citizenship; Priscilla probably was freeborn. They could settle down in Ephesus in their trade, perhaps support themselves from independent resources, and lay the groundwork for Paul, when and if he could get to Ephesus (cf. Acts 18:21). I can see no other possible reason for rooting them up from their important work in Corinth.

Priscilla and Aquila were in Ephesus during all of Paul's extended stay in that city. The Church met in their home. Then suddenly a few months later Priscilla and Aquila were in Rome when Paul wrote the epistle to the Romans, toward the end of his third missionary journey. Why? I can think of only one satisfactory reason: Paul was using the same strategy for Rome that he had used for Ephesus. He was sending Priscilla and Aquila on ahead in order that the groundwork would be laid for his arrival. What he did not know at the time was that a two-year delay would be occasioned by his imprisonment in Caesarea.

We are often told that Paul was a woman-hater. Where does this idea come from? I suppose it arises partly from some of the things that Paul says about women in First Corinthians and in his letters to Timothy. But are we right in judging Paul by what he said in these writings? The one was addressed to Corinth, the other to Ephesus. Corinth was a wicked city, and the women in Corinth, for the most part, had a terrible name, so that the word "Corinthian" had come to mean harlot. Ephesus was not so overtly wicked, but its religious life was just as objectionable from a Christian viewpoint. So when Paul expressed his feeling that he did not want women to be active in the Church, that he did not want them to teach or to pray in public, that he wanted them to keep their heads covered, I think we must understand these things against the background of the cities involved.

There is another side to the story of Paul and his attitude toward women. This is expressed by Priscilla and the work she was doing. It is expressed by Lois and Eunice of Lystra, by Lydia of Philippi, by Euodia and Syntyche of Philippi, by Tryphaena and Tryphosa of Rome, and by other women mentioned either by name or in general statements in Paul's letters. For a woman-hater, Paul certainly had a long list of female fellow workers!

Priscilla and Aquila and Apollos. Apollos is introduced to us by Luke as "a Jew . . . a native of Alexandria . . . an eloquent man, well versed in the scriptures" (Acts 18:24). Alexandria was one of the largest cities of the Empire, and it had a large and vigorous Jewish quarter. The Jews of Alexandria seem to have been characterized by a love of philosophy and by an allegorizing tendency in interpreting the Scriptures. It seems likely that there was a John-the-Baptist sect of Jews in Alexandria, and that Apollos was influenced by this movement.

When Apollos arrived in Ephesus, he participated in the worship of the synagogue, and it was there that Priscilla and Aquila heard him. They were not only impressed with his eloquence and knowledge of the Old Testament, but also with his knowledge of details of the life of Jesus. He knew only the baptism of John, however, and was apparently ignorant of the facts of the baptism of Christ which is baptism of the Holy Spirit (cf. Acts 18:25). If I may be permitted to expand this, as I understand it, Luke is telling us that Apollos knew the messianic hopes of the Jews; he knew the declaration of John the Baptist that the Kingdom of God was at hand, therefore these hopes were to be realized; he knew that Jesus was designated by John as the One who should come; he may have known the story of the crucifixion of Jesus. But he did not know the fundamental nature of the Church. He did not know that baptism by the Holy Spirit was necessary for entrance into the Kingdom, or that the Church was the body of those who had received this baptism. He probably did not know that the death of Jesus Christ was redemptive in atonement for sins, or that it was by faith in this divine act that man received the benefits of God's gracious redemption.

Priscilla and Aquila realized that Apollos was a gem in need of a bit of polishing, and "they took him and expounded to him the way of God more accurately" (Acts 18:26). They must have been satisfied that he understood what they were trying to teach him, for they encouraged him to go to Greece, and wrote letters of recommendation on his behalf (Acts 18:27-28). Some indication of the work done by Apollos in Corinth can be drawn from a statement which Paul makes in First Corinthians: "I planted, Apollos watered" (I Corinthians 3:6). Paul might have said, "I started the church in Corinth; Apollos continued to nourish and develop it."

There are some scholars who think that Apollos was responsible for a factious spirit in the Church of Corinth. It is obvious that Paul wrote First Corinthians because there was trouble in that Church. "For it has been reported to me by Chloe's people that there is quarreling among you, my brethren. What I mean is that each one of you says, 'I belong to Paul,' or 'I belong to Apollos,' or 'I belong to Cephas,' or 'I belong to Christ.' Is Christ divided? Was Paul crucified for you? Or were you baptized in the name of Paul?" (I Corinthians 1:11-13).

Now it could be that Apollos, the Alexandrian, with his love of philosophy and his allegorizing of the Scriptures, had started the people of the Church in Corinth thinking in a slightly different way than Paul had led them to think. To be committed to the inspiration of Paul's writings is not to be committed to the infallibiliy of Paul's preaching—if this were so, then we should have to accept Peter's infallibility as well; and that would include Peter's dissimulation at Antioch when Paul rebuked him. No, Paul was not infallible as a preacher; he was only a human being. He developed and used the gifts that were in him, and I am sure Apollos did the same. It is possible that Paul had something of Apollos' preaching in mind when he wrote, "When I came to you, brethren, I did not come proclaiming to you the testimony of God in lofty words or wisdom" (I Corinthians 2:1). Perhaps Paul is reflecting something of the difference between the two men when he says: "I fed you with milk, not solid food; for you were not ready for it; and even yet you are not ready. . . . For when one says, 'I belong to Paul,' and another, 'I belong to Apollos,' are you not merely men?" (I Corinthians 3:2-4). Some think that Apollos was deficient in his doctrine of the Holy Spirit, which would account for Paul's emphasis upon the subject in his Corinthian correspondence.

It seems to me, however, that the party spirit that developed in the Church at Corinth did not result from any deliberate act on the part of Apollos. Rather, it was the result of human factors common to all men. Some liked Apollos' preaching; some liked Paul's. That happens in churches, does it not? Some like the "simple gospel"; some like philosophy. Some like simple language; some like rhetorical preaching.

Paul's reaction, as I understand it, was an effort to override the personal elements. Listen to him carefully: "This is how one should regard us, as servants of Christ and stewards of the mysteries of God. Moreover it is required of stewards that they be found trustworthy. But with me it is a very small thing that I should be judged by you or by any human court. I do not even judge myself. I am not aware of anything against myself, but I am not thereby acquitted. [This statement helps us put the accent on the right words; Paul is not emphasizing the "I's."] It is the Lord who judges me. . . . I have applied all this to myself and Apollos for your benefit, brethren, that you may learn by us to live according to scripture, that none of you may be puffed up in favor of one against another" (I Corinthians 4:1-6).

You see, Paul is not suggesting that he is right and Apollos wrong. Rather he is saying, in effect, "Now I am bringing this out into the open so that you can see that Apollos and I are mere men trying to do the job God gave us to do." Paul does not criticize Apollos and his method of preaching; he does not defend his own method other than to claim that it is suited to the spiritual maturity (or immaturity) of his hearers. He simply stresses the importance of preserving the unity of the Church in Christ Jesus while forgetting the human leaders.

Further on Paul says, "As for our brother Apollos, I strongly urged him to visit you with the other brethren, but it was not at all God's will for him to go now. He will come when he has opportunity" (I Corinthians 16:12). Does this sound like a man who is trying to defend his own viewpoint and who is afraid to have his opponent come into the church and stir things up anew? It sounds rather like a man who feels that the best thing that could happen would be to have Apollos return and straighten up the Corinthians on this matter of human leadership and divided loyalties.

We know nothing else about Apollos. Some think that he wrote the Epistle to the Hebrews; Martin Luther did, for example, and A. B. Bruce was content to say, "Apollos is the kind of man wanted" for such an assignment.

Priscilla and Aquila, husband and wife! As McGiffert says, "They furnish the most beautiful example known to us in the Apostolic Age of the power for God that could be exerted by a husband and wife working in unison for the advancement of the Gospel."[11] Their home was always open for the Church that met in their house. They were always ready to go wherever God needed them. They were willing to lose themselves in the footnotes of history. But their influence was clearly felt in the greatest cities of their day. Here is an example for any young couple to follow.

[11] A. C. McGiffert, *A History of Christianity in the Apostolic Age* (revised edition; New York: Charles Scribner's Sons, 1906), p. 428.

CHAPTER XV

Timothy and Titus

THIS STUDY SHOULD be dedicated to mothers and grandmothers, for it is the story of a young man, perhaps little more than a boy when we first meet him, who was brought up in the faith by a believing mother probably over the opposition of an unbelieving father. The mother was aided in her faith by her mother, the boy's grandmother. One day the Lord laid His hand on this young man for full-time Christian service, and the mother, in splendid faith and sacrifice, gave him to the Lord. The young man was Timothy, and his story can be told in connection with his associates in Christian work.

Timothy and Paul. In his customary manner, Luke gives us a brief description of Timothy when he first appears in Acts: "And he [Paul] came also to Derbe and to Lystra. A disciple was there, named Timothy, the son of a Jewish woman who was a believer, but his father was a Greek. He was well spoken of by the brethren at Lystra and Iconium" (Acts 16:1-2). The way the statement is worded, Timothy may have been living at either Lystra or Derbe.[1] The time was early in the second missionary journey, perhaps A.D. 50. Luke's sentence structure—an important point when reading an author who is so careful in such matters—suggests not only that Timothy's father was a Greek, whereas his mother was a Jewess, but also that Timothy's father was not a believer. Since Timothy had not been circumcised (cf. Acts 16:3), we may suppose that the father was not sympathetic to the mother's religious views and perhaps had even forbidden the religious rite.

Paul had visited Lystra and Derbe on his first missionary journey a few years earlier. At that time he was accompanied by Barnabas, and

---

[1] F. F. Bruce, for example, chooses Lystra on the basis of its occurrence in both sentences (*The Book of the Acts,* p. 321). It would be equally logical to assume that Derbe was Timothy's home, since his reputation at Lystra and Iconium is mentioned. See also Acts 20:4. The point is hardly worth debating.

at Lystra they had performed a miracle on a man who had been crippled from birth (Acts 14:8-10). The wonderful work of mercy quite naturally caused widespread excitement, and created a keen interest in the apostles. Paul of course used this as an opportunity to preach the gospel. Luke does not fill in the details, but it is obvious that effective preaching led to conversions as well as to opposition; news of what was happening reached Antioch and Iconium; Jewish opposition to the apostles came from these cities and stirred up mob action, and as a result, Paul was stoned and dragged out of the city for dead (cf. Acts 14:19-20). Some of the converts gathered about him, and he revived and entered the city; the next day he and Barnabas went to Derbe.

Luke does not mention the conversion of Timothy's mother, Eunice, but it is reasonable to believe that it occurred at that time. Some have suggested that Paul may have been taken to her home, and his wounds may have been bathed and bandaged there. The suggestion is based on Paul's reminder to Timothy that he had observed Paul's persecutions and sufferings, and what befell him at Antioch, at Iconium, and at Lystra (cf. II Timothy 3:11).[2] It is an attractive suggestion, and we would like to think that young Timothy came to know the gospel at that time. However, this is far from certain. We can safely conclude that Timothy's grandmother Lois was also converted to the faith at that time or soon thereafter, and finally he himself (cf. II Timothy 1:5).

It is generally assumed that Timothy was converted to Christianity by Paul. This is based on the way Paul refers to his young colleague; for example, "my true child in the faith" (I Timothy 1:2), and "my beloved and faithful child in the Lord" (I Corinthians 4:17). Once again, however, I would suggest that we do not accept as an established fact what is only a very good suggestion. In II Timothy 3:15 there is a suggestion that Timothy may have received his faith from his mother. Paul's references to Timothy as his "child in the faith" would

[2] The question of Pauline authorship of the Pastoral Epistles (I and II Timothy and Titus) is very complex, and many scholars are firmly convinced that Paul did not write them. I follow the traditional view, hence use material in the Pastorals for these studies. All scholars, I believe, would admit that the Pastorals contain an early tradition, and whether it had been written down by Paul or by someone else would not greatly affect the use we are making of it here. For a full discussion, with references to recent literature, see Donald Guthrie, *The Pastoral Epistles* (London: The Tyndale Press, 1957), pp. 11-53, 212-228.

be sufficiently explained, I believe, by the fact that Paul trained Timothy in Christian doctrine and practice.

How old Timothy was at the time we are not told. Nearly twenty years later Paul addressed Timothy as a young man—but what is a "young man"? To a twenty-year-old, a man of forty is not young; to a man of sixty or seventy, the forty-year-old man is still young. We suppose that Timothy was in his teens when Paul first visited Lystra and Derbe; that he was perhaps in his early twenties at the time of Paul's second visit—which would make him forty or forty-five when the Pastoral Epistles were written.

When Paul returned to Timothy's home town on his second missionary journey, he was impressed with the reports of Timothy's Christian faith and life, and desired to take Timothy along with him. On the first journey, we remember, Paul and Barnabas had started out with young John Mark as their helper. Timothy would stand in the same relationship to the team of Paul and Silas. Timothy's mother agreed, obviously, and the Church ordained the young man by the laying on of hands (compare II Timothy 1:6 with I Timothy 4:14).

Because Timothy was the child of a mixed marriage, Paul circumcised him (Acts 16:3). This action has caused a great deal of discussion on the part of Biblical scholars, and many think that Paul at this point displayed a serious inconsistency. Just a year or so earlier, at the time of the debate in Jerusalem over the Judaizer problem, Paul had refused to permit Titus to be circumcised (cf. Galatians 2:3). Paul was standing on the principle that a Gentile should not be required to take upon himself the obligations of the Law of Moses.[3] Now Paul was violating that principle, it is charged, by circumcising Timothy.

It seems to me that two entirely different principles are under consideration. Titus was a Gentile born to Gentile parents. Circumcision in his case would be a violation of Paul's principle concerning Gentiles. Timothy, on the other hand, was part Jew. Moreover, Paul wanted to use him in Jewish evangelism in the synagogues. As a Jew, even of a mixed marriage, Timothy would be an offense to other Jews if he did not keep the Mosaic Law, and this would become an unnecessary

---

[3] It should be pointed out that circumcision in itself was not the issue. The implication of the act was what mattered, for by submitting to this rite the male was obligated to perform all of the Law. Whether a present-day Christian Gentile should have his male children circumcised as a matter of personal hygiene is entirely another question and has no theological implication.

stumbling block to his fellow Jews. Paul therefore applied a different principle, which is described by him as follows: "To the Jews I became as a Jew, in order to win Jews; to those under the law I became as one under the law . . . that I might win those under the law. . . . I have become all things to all men, that I might by all means save some. I do it all for the sake of the gospel . . ." (I Corinthians 9:20-23). Timothy, a Jew by birth and therefore no hypocrite in taking on himself voluntarily the obligations of Judaism, was a demonstration of this principle.

We can trace Timothy's itinerary with some detail. He went to Europe with Paul, Silas, and Luke, but was apparently not jailed with Paul and Silas in Philippi (Acts 16:19). Luke seems to have stayed in Philippi when the other three moved west along the Egnatian Road to Thessalonica. When Paul and Silas were sent off to neighboring Beroea by night, Timothy seems to have remained in Thessalonica, but later joined the apostles in Beroea (cf. Acts 17:10,14); Timothy and Silas stayed there when Paul moved on to Athens. Later Paul sent Timothy to Thessalonica (it would seem that Timothy had meanwhile rejoined Paul at Athens, but this is not clear), in order to get news about his recent converts and to establish them in the faith (I Thessalonians 3:1-2). After that, Timothy and Silas joined Paul in Corinth (Acts 18:5), and Paul sent the first of his letters to the Thessalonians (I Thessalonians 3:6), rejoicing over the news which Timothy had brought. It is possible that Timothy acted both as Paul's amanuensis and emissary, writing the letter for Paul and delivering it; then returning with a reply that occasioned the second letter to Thessalonica.

The next time we hear of Timothy he was in Ephesus with Paul, and Paul was sending him and Erastus to Macedonia, where Thessalonica is located (Acts 19:22). Still later, Paul sent Timothy from Ephesus to Corinth to handle some of the difficult matters in that Church (I Corinthians 4:17). The last time Timothy is mentioned in Acts is at Troas with the group that was planning to carry an offering from the Gentile churches to the needy Jewish Christians at Jerusalem (Acts 20:4).

According to the salutations of the Prison Epistles, Timothy was with Paul during the first Roman imprisonment (cf. Colossians 1:1; Philippians 1:1; Philemon 1). Then, if we are correct in following the tradition that Paul was released from prison, Timothy went to Ephesus with Paul and was left there to carry on the work in that city

(I Timothy 1:3). He was imprisoned, where and when we do not know, and subsequently released (Hebrews 13:23), and later, according to tradition, martyred at Ephesus under Domitian after having served as the first bishop of Ephesus.[4]

Timothy was doubtless the closest of Paul's associates, with perhaps the exception of Luke. He is mentioned in the opening salutation of six of Paul's epistles as co-author, and two others are addressed to him. He was young, somewhat timid, possibly not physically strong (cf. I Timothy 5:23). Some scholars seem to think that he experienced a moral degeneration in the years he was on his own, and that Paul had to warn him against temptations of the flesh, the love of money, and laziness. I do not get this impression; rather, it seems to me that Paul is reacting as a father would react to the snares and temptations of the world. When I encourage my children it is not because I have lost confidence in them, but rather because I feel that we all need to be reminded constantly to be on guard against the wiles of the devil. In such a way Paul exhorted Timothy.

Timothy and Titus. Titus is one of the outstanding men in the New Testament Church, and yet he is not mentioned by name in the Book of Acts. The only satisfactory explanation of this omission would be either that Titus was another name for Luke, or that Titus was a relative of Luke and was not named because of family modesty. Are there any indications that would support either of these theories? A cursory reading of II Timothy 4:10-11 quickly proves that Titus (who had gone to Dalmatia) was not Luke (who was with Paul in Rome). When there was trouble in the Church at Corinth, Paul sent Titus to work it out, and he wrote, "With him we are sending the brother who is famous among all the churches for his preaching of the gospel" (II Corinthians 8:18). Again he said, "I urged Titus to go, and sent the brother with him" (II Corinthians 12:18). This is not much to build on, but the supposition that Titus was Luke's brother is attractive —at least to me.

Titus was of Gentile parents (Galatians 2:3), and was taken to Jerusalem by Paul at the time of the Judaizer controversy (Galatians

---

[4] Eusebius, *Ecclesiastical History* 3.4; Nicephorus, *Ecclesiastical History* 3.11. The latter reference is from *The Fathers of the Church,* edited by R. J. Defarrari, vol. 19, *Eusebius Pamphili, Ecclesiastical History* (New York: Fathers of the Church, Inc., 1953), p. 142, n. 6; I have been unable to verify the reference.

2:1). Titus was "Exhibit A"—evidence that could be examined; living proof that a Gentile who had not come under the Law of Moses could still demonstrate the fruits of the Spirit that were the sign of a regenerate man in Christ.

Titus comes into our story about Timothy in connection with the problems in the Corinthian Church. Timothy, we learned, had been sent to Corinth by Paul to take care of grave difficulties in that Church, difficulties of moral, doctrinal, and administrative nature. To read the letters to the Corinthians is to discover how complex the problems were. And Timothy failed in the mission. He failed not because of any lack of ability, but because of lack of experience: he was just too young. The Church in Corinth despised his youth, and were hostile because Paul himself had not visited them (see I Corinthians 4:17-18 and compare I Corinthians 16:10-11). Perhaps that was why Paul on a later occasion said to Timothy, "Let no one despise your youth" (I Timothy 4:12).

If we take the trouble to check the chronological details, we shall find that this was about A.D. 55. Timothy had been in Paul's company almost constantly for about five years. He had traveled widely, had undergone all sorts of experiences with Paul and with Silas; he had even been sent on missions alone by Paul, such as those to Thessalonica. He was by this time probably twenty-five years old, and a veteran of five years' service. In our modern day, we take young fellows and girls who have had little or no training in Christian service and send them into some of the most difficult situations in the world—then we wonder why they sometimes fail. They fail because we are expecting young people to do the work of mature and experienced workers. With far more preparation and experience, Timothy failed. But failure under such circumstances is no disgrace.

Titus, however, succeeded. Paul was comforted by the news that Titus brought and by the fact that he had been so well received in the Corinthian Church (cf. II Corinthians 7:5-7). Titus was probably somewhat older than Timothy (compare Titus 2:15 with I Timothy 4:12), and he had had a few more years' experience. Possibly he had certain personal qualifications that Timothy lacked, as, for example, self-confidence or boldness. It is even possible that Timothy had, knowingly or unknowingly, prepared the way for Titus; the Corinthians had had time to regret how they had treated Timothy and may have determined to act toward Titus in a more Christian manner. Whatever the reasons, we know that an affection developed between Titus and the Corinthian Church that brought joy to Paul's heart (cf. II Corinthians 7:13-14; 8:16).

After Paul was released from the Roman imprisonment, he took Titus and Timothy on some part of his further travels. He left Timothy in Ephesus, as we have seen; and he left Titus in Crete (Titus 1:5). That in itself is to me an amazing testimony of Paul's confidence in these two men. Ephesus was, by Paul's own estimate, one of the most strategically important cities of the Empire. It was not without its difficulties, particularly with reference to the hostility of those who were devoted to the goddess Artemis. Later, as we find from Second Timothy and corroborated by Revelation 2:2-6, strong reaction set in against the gospel. Yet Paul was willing to entrust the situation to Timothy. Likewise Crete was one of the more difficult regions in the Empire, as we know from references in the literature of the day. Paul was willing to place the work there in the care of Titus.

Timothy and the Church. We are beginning to get, through the experiences of Timothy, a different view of the Church. Up until this point, we have been seeing the Church of the first generation. It was the Church of the apostles, the Church of those who had known Jesus according to the flesh, or had (in the case of Paul) been granted a personal experience of the risen Christ. But with Timothy, and doubtless also with Titus, we are moving into the next generation: this is "second generation Christianity," with all its new problems. The Church that we see in the experiences of Timothy is the Church in its on-going history, after the apostles have begun to depart from the scene.

Of course the apostles were not yet gone; but Paul was anxiously making preparations for the day when he would be. He was setting up Timothy and Titus (and were there others, of whom these are typical?) in strategic locations because he knew that the hour of his departure was at hand. He was writing letters to them (and shall we not assume that he expected others to read these letters?) in order to strengthen them for the work of the next generation.

Timothy was not an apostle; that is made clear in Colossians 1:1. He was never looked upon as a successor to Paul, and he was never portrayed as having the authority of an apostle. Read the letters to Timothy and Titus, and notice that such authority remained in the apostolic office and was not conferred on younger ministers. Yet there is authority (cf. I Timothy 4:11, 14): it is the authority of the gospel.

Through Timothy we learn something about the nature of the Church. It is God's family (I Timothy 3:5, 15). Its members are called "brothers" (I Timothy 4:6), "believers" (I Timothy 4:12; 5:16), and "holy ones" (or "saints," I Timothy 5:10). These words define their relationship to one another: they are brothers; their relationship to God: they are believers; and their relationship to the world: they are holy, set apart from sin for lives of purity.

In the Church are certain officers, whose duties and qualifications are described in the Pastoral Epistles. We call them "bishop," "priest" or "presbyter," and "deacon." I think these high-sounding names have confused us. Originally they were common Greek words that could be translated "overseer" or "supervisor," "elder," and "minister" or "servant." But hierarchies do not develop from such commonplace words, therefore we have bishops, priests, and deacons. Two other "offices" are described in the letter to Timothy, but we tend to ignore them. These are "women" or "wives" and "widows." As we read through the qualifications from I Timothy 3:1 to 5:22, particularly if we read them in some modern language translation, we get the feeling that we are not reading about ecclesiastical offices, but about normal family life. "Bishops" are described in their relationship to their households and their children, "deacons" likewise; their "women," or better, "wives" (cf. I Timothy 3:11-12) are to refrain from gossipy slander; the duties of the "widows" concern the religious obligations they have to their own children (I Timothy 5:4). Do not misunderstand me; I am not opposing organization within the Church, nor am I seeking to belittle the offices instituted by God. But I think these offices, in some cases, have gotten far away from the divine intention. Let the Church be the family of God and the officers the members of that family.

We learn quite a bit about the beliefs of the Church in the Pastoral Epistles, but I shall reserve that for another study.

Finally, and notably, we observe that Paul is very much concerned about false teachers and apostasy. "Understand this," says Paul, "that in the last days there will come times of stress. For men will be lovers of self, lovers of money ... lovers of pleasure rather than lovers of God, holding the form of religion but denying the power of it" (II Timothy 3:1-5). "Now the Spirit expressly says that in later times some will depart from the faith" (I Timothy 4:1). As long as apostolic eyewitnesses are present, they can controvert error by their personal testimony, but what can Timothy do? What can you and I do?

Our first responsibility, as was Timothy's, is to guard the faith that is in us. "You then, my son, be strong in the grace that is in Christ Jesus" (II Timothy 2:1). If you are concerned by apostasy in the world, look to your own spiritual life. Make sure that it is strong.

The second responsibility that Paul laid upon Timothy was to train up faithful successors. "What you have heard from me before many witnesses entrust to faithful men who will be able to teach others also" (II Timothy 2:2).

The third responsibility was to trust God. "God's firm foundation stands, bearing this seal: 'The Lord knows those who are his,' and 'Let every one who names the name of the Lord depart from iniquity'" (II Timothy 2:19).

The fourth responsibility, and by no means the least important, was to stay out of arguments. "Have nothing to do with stupid, senseless controversies; you know that they breed quarrels. And the Lord's servant must not be quarrelsome but kindly to every one, an apt teacher, forbearing, correcting his opponents with gentleness. God may perhaps grant that they will repent and come to know the truth . . ." (II Timothy 2:23-25). Righteousness, faith, love, and peace will have far greater effect upon the opponents than argument (cf. II Timothy 2:22).

All these responsibilities can be summarized in one charge: "Preach the word, be urgent in season and out of season, convince, rebuke, and exhort, be unfailing in patience and in teaching" (II Timothy 4:2).

This is the Church and its responsibility in the post-apostolic age, as I see it in Timothy: officers to divide up the duties according to ability, and not just to be officious; preachers to preach the word handed down by the apostles, and witnesses to tell what they have experienced personally; and always teachers, everywhere teachers, to train up the next generation in the faith.

You and I shall never stop the attacks on faith that our young people must face in the world. That is an impossibility. And if we seek to shun our responsibility by sheltering our young people in some other-worldly school or college, we merely delay the day when they must face the anti-Christian forces in the world. Our only defense of the faith is to stengthen the faith that is in us and to train our children and their friends in the Word of God. Our responsibility ends when we have passed on the truth to the next generation. After that, we must trust God to do the rest—and He is faithful.

CHAPTER XVI

Thomas Who Believed

WE USUALLY SPEAK of Thomas as a doubter: "doubting Thomas." I would like to present him as the believer. The words of his faith constitute the fullest statement of faith expressed in the Gospels: "My Lord and my God" (John 20:28).

We are not sure of his name. You say, "Why, it was Thomas!" But that is only because we have made the word "Thomas" into a name —at first it was only a common noun. The Gospel writer knew that, and translated the word for us: "which means Didymus" and Didymus means "twin." Need we point out that one does not usually name a child "Twin"? What would you name the other one?

An early and widespread tradition tells us that his name was Judas. If, so, there were three of the Twelve with the same name: Judas Iscariot, Judas "not Iscariot," and Judas "the Twin." That would not be improbable, for Judas was a very common name. Another tradition that is preserved in the writings of the Church in the Middle Ages tells us that Thomas was the twin of Jesus. How such a notion started is probably to be explained from the words of the Lord Jesus in the Acts of Thomas, where Jesus appears in the likeness of Thomas and, when asked if He is Thomas, replies, "I am his brother!"[1] It is easy to see how such an idea, once started, could have become the source of much confusion. Thomas is usually portrayed as the Apostle to India; the earliest tradition, however, locates his field of labor in Parthia (modern Iran). So much for tradition.

Thomas and Jesus. Thomas was a doubter; I would not deny that. But even his doubts must be set against the background of his faith. Thomas was one of the Twelve, but before he became one of the Twelve, he had to be one of the disciples. Let the implications sink in, and you will realize that somewhere along the way, and it must have

[1] Acts of the Holy Apostle Thomas, *The Ante-Nicene Fathers,* vol. 8, p. 537.

been early in Jesus' ministry, Thomas had heard the call of Jesus and had cast his lot in with Him. Jesus had observed him carefully, as He had observed the others, and after a night in prayer had chosen Thomas as one of that group to whom would be given the tremendous and awful responsibility of evangelizing the world. This should convince us of the worth of this man.

There are three short references to Thomas, all of them in John. The first is in the eleventh chapter, in connection with the illness of Lazarus and the events pertaining to it. Jesus and His apostles were beyond the Jordan, safely beyond the reach of those who were seeking to destroy Him; for, as we know, Jesus had a sense of timing whereby His death must occur on the day of the great sacrifice, the Passover. Word had been sent to Jesus that Lazarus was ill, and Jesus had delayed going to Bethany. Then He announced to the disciples that "Lazarus is dead . . . let us go to him" (John 11:14-15). At this point, Thomas comes into the picture, saying, "Let us also go, that we may die with him" (John 11:16).

It is clear that Thomas did not understand Jesus, and I am not sure I understand Thomas. Thomas may have thought that by the expression, "Let us go to him," Jesus was implying that they should join Lazarus in death. Such an idea he would have gotten, I think, from Jesus' teachings about the suffering and death that must occur at Jerusalem. Or it may be that Thomas was simply referring to the danger that a trip to the vicinity of Jerusalem would incur: it would be sealing their own death warrants. But regardless of what Thomas implied, there can be no doubt that Thomas was declaring his loyalty to the Master, and his willingness to die, if necessary, for the Master.

I rather like Thomas for this, don't you? There is no bravado; no boasting that he was able to face dangers that would cause the rest of them to run. Quite the opposite, Thomas includes the rest in the decision: "Let us also go." There is a gloomy outlook, true; but there is a quiet and deep devotion. If Jesus feels that He must return to the place of danger, let us not desert Him. Let us stay with Him, even if it means our death.

The second reference to Thomas is found in the fourteenth chapter of John. This was only a short time after the resurrection of Lazarus, and the dinner given in honor of Jesus had brought a crowd of people to see Lazarus also (cf. John 12:9). The following day had been exciting, with the triumphal entry of Jesus into Jerusalem; that had been followed by two days of activity in Jerusalem, as Jesus sought desperately to bring the city to its senses, while the religious leaders sought to trap Him into some statement or action that could be used as a capital charge against Him. The sands of time were running out rapidly, and Jesus had gathered His own in the Upper Room for the parting words of instruction.

"Let not your hearts be troubled," He said; "believe in God, believe also in me. In my Father's house are many rooms; if it were not so, would I have told you that I go to prepare a place for you? And when I go and prepare a place for you, I will come again and will take you to myself, that where I am you may be also. And you know the way where I am going" (John 14:1-4). Thomas interrupted: "Lord, we do not know where you are going; how can we know the way?"

I am puzzled to know what lay behind Thomas' question. He may not have understood what Jesus was talking about—but I find that hard to believe. In view of the events of the preceding days, added to the teachings of Jesus, it seems that they all should have known that Jesus was talking about His imminent death. Still, there is that word spoken later, "Ah, now you are speaking plainly, not in any figure!" (John 16:29). But then again, Thomas may have understood that Jesus was referring to His death, and may have been seeking more light on the "where" and the "way." If Jesus had intended to follow up this line of inquiry, He was interrupted by Philip's question (John 14:8 ff.). Most of us, I am sure, wish that Jesus had said more about His Father's house—but He told us all He wants us to know, and all we need to know.

The third reference to Thomas is in the twentieth chapter of John. The resurrection of Jesus had taken place. It was the evening of resurrection day, the first Easter Sunday, and there was much excitement among the Eleven—Judas had removed himself not only from the apostolic band but from this life as well—for there were strange reports that Jesus was alive. He had been seen by Peter. Two disciples from Emmaus reported walking and talking with Jesus. The women's stories about the empty tomb and the angelic messages were being recounted. And as a result, the apostles, who had been scattered by the terrible tragedy of the cross, had gathered together, still fearsome of the spirit of hostility in the city. Suddenly, Jesus was in their midst. His first words were, "Peace be with you." Then He showed them the tokens of His passion, His hands and side.[2] Thomas was not present.

When the disciples found Thomas, they told him, "We have seen the Lord." Thomas said, "Unless I see in his hands the print of the nails, and place my finger in the mark of the nails, and place my hand in his side, I will not believe" (John 20:25).

Thomas and his doubts. Have you ever thought about the different kinds of doubt? There is one word,[3] sometimes translated "doubt," that means "perplexity, inability to comprehend." Like the Latin word *dubitare,* from which we get our word "doubt," it has a basic meaning related to "way," except that the Latin literally means "to go two ways," whereas the Greek means, "without a way." This is the word used of the women at the empty tomb: they were "perplexed" (Luke 24:4); this is the word used of the disciples when Jesus announced, "One of you shall betray me" (John 13:21); a similar but stronger word is used of Herod, when he heard reports that John the Baptist was alive again (Luke 9:7), and again of the crowd in Jerusalem when they heard the apostles speaking with tongues (Acts 2:12). In all cases, they were stopped, they did not know which way to turn for a solution to the situation confronting them.

A second word for "doubt" has more the meaning of "weakening or loss of faith."[4] Faith was already present, but then began to fail. The word is used of Peter, after he had started to walk on the water, and then asked himself, "What am I doing here?" Jesus said to him, "Why did you doubt?" (Matthew 14:31). The word is also used of the disciples, when they met with the risen Lord: "And when they saw him, they worshiped him; but some doubted" (Matthew 28:17).

The third word originally meant "to discriminate, decide," and in Hellenistic Greek came to mean "to be divided in mind, hesitate, doubt."[5] It is used when God instructed Peter concerning the men sent by Cornelius: "accompany them without hesitation"—I suppose we might translate it, "without allowing your critical judgment to hold you back by doubting My word" (Acts 10:20).

[2] Traditionally, there were five wounds: the hands, the side, and the feet. Strangely enough, Scripture nowhere mentions any nailing of the feet of Jesus!

[3] In Greek, *aporô.* Quite similar in meaning is *diaporô.*

[4] The Greek word is *distázō,* which is somewhat like the Latin *dubitare* in its formation from the word for "two."

[5] In Greek, *diakrínō.*

None of these words is used about Thomas, and none of them truly fits the situation.

If we turn to the idea of "unbelief," we find again that there are several kinds of unbelief, although in this case we do not find the distinction in the use of different Greek words. Rather, the differentiation must be sought in how the word is used.[6] There is a kind of unbelief that might be termed scientific skepticism. It says, "I do not believe, because there is insufficient evidence to convince me." It is a judgment that may be challenged by others who are convinced that there is sufficient evidence, but we must recognize the fact that the scientist has been trained to verify his observations, and the once-for-all (the miracle, the unique Son, the single resurrection, etc.) is not repeatable and therefore not verifiable by the scientist. The historian, on the other hand, must accept hearsay evidence; his verification is only an effort to check the accuracy of the witnesses. This skeptical unbelief is perhaps illustrated by the disciples, when the women reported their experiences at the garden tomb to the apostles: "but these words seemed to them an idle tale, and they did not believe [literally, they disbelieved] them" (Luke 24:11).

A second kind of unbelief is deliberate rejection. Paul uses the noun form of the word, "unbelievers," quite often in his Corinthian letters, to designate non-Christians (see I Corinthians 7:12-15; II Corinthians 6:14-15, etc.), but the deliberateness of the rejection is more sharply etched in a statement such as that reported at the close of Acts: "And some were convinced by what he said, while others disbelieved" (Acts 28:24). Paul's use of a quotation from Isaiah (6:9-10) serves to define further the kind of disbelief that is intended.

A third kind of unbelief is perhaps best illustrated by the father of the demon-possessed boy. Jesus said to him, "All things are possible to him who believes," and the father replied, "I believe; help my unbelief!" (Mark 9:23-24). It is almost like saying, "I have faith; but I haven't yet come to the place where I have real faith." There is nothing essentially wrong with this kind of unbelief, provided we do not become established in it. But if we become content with unbelief, we shall one day find ourselves confronted with the horrible judgment prepared for the cowardly, the faithless, murderers, liars, and others like them (see Revelation 21:8).

[6] In Greek, the word is *ápistos* ("without faith") and its derivatives.

What was Thomas' characteristic? It was not doubt. It could hardly be called skepticism. In the light of what happened when he was confronted with the evidence, we cannot call it deliberate disbelief. The best term is simply unbelief. Jesus confronted Thomas, and said, "Put your finger here, and see my hands; and put out your hand, and place it in my side; do not be faithless, but believing" (John 20:27).[7]

Thomas and his faith. The resurrection of Jesus Christ is central in the faith of the Christian Church. Carefully defined and clearly understood, it would be possible to say that without the resurrection of Jesus Christ there is no Christian faith. This is what the Apostle Paul says in his great chapter on the resurrection. Read it carefully: "If Christ has not been raised, then our preaching is in vain and your faith is in vain. . . . If Christ has not been raised, your faith is futile and you are still in your sins" (I Corinthians 15:14, 17).

This has always been the unwavering and unquestioned faith of the Church. There has never been a doctrinal controversy on the subject of the resurrection of Christ.[8] The Church discussed the natures of Christ, the Trinity, the procession of the Holy Spirit, and many other subjects, but it was unanimous in the declaration that on the third day Christ rose again. The person who denies the resurrection of Christ places himself outside the faith of the historic Christian Church just as surely as does the man who denies the incarnation.

In the hazy thinking and careless usage of words that characterize too much of modern religious thought and writing, immortality is often confused with resurrection. Immortality is a state of being not mortal, not subject to death. Resurrection is an act, a change, a rising from the dead to newness of life. What could the statement "on the third day He was immortal" possibly mean? If He was immortal on the third day, He was equally immortal on the second and the fourth. Moreover, what is the significance of the resurrection appearances of Jesus to His apostles? And that brings us back to Thomas. Thomas was

---

[7] The play on words in Greek (*ápistos* and *pistós*) would be better brought out if translated, "do not be believing-less, but believing" or "do not be without faith, but with faith."

[8] An examination of R. Seeberg's two-volume *Text-Book of the History of Doctrines* (Philadelphia: Lutheran Publication Society, 1904), for example, will show that the word "resurrection" is not even in the index. The only discussions on the subject of resurrection that took place concerned the nature of our bodies in the final resurrection. I do not consider modern unbelief to be in the category of a doctrinal controversy.

not convinced by the accounts that he heard. He wanted evidence
before he was willing to commit himself in faith. What kind of evidence was available?

First, either Jesus died on the cross, or He did not die. If He did
not die, then what happened to Him? The "swoon" theory supplies
the answer: He revived in the cool of the tomb. Pushing aside the
stone,[9] He made His way to the apostles, who nursed Him back to
health. Apart from the hypocrisy involved in apostles who would
report His resurrection knowing the truth, how does this fit with the
experience of Thomas?

Second, if Jesus died on the cross, either His body was found in
the tomb, or the tomb was found empty. His body was not found
in the tomb: that is the testimony of the women and also of Peter
and John (see Mark 16:5; John 20:6); further, it is corroborated by
the fact that His enemies did not produce the body.

Third, if an empty tomb was found, it was either the wrong tomb
or the right one. The right one was identified by a seal and a guard of
soldiers (Matthew 27:66). Independent groups or individuals found
their way to a common point: Mary Magdalene, very early in the
morning, then Peter and John, and still later the women mentioned
in Mark (see John 20:1 ff.; Mark 16:1 ff.)—and their testimony concurs. They could not all have made the same mistake. Moreover, the
testimony of the soldiers substantiates this point (Matthew 28:11).

Fourth, if the tomb was found empty, the body either was taken or
rose. If it was taken, it was taken either by enemies or friends; if by
enemies, they would have produced it and silenced the apostolic
preaching of the resurrection; if by friends, then we have, as many
have recognized, the psychological impossibility of apostles suffering
martyrdom for what they knew was not true. The story that the
disciples had stolen the body was tried at the very outset (see Matthew
28:11-15), and convinced no one. Except for some cheap pulp writings
or some anti-Christian movements, this theory has been given up.
And again, we must ask, what about Thomas? Can we suppose that
he who refused to be convinced by apostolic testimony could be convinced by apostolic fraud?

That brings us to the last step of the logical process: Jesus Christ

[9] The theory was first proposed in ignorance of the nature of such stones.
They roll in deep-cut grooves, and fall into a socket when closed. It would
take two healthy men to move such a stone, as the women knew (Mark 16:3).

rose from the dead. Either He was seen thereafter, or He was not seen. Peter says he saw Him; the two from Emmaus claim they saw Him; the women saw Him; the rest of the apostles saw Him. Paul, having started out as a bitter opponent of the movement, declared that Jesus appeared "to more than five hundred brethren at one time," most of whom were still alive when he wrote those words (I Corinthians 15: 6). But what about Thomas? Thomas refused to believe the testimony of anyone else—even that of his closest friends. Then came the night when Jesus appeared to him, challenged him to put his unbelief to the test by touching the wounds still visible, and Thomas yielded: "My Lord and my God!"

I suppose one other objection should be faced here. All that I have said is based on the Gospel record; but how do we know that this record is true? This is a study in itself.[10] Suffice it to say here that as a result of nearly two centuries of critical study, the Gospels are as firmly entrenched as ever. Critical scholars have now despaired of trying to find a "historical Jesus" (by which they mean non-supernatural) by critical study of the Gospels; they admit that these Gospels are products of the first century and represent the convictions of the Early Church; they now concentrate their efforts on trying to explain the faith that produced the Gospels. It seems fair to say that the evidence for the resurrection of Jesus Christ is as historically trustworthy as any evidence for any event in the past. If on the basis of critical judgment applied to the study of historic documents we cannot believe in the resurrection of Jesus Christ, then we cannot believe anything. Alexander's Empire can be explained away as the projection into the past of Hellenistic ideals, and Napoleon's campaign to Egypt as an attempt by his followers to make him as great as Alexander.

Thomas and his followers. Thomas faced the problem of faith for all honest unbelievers. Jesus knew that there would be others like Thomas: "Have you believed because you have seen me? Blessed are those who have not seen and yet believe" (John 20:29).

Some doubters do not deserve to be classed with Thomas: those who are superficial and are not interested in the evidence; sophomoric persons who are proud of being skeptics and do not want to see any

[10] See, for example, F. F. Bruce, *The New Testament Documents: Are They Reliable?* (fifth revised edition; Grand Rapids, Mich.: Wm. B. Eerdmans Publishing Co., 1960), 120 pp.

evidence that will force them to change their minds; and the disbelievers, who flatly reject all evidence.

But there are others who can be called honest doubters. They do not believe the evidence is sufficient, or they have not considered the evidence. They are willing to consider it, and Thomas would be the first to invite them to sit down while he tells them his experience.

You and I shall probably never have the opportunity in this life of seeing the Lord Jesus Christ. Paul claimed that he was given such an experience—we have seen this in an earlier study—and there have been others who have claimed to have had a vision of Christ. But for most of us, God requires us to rest content with the apostolic testimony. I believe in the resurrection of Jesus Christ because I believe in the reliability of the record; because I believe the testimony contained in the record is that of reasonable men, rational men, who were convinced against their first doubts that their Lord was alive again. I believe their testimony is not only historically supported, but also psychologically supported, for their subsequent course of life and action can only be explained on the basis of their experience. I believe in the resurrection because it is consistent with the nature of God, who could not let such a One as Jesus be conquered by death. Finally, I believe in the resurrection of Jesus Christ because only such a faith can account for whatever spiritual power I can find in my own self. Is this your faith too?[11]

[11] For an excellent article, see W. M. Smith, "Resurrection," *Baker's Dictionary of Theology*, pp. 448-456.

CHAPTER XVII

John the Theologian

WHEN I VISITED Ephesus, I found that a portion of the modern city is known as Ayasuluk—a corruption of the name Hagios Theologos, "Holy Theologian." This name was given to Saint John, who lived in Ephesus, according to a strong tradition, in the closing years of his life.

Theologians today are not high on the list of the world's most popular figures. Let a preacher announce that he is planning to give a series of theological lectures, and the people stay away in droves. Scientists, on the other hand, are quite popular. Yet the strange and simple fact is that theologians are, or ought to be, scientists. That statement needs explaining, I know. A scientist is one who has learned to apply scientific method, which is to observe, record, compare, control, and draw whatever conclusions are valid. The theologian ("theology," as the word implies, is the orderly study of God) should observe, record, compare, control, and draw conclusions concerning what he can learn about God.[1]

The Bible, we are told, does not contain theology. In a sense, this is true. Neither does the world contain geology or chemistry. But the world does contain the data which the scientist can arrange into the science of geology or chemistry; and the Bible and the world likewise contain the data which the theologian can arrange in orderly and systematic manner—which is theology. Theology, by its very nature, is fraught with the dangers of subjectivism. The theologian, if he is not extremely careful, will record his impressions or opinions about God and the spiritual world, and think that these are objective data; and the scientist, of course, becomes impatient with him.

The theologian, therefore, should have a long life, for he has many observations to make; he should be intimately acquainted with God,

---

[1] There is a different viewpoint, according to which the theologian is a philosopher. The difference, in my estimation, arises from a man's methodology: if he works at the problem from deductive processes and speculation, he is more of the philosopher; if he works inductively from what God has revealed, he is more of the scientist.

165

not only in mystical immediacy, but also in some way that is sensuously verifiable; and he should be gifted in ability to make known his conclusions in such a way that others will understand him.

John had these qualifications.[2] He lived to about one hundred years of age. He was a mystic, and yet he knew the Incarnate Son of God in the flesh (cf. I John 1:1). His Gospel is, beyond any argument, a beautiful book, a book that presents theological concepts in the simplest form, a book that men have read and loved and understood—at least sufficiently to give them satisfaction of soul.

John and the Holy Spirit. The most extensive, and in fact the only satisfactory teachings on the Holy Spirit in the Gospels are in the Gospel of John. This omission in the other Gospels may seem strange in the light of the emphasis placed upon the subject of the Holy Spirit in the Early Church as portrayed in the book of Acts. I cannot explain it; I can only record it. I cannot explain it any more than I can explain the fact that the great creeds of the Church are deficient in their statements concerning the Holy Spirit. The Westminister Confession, for example (adopted A.D. 1643), had no satisfactory statement on the Holy Spirit, and the Presbyterian Church, which adopted the Westminster Confession in 1729, added the chapter on the Holy Spirit in 1903.

On the last night before His death, Jesus said, "These things I have spoken to you, while I am still with you. But the Counselor, the Holy Spirit, whom the Father will send in my name, he will teach you all things, and bring to your remembrance all that I have said to you" (John 14:25-26). Perhaps John did not particularly notice those words when they were spoken—no one else recorded them—but sixty-five years or so later, he remembered them as clearly as if they had just been uttered. Why? To reply that this is how the mind works, that as we grow older we tend to remember details of our earlier life, is only part of the answer. John remembered because the Holy Spirit helped him to remember. That is what the Holy Spirit is for.

[2] This is not the place to enter into a discussion of the Johannine problems. I am personally convinced that the simplest and most satisfactory solution to the problem is to accept the traditional view that John the son of Zebedee, the "disciple whom Jesus loved," wrote the Gospel of John, the Epistles, and the Apocalypse. This chapter proceeds on that assumption. For a discussion of the problem see R. V. G. Tasker, *The Gospel According to St. John* (Grand Rapids, Mich.: Wm. B. Eerdmans Publishing Co., 1960), pp. 11-20, and William Temple, *Readings in St. John's Gospel* (London: Macmillan and Co., 1950), pp. ix-xxxiii.

This certainly does not mean that the Holy Spirit leaves us free from any responsibility or effort to memorize. Students in my Hebrew classes who feel that they can depend upon the Holy Spirit to take the place of memorizing vocabulary soon discover the heretical nature of such a theory. Moreover, it does not mean that John's records of Jesus' teachings will be in the exact words that Jesus used. Six decades had perhaps taken away some of the words, but had added understanding and depth of meaning. "Memory, reflection, and the incubative work of the Spirit enabled the writer to penetrate to the heart of the Lord's person and mission and so elicit truth which he perceived only dimly, if at all, in his earlier days."[3]

Jesus had said also, "I will pray the Father, and he will give you another Counselor, to be with you for ever, even the Spirit of truth" (John 14:16-17). John had lived long enough to see the forces of falsehood begin to oppose the truth of the gospel. Men were denying that Jesus was the Christ, that He was possessed of the Father (I John 2:22-23); men were teaching that gratification of the fleshly appetites was not sin, that the fleshly nature of man was not real, that only the spiritual nature was real (I John 3:4-9); men were teaching that the Son of God could not therefore have taken a true human nature (I John 4:2-3). But the Holy Spirit, the Third Person of the Godhead who was sent to dwell in all who believe in Christ, is the Spirit of truth. He was the source of John's spiritual discernment of truth and error (I John 4:13; 5-7; cf. 2:26-27).

Some will say that this is not a very sure defense of truth; that it is too "subjective," and cannot be trusted. Two things need to be kept in mind: The Spirit who guides us in truth, who helps us discern between truth and error, is the same Spirit who inspired the Holy Scriptures; therefore truth will always be consonant with Scripture. In the second place, the guidance of the Spirit today extends to the entire Church, hence every individual is obligated to check his spiritual discernment with that of other Christians—including those of previous generations whose testimony is recorded in the great creeds and theological works of Christendom.

Jesus had further said concerning the Spirit, "And when he comes, he will convince the world of sin and of righteousness and of judgment" (John 16:8). He is the *Holy* Spirit, or the Spirit of holiness.

[3] Everett F. Harrison, "The Gospel and the Gospels," *Bibliotheca Sacra* 116 (April, 1959), p. 114.

John had had many years in which to learn the lessons of holiness. He knew that Jesus had once told Nicodemus, "Unless one is born of water and the Spirit, he cannot enter the kingdom of God" (John 3:5). He knew that access to the Kingdom under the symbol of the Holy City was denied to all evildoers (Revelation 21:8; 22:15). He knew that "any one born of God does not sin, but He who was born of God keeps him, and the evil one does not touch him" (I John 5:18). To John this was no mere academic discussion. He knew from experience that the One who was most completely possessed of the Holy Spirit could not be convicted of any sin. Jesus was holy as God was holy, and the Holy Spirit was the Spirit of Jesus.

Yet once more, Jesus had said, "When the Counselor comes, whom I shall send to you from the Father, even the Spirit of truth, who proceeds from the Father, he will bear witness to me" (John 15:26). The Spirit does not witness to Himself. For this reason Christians sometimes ask, "How do I know whether I have the Holy Spirit?" The Spirit witnesses to Jesus, just as the apostles witnessed to Jesus (cf. John 15:27).

The Holy Spirit is no mere doctrine: He is an experience. Every Christian in the Early Church knew that he possessed the Spirit of God, for he had an experience of the presence of the Spirit. That very same Spirit who dwelt in Jesus dwells in you and me, and we know it—or else He is not present (I John 3:24). He works through the Scriptures as we read or meditate upon them. He reminds us of God's will when we are tempted to wander away into sin. He tells us of Christ and His redeeming work. He warns us of error when we hear some false gospel. He helps us discern between error and truth. He does all these things—if we let Him. But we must learn to become sensitive to His leading. The Apostle John had developed that sensitivity; that is why John was Christlike, for he had let the Spirit of Christ dwell in him. Did John speak in tongues? Did he have the gift of healing? Very little is said about these gifts in connection with John. But he did have the best gift of the Spirit, the gift of love. He learned that "if God so loved us, we also ought to love one another" (I John 4:11). In fact, "Love one another" could be described as John's life-text.

John and the Son of God. John was one of the first to heed the words of John the Baptist and follow Jesus (John 1:35-39). John was the last (and perhaps the only) disciple at the foot of the cross (John 19:26). Between those two events, John was with Jesus during most of His ministry. As one of the "inner circle" of the apostles (Peter, James, and John), he witnessed some of Jesus' works and experiences that the rest of the Twelve did not behold. Perhaps that is why he was the first to believe in the resurrection (John 20:8).

John was one of the sons of Zebedee (Matthew 4:21), and from the fact that Zebedee had "hired servants" (cf. Mark 1:20) it is assumed that he had a sizeable fishing business on the Sea of Galilee. Zebedee's wife was Salome[4] (compare Mark 15:40 with Matthew 27:55-56), who was one of the women who ministered to Jesus and the disciples and one of those who went to the tomb to care for His body. According to what seems to me to be the normal reading of John 19:25, there were four women at the foot of the cross (it would be contrary to all experience for two sisters to have the same name); and if this is compared with the passages in Matthew and Mark just cited, we may reasonably infer that Salome was the sister of Mary the mother of Jesus. If so, then John was a cousin (or near relative) of John the Baptist, as well as a cousin of Jesus. This may explain some of the evidences of familiarity displayed by James and John and by their mother. We have already seen that Jesus did not tolerate demands based on earthly relationships.

In the Fourth Gospel, John does not refer to himself or his brother by name, but five times he does refer to "the disciple whom Jesus loved";[5] the only identification that meets the requirements in all of these texts is John himself. Some think that it would display gross egotism to call oneself "the disciple whom Jesus loved." But let us think about it a bit. Jesus did show some sort of preference for Peter, James, and John, when He took them with Him on certain occasions. Jesus did choose Peter and John to prepare for the Passover that was to become the Last Supper (Luke 22:8). Jesus did commend His mother into the care of John (John 19:26-27). There are indications that Jesus did love John in a way that was just a little different from His love for the others.

But let us look at this from a different angle. Jesus had given to

---

[4] To be distinguished, of course, from the daughter of Herodias who was instrumental in having John the Baptist beheaded. The name is pronounced suh-lō′me.

[5] John 13:23; 19:26; 20:2; 21:7, 20.

James and John the name "sons of thunder" (Mark 3:17). What led to that name we are not told; but some of the events that occurred later may give us a clue. One day—and it was late in the ministry, toward the time of the crucifixion—Jesus and His disciples were on their way to Jerusalem, and He sent disciples on ahead into a Samaritan village to make arrangements probably for their lodging. The village refused to give them hospitality. James and John said, "Lord, do you want us to bid fire come down from heaven and consume them?" Jesus turned and rebuked them (Luke 9:54-55). Another time, John said, "Master, we saw a man casting out demons in your name, and we forbade him, because he does not follow with us." Again Jesus rebuked him with the words, "Do not forbid him; for he that is not against you is for you" (Luke 9:49-50). On still another occasion, Salome brought her sons James and John to Jesus, and said, "Command that these two sons of mine may sit, one at your right hand and one at your left, in your kingdom" (Matthew 20:21; cf. Mark 10:35-41). Once again a rebuke was in order, and Jesus administered it kindly but firmly.

That John thought of these events many times I have no doubt—and I suppose that whenever he did, he grew red around the ears. He probably thought, "How He loved me, to put up with such a man!" John never told any of these stories in his Gospel—but he did write, "If we say we have no sin, we deceive ourselves . . ." (I John 1:8).

Son of God! John walked with Him, lived with Him, listened to Him. John heard Him make statements that sounded like the great "I Am": Jehovah Himself (cf. John 8:58). John saw Him perform miracles the like of which the world had never heard (cf. John 9:32). John heard Him pray in Gethsemane. John saw Him die on Calvary. John saw the grave cloths in the empty tomb. And John wrote, "The Word became flesh and dwelt among us, full of grace and truth; we have beheld his glory, glory as of the only Son from the Father" (John 1:14), and again, "That which was from the beginning, which we have heard, which we have seen with our eyes, which we have looked upon and touched with our hands . . . that which we have seen and heard we proclaim also to you, so that you may have fellowship with us; and our fellowship is with the Father and with his Son Jesus Christ" (I John 1:1-3).

To John the essence of antichrist was the denial of the Sonship of Jesus Christ: "Who is the liar but he who denies that Jesus is the

Christ? This is the antichrist, he who denies the Father and the Son" (cf. I John 2:18-24). To John the great divide was the witness to the incarnation: "Every spirit which confesses that Jesus Christ has come in the flesh is of God, and every spirit which does not confess Jesus is not of God" (I John 4:2-3).

To John the way God made His love known to the world was the incarnation: "In this the love of God was made manifest among us, that God sent his only Son into the world, so that we might live through him" (I John 4:9). The propitiation for our sins, the satisfaction of divine justice necessary because of our guilt, the removal of divine wrath against all unrighteousness, was possible only by the act of God's love: "In this is love, not that we loved God but that he loved us and sent his Son to be the expiation [or better, propitiation][6] for our sins" (I John 4:10). "He appeared to take away sins, and in him there is no sin" (I John 3:5).

John wrote his Gospel to set forth his convictions: "these are written that you may believe that Jesus is the Christ, the Son of God, and that believing you may have life in his name" (John 20:31). Some would tell us that the Son of God of the Fourth Gospel is not the simple Carpenter of the Synoptics. But did John make Jesus, or did Jesus make John? Did the son of Zebedee turn the Carpenter of Nazareth into the Son of God, or did the One who came that we might have life turn the Galilean fisherman into the Holy Theologian? For myself, I find it easier to believe the second alternative.

John and God the Father. In the symbolism of the Christian Church, John is often portrayed as an eagle, which is meant to imply that as the eagle is said to be the only bird able to look directly into the sun, so the Apostle John is the only evangelist able to look directly upon God. I am not sure that either the symbolic identification or the explanation is true—but there is a great truth behind the symbolism. Philip spoke for all of us: "Lord, show us the Father, and we shall be satisfied." Jesus answered, "He who has seen me has seen the Father" (cf. John 14:8-9). John has attempted to portray Jesus in such a way that we shall see the Father. It can be summarized, I think, in one word: love.

"God so loved the world that he gave his only Son, that whoever

[6] For a study of this great theme, and in particular the words used to describe it, see Leon Morris, *The Apostolic Preaching of the Cross* (Grand Rapids, Mich.: Wm. B. Eerdmans Publishing Co., 1955), pp. 125-185, especially pp. 177-180.

believes in him should not perish but have eternal life. For God sent the Son into the world, not to condemn the world, but that the world might be saved through him" (John 3:16-17). Love is the only sufficient reason for the redemptive work of God in Christ. You and I have no claim on God. He owes us nothing. We are not by natural birth His children—that is a Stoic idea that has forced its way into Christian (or should we say sub-Christian?) thought. At this point the scientist is absolutely right when he ridicules the notion that this microscopically insignificant bit of the vast universe should presume to identify himself with the Creator. But what the scientist has not been able to discover, God has revealed in Jesus Christ: God loves us. And by receiving this incarnation of God's love into our hearts and lives, we can become God's children (cf. John 1:12).

Some men object to this doctrine. They seem to think that God must treat all men exactly alike. But it is not God who is to be condemned for His love, but man for his unbelief: "He who does not believe is condemned already, because he has not believed in the name of the only Son of God. And this is the judgment, that the light has come into the world, and men loved darkness rather than light, because their deeds were evil" (John 3:18-19).

Only love is sufficient to explain the sacrifice of Jesus. Why did God let His Son die? What kind of divine justice is it that allowed wicked men to torture and kill One who went about doing only good? Or was God unable to stop it? Men struggle with the problem, seeking an answer; but the answer that God has given is sufficient: He loved us, even while we were sinners. "In this the love of God was made manifest among us, that God sent his only Son into the world, so that we might live through him" (I John 4:9). Jesus willingly went to the cross because He knew that only in this way would the Father be glorified. "Now is my soul troubled. And what shall I say, 'Father, save me from this hour'? No, for this purpose I have come to this hour. Father, glorify thy name" (John 12:27-28). After John had pondered the mystery of divine condescension for many years, he realized at last, "We have seen and testify that the Father has sent his Son as the Savior of the world. . . . So we know and believe the love God has for us" (I John 4:14, 16).

Love is sufficient to express obedience to divine commandments. "This is my commandment, that you love one another as I have loved you. . . . This I command you, to love one another" (John 15:12, 17).

Every law in the Decalogue can be obeyed by simply this: Love one another. The summary of the Law was expressed by Jesus in the two commandments, to love God, and to love your neighbor. John says, "Beloved, let us love one another; for love is of God, and he who loves is born of God and knows God. He who does not love does not know God; for God is love" (I John 4:7-8).

To John the example of divine love is sufficient to compel human love. "Beloved, if God so loved us, we also ought to love one another" (I John 4:11). To John the demonstration of love was a manifestation of God: "No man has ever seen God; if we love one another, God abides in us and his love is perfected in us" (I John 4:12). In fact, so essential is the demonstration of love on our part that John writes with great emphasis, "If any one says, 'I love God' and hates his brother, he is a liar; for he who does not love his brother whom he has seen, cannot love God whom he has not seen. And this commandment we have from him, that he who loves God should love his brother also" (I John 4:20-21).

When man and woman are joined in perfect love, there is unity. Oneness is the ultimate realization of love. Because of the love of the Father for the Son and the Son for the Father, Jesus could say, "I and the Father are one" (John 10:30). Using a different figure, Jesus described this perfect unity as vine and branches, and immediately He passed from speaking of abiding in the vine to speak of abiding in love (cf. John 15:1-10).

The most perfect expression of this unity in love is found in Jesus' prayer. "I have manifested thy name to the men whom thou gavest me out of the world. . . . I have given them thy word; and the world has hated them because they are not of the world, even as I am not of the world. I do not pray that thou shouldst take them out of the world, but that thou shouldst keep them from the evil one. . . . I do not pray for these only, but also for those who are to believe in me through their word, that they may all be one; even as thou, Father, art in me, and I in thee, that they also may be in us, so that the world may believe that thou hast sent me. The glory which thou hast given me I have given to them, that they may be one even as we are one, I in them and thou in me, that they may become perfectly one, so that the world may know that thou hast sent me and hast loved them even as thou hast loved me" (John 17:6-23).

This is John the Theologian. Many have summarized his theology in the key words: light, life, love. Life, I think, would characterize what he tells us about the Holy Spirit, for He is the source of life. We are born anew by the Spirit. We live by the Spirit. We have holiness of life by the Spirit. Light characterizes the Son, the true Light that came into the world. In His light we see light. God the Father is invisible, but the Son has manifested Him. Love characterizes the Father. God is love. We do not even know God if we do not know what love is, and to say that we love God without loving our brother human being is hollow mockery. Yet these three are one, and what is said of any one Person can be said of the others. We therefore say that these three are one God.

You thought theology was supposed to be dry and lifeless? Not so. Theology brings God into daily life. It derives concrete realizations from the abstract. It gathers together diverse teachings into useful categories and applies them to life situations. At least that is what John the Theologian did with theology.

CHAPTER XVIII

The Triumphant Christ

WE PREVIOUSLY DEVOTED a study to the human nature of Jesus Christ, pointing out at the time that there is also a divine nature to be considered (see Chapter IV). I have saved the study of the divine nature of Jesus Christ to the end because it can best be understood against the background of the Early Church. For the Early Church is, as I hope we have seen, the work of Jesus Christ the Son of God through the Holy Spirit whom He sent following His own death, resurrection, and ascension to heaven. To try to explain the Church as merely the work of men who had caught the vision of what the Galilean Carpenter was trying to teach them is to fail to understand either the Galilean or those who claim to be His apostles.

Christ in the midst of the churches. In His great commission, when the risen Jesus sent His apostles out into the world to make disciples of all nations, He added the promise, "and lo, I am with you always, to the close of the age" (Matthew 28:20). In the exquisite, if often misunderstood, symbolism of the Book of Revelation, this promise of Jesus' abiding presence is expressed in a different way. There John says, "I turned to see the voice that was speaking to me, and on turning I saw seven golden lampstands, and in the midst of the lampstands one like a son of man" (Revelation 1:12-13). John fell as one dead before the vision, but the Speaker, who identified Himself as the One who died and is alive for evermore, explained the symbolism: "the seven lampstands are the seven churches" (Revelation 1:20). Christ, then, is portrayed symbolically as standing in the midst of the churches.

Too often we seem to have the idea that Jesus has gone to heaven, where He is seated on the right hand of God, and whence some day He shall return to earth; meantime we are left to run things in our own wisdom and strength. Now it is true that Jesus has returned to heaven and maintains a session of intercession. It is also true that He is coming again. But it is not true that He has left us alone in the meantime. He has sent us One who is like Himself, who has all the power of the Godhead, who remains with us and in us during all this age; and these two are so completely identified that we can speak either of the Holy Spirit or the Spirit of Christ.

The seven churches are seven historic churches: Ephesus, Smyrna, Pergamum, Thyatira, Sardis, Philadelphia, and Laodicea. I have visited each of these sites. They are not just mysterious names put in a strange book; they are the locations of churches started when Paul was in Ephesus, and continuing during the ministry of Timothy and John and for centuries afterwards. They form approximately a circle, moving clockwise from Ephesus, the most distant being less than one hundred miles.

The Lord Jesus once said, "I will build my church" (Matthew 16:18). In the Book of Acts we see Him building His Church, working in and through men such as Peter, Stephen, Paul, Barnabas, and others. But that was only the beginning. The Book of Acts, as many have noted, has no true ending. In a sense we might say that it is still being written, for Christ is still building His Church.

The first of the seven churches in Revelation is the Church at Ephesus. Jesus tells John to write to the "angel"—the Greek word also means "messenger," and almost certainly refers to the pastor or minister—of the church and say, "I know your works" (Revelation 2:2). These words are spoken by the One "who holds the seven stars in his right hand, who walks among the seven golden lampstands." The "stars" are the "angels" or "messengers" (Revelation 1:20), and the lampstands, as we have seen, are the churches. The number seven, used so frequently in Revelation, suggests the idea of completion—not that the seven churches are the only churches, but that they are symbolic or representative of all churches. In other words, putting the symbolism into prosaic language, Jesus says, "I who hold the messengers in my hand and who walk in the midst of the churches—I know your works."

That is a beautiful thought, is it not? He knows the toil, the patient endurance, the impatience with false teachers (Revelation 2:2). He knows the tribulation and poverty (Revelation 2:9). He knows every detail of the life of every church.

But it is also a frightening thought, for He who knows the faith and patience, love and good works, also knows the unbelief, the lack of vitality, and the lukewarmness. He who stands in the midst of the lampstands, holding the stars in His right hand, is also the One out of whose mouth issues the two-edged sword (Revelation 1:16). The sword coming from the mouth can only be the Word, and its two edges can only symbolize its ability to cut both ways, in praise and in blame.

The Church in Ephesus was a church of toil and patience, but it was also a church that had abandoned the love it had at first (Revelation 2:4). That is a terrible thing to have to say to a church or to an individual. It indicates the lack of a sense of judgment. When you abandon what formerly you loved, it means either that you had poor judgment when you developed that love, or that you have poor judgment in leaving it. In other words, you sit in judgment on yourself either way. It indicates a lack of maturity, a basic inability to make up your mind, an absence of a true sense of values, a vacillating spirit. What can be done about it? "Remember then from what you have fallen, repent and do the works you did at first" (Revelation 2:5). Think back to the beginning, think of what led to that first love; then repent, turn your mind about, think the way you once thought; go back to the works you did in that previous way of thinking. And what if you do not? "If not, I will come to you and remove your lampstand from its place, unless you repent" (Revelation 2:5). The lampstand is the church. Christ is saying, if the church refuses to do the work of the church, if it refuses to demonstrate the love of the church, it is no church. By removing the lampstand, He takes away its right to call itself a church.

Approximately forty years earlier, Paul had expressed his great concern about the Church at Ephesus. "I know that after my departure fierce wolves will come in among you, not sparing the flock; and from among your own selves will arise men speaking perverse things, to draw away the disciples after them. Therefore be alert . . ." (Acts 20:29-31). No church can say that it has not been warned. What Paul said to the elders of the Church at Ephesus the Holy Spirit is saying to every church. What Christ said to the angel of the Church at Ephesus, the Spirit is saying to all churches. "He who has an ear, let him hear what the Spirit says to the churches" (Revelation 2:7).

What has been said about Ephesus can be said, *mutatis mutandis,* about the other churches. The letters to the seven churches are letters that search out specific points of praise or blame, so that "all the churches shall know that I am he who searches mind and heart, and I will give to each of you as your works deserve" (Revelation 2:23). We call this judgment. Judgment begins at the house of God.

Some men do not like the idea of judgment, and quite often the preacher hears an objection to sermons on the subject. I think that is because of a faulty notion of what judgment is. When we say, "He is a man of good judgment," no one shudders; but when we say, "God is a God of judgment," men cringe. But are we not saying the same thing? Men sometimes think of judgment as the final act, the ax that falls on the neck of mankind, ending the drama. There is indeed a finality in the Last Judgment, but we should think first of judgment as a process. God is a good Judge who discriminates between the good and the bad, between that which has value and that which has no value, between the ephemeral and the eternal. He judges His Church, not just at the end but at each stage along the way. Like a careful viticulturist, He prunes away that which is not good, in order that the good will be better. Like a skilled surgeon, He removes that which is diseased in order that life may be preserved.

There are those who seem to think of heaven as a cosmic junkyard, as though God is interested in collecting broken and rotten lives. Anyone who has been a failure can, if he will only attend the evangelist's rally, get into heaven. This is a travesty on the grace of God and a denial of His judgment. God saves sinners—but there will be no sinners in heaven, only ex-sinners. In beautiful symbolism, heaven is described for us, and we read: "They shall bring into it the glory and the honor of the nations. But nothing unclean shall enter it, nor any one who practices abomination or falsehood, but only those who are written in the Lamb's book of life" (Revelation 21:26-27). God's judgments in this age are gracious acts, whereby we who name His name are prepared for the Holy City.

Christ in the midst of the churches is also the Christ of rewards. To each of the churches He has some word concerning the reward He will give to those who overcome. Not all of His rewards are reserved for the age to come; even in this life we experience the benefits of serving the Lord in His Church.

Christ on the throne. In His great commission, Jesus said: "All authority in heaven and on earth has been given to me" (Matthew 28:18). This is expressed symbolically in the Book of Revelation in the following terms: "I was in the Spirit, and lo, a throne stood in heaven, with one seated on the throne! . . . And I saw in the right hand of him who was seated on the throne a scroll written within and on the back, sealed with seven seals; and I saw a strong angel proclaiming with a loud voice, 'Who is worthy to open the scroll and break its seals?' . . . And between the throne and the four living creatures and among the elders, I saw a Lamb standing, as though it had been slain . . . ; and he went and took the scroll from the right hand of him who was seated on the throne. . . . And they sang a new song, saying,

'Worthy art thou to take the scroll and to open its seals,
for thou wast slain and by thy blood didst ransom men for God
from every tribe and tongue and people and nation,
and hast made them a kingdom and priests to our God,
and they shall reign on earth'" (Revelation 4:2; 5:1-2, 6-7, 9-10).

The seven-sealed book is the book of destiny; it is the book of the future, the history that must yet take place on the earth. Who is able to open the book and lay bare the secrets? Who is able to control the destiny of the world? No one. No one in heaven, or on earth, or in the underworld. No one but the Lamb that had been slain, the Lion of Judah, the Root of David (cf. Revelation 5:3-5).

Men have varying views of history. Some are naïvely optimistic: things are getting better all the time. Give man enough knowledge, enough science, enough technical achievement, enough medical wisdom, and he will solve all his problems and bring in the golden age. Some are pessimistic: civilizations reach their peaks and then decline. No civilization can maintain the vitality necessary to dominate forever. History must ever be a series of rise-and-decline. Some look upon history as an endless cycle, a universal carrousel ride with its perpetual "here we go 'round again." History repeats itself. The Bible takes the truth in each of these systems and combines it into a complex idea that says that without God man is doomed to decline, but with God's redemptive power man shall reach the skies. God is in it with us, for when Jesus Christ came into this world God became incarnate, and He has never relinquished that human nature. He took it to heaven, and in so doing, He made it possible for man to become like God. He is totally involved in history, for the Church is His body, and whatever happens to the Church happens to Him; moreover, whether or not men admit it, He sits on the throne and rules the nations with a rod of iron.

The inability of anyone else to solve the riddle of the seven-sealed book is moral inability: "No one was found worthy to open the scroll or to look into it" (Revelation 5:4). Think about that for a minute or two, and you will realize how true it is. The problems of this world are moral problems. Wars, social inequities, class hatred, lust—these, and all other matters that constitute the riddle of history, are moral problems. The Christian businessman tells his pastor, "I cannot compete in this world and hold to my Christian convictions. I have to lie and cheat, I have to cut the corners, or I'll go out of business." On a vaster scale, the leaders of nations cannot operate according to the principles of the Kingdom of Heaven—the incident of the U-2 demonstrated that. While men or nations lie and deceive, all must use the same principles, or perish. Perhaps this is what Jesus had in mind when He said, "If my kingship [or kingdom] were of this world, my servants would fight" (John 18:36). This may have been what He meant when He said, "Behold, I send you out as sheep in the midst of wolves; so be wise as serpents and innocent as doves" (Matthew 10:16.[1] This is a sinful world, and there is no way out of the mess except to get rid of the sin—and that is possible only by the way of the cross. It is the Lamb that was slain who is able to break the seals and open the book.

When the seals are opened and the scroll is unrolled, what do we see? What is to be the history of the world? Well, at first it is not pleasant to behold: there is war, famine, pestilence (cf. Revelation 6:1-8, note verse 8); there is terrible persecution, and fearsome calamities (Revelation 6:9-17)—these are described as "the wrath of the Lamb." When we were looking at the picture of Christ in the midst of the churches, we saw that He visits judgments upon His own. Those judgments are in order to cleanse, to purify, to make His Church glorious, without spot or wrinkle. But in the symbolism of the

---

[1] It is possible, if the western world collapses under the godless impact of communism, that historians will one day write, "They tried to apply idealistic principles in a world that refused to adopt the same ideals." And the blindest of the blind are those ministers, who should be the interpreters of God's Word, who accept and repeat all that Jesus said about principles that are intended to apply to the Church, but who refuse to accept what Jesus said about the unbelief and the sin of the world, or the fundamental separation between the Church and the world. It is not wise for sheep to pretend that wolves are sheep!

central portion of Revelation are set forth the judgments of God on the world.

As a general principle it can be said that the judgments of God are bound up with His laws, particularly with the inexorable law of cause-and-effect. Men have war because they have rejected the way of peace. Men have famine because of the selfishness and greed of men. When empires refuse to treat their colonials like human beings, when they refuse to place confidence in them, train them, and prepare them for self-rule, empires can expect the colonies one day to rise in revolt. When the white man exalts himself as lord of the human race and treats his fellow men of different pigmentation as beasts of burden, he can expect them one day to rise up against him and seek to destroy him. When greedy capitalists exploit labor and manifest a public-be-damned attitude, they can expect a public reaction and a revolt of labor. When nations oppress nations they can be certain that war will follow.

These are the judgments of God, and they are just. When the bowls of wrath are being poured out on earth, the angel is heard to say,

"Just art thou in these thy judgments,
thou who art and wast, O Holy One.
For men have shed the blood of saints and prophets,
and thou hast given them blood to drink.
It is their due!" (Revelation 16:5-6).

But don't close the book! Read it through to the end. Men have missed the value of the Book of Revelation because they have gotten lost in the maze of details and have failed to see the progress. After the judgments comes triumph. After the failure of man comes success. "Then I saw heaven opened, and behold, a white horse! He who sat upon it is called Faithful and True. . . . On his robe and on his thigh he has a name inscribed, King of kings and Lord of lords. . . . Then I saw an angel coming down from heaven, holding in his hand the key of the bottomless pit and a great chain. And he seized the dragon, that ancient serpent, who is the Devil and Satan, and bound him for a thousand years. . . . Then Death and Hades were thrown into the lake of fire. . . . Then I saw a new heaven and a new earth . . ." (Revelation 19:11,16; 20:1-2,14; 21:1).

This is the story of the seven-sealed book. After the wars and the famines, after the horrors caused by man in his godless efforts to rule the world, comes the victory of the King of kings and the glory of His Kingdom.

Christ in the Holy City. The Lord Jesus, on the last night before He was betrayed, told His disciples, "When I go and prepare a place for you, I will come again and will take you to myself, that where I am you may be also" (John 14:3).[2] In the beautiful language of Revelation, this is set forth as follows: "I saw the holy city, new Jerusalem, coming down out of heaven from God, prepared as a bride adorned for her husband; and I heard a great voice from the throne saying, 'Behold, the dwelling of God is with men. He will dwell with them, and they shall be his people, and God Himself will be with them . . .'" (Revelation 21:2-3).

It is a beautiful city. All attempts to describe it fail because of the limitations of language. John saw it "having the glory of God, its radiance like a most rare jewel, like a jasper, clear as crystal" (Revelation 21:11). He saw a wall of jasper, and gates of pearl, a city of gold with streets of pure gold. The city was as high as it was wide and long —was it a cube, or a pyramid?—and it had a river flowing from the throne, nourishing the tree of life that grew along its banks. There was no need of the sun or moon or any artificial means of light, for the Lord God is its light (Revelation 21:11—22:5). Some men find it hard to get an intelligible picture from this description. This is because we are trying to visualize in our minds what we have never seen with our eyes. Perhaps the language is more symbolic than we think. Perhaps John himself was at a loss for words, trying to record the glories of the Holy City in expressions drawn from earth's vocabulary.

It is God's city. Centuries ago Abraham set out to find the city "whose builder and maker is God" (Hebrews 11:10). This is it. The wall of the city has twelve gates, "and on the gates the names of the twelve tribes of the sons of Israel were inscribed" (Revelation 21:12). The wall also has twelve foundations, "and on them the twelve names of the twelve apostles of the Lamb" (Revelation 21:14). It is only

---

[2] Some scholars do not think this passage refers to the Lord's return at the end of the age. I shall not debate the point, for whether in this passage or some other, the Scripture clearly teaches the return of Christ for His own at the end of the age.

one city, and only one wall; and a wall would be of no use without gates, and gates would be meaningless without a wall. It is one city, but Jew and Gentile, old and new alike have been brought together and fashioned into one to form the wall. They are one in Christ.

There is no temple in the city (cf. Revelation 21:22). When the Book of Revelation was written (perhaps A.D. 96), Jerusalem had long since been destroyed. The Temple was a heap of rubbish and ash. I have no doubt that many Jews were saying, "How can we worship the Holy One without the Temple? Without the Temple there can be no sacrifice, and without the sacrifice there can be no atonement." But what is the Temple? and what is the sacrifice of bulls and goats? These things are symbols behind which stand the greater realities. The Temple is the symbol of God's presence. There is no need of a temple in the Holy City, "for its temple is the Lord God the Almighty and the Lamb" (Revelation 21:22). And there is no further need of the sacrifice of bulls and goats, which can never take away sin, for the Lamb has been slain once for all and sin is no more.

It is a holy city. There will be no unholiness there, and no unholy beings. There will be multitudes of redeemed sinners, but all their sins will have been washed away. "Nothing unclean shall enter it, nor any one who practices abomination or falsehood, but only those who are written in the Lamb's book of life" (Revelation 21:27). "There shall no more be anything accursed, but the throne of God and of the Lamb shall be in it, and his servants shall worship him" (Revelation 22:3). God is holy, and His word has ever been, "therefore you shall be holy" (cf. Leviticus 19:2).

Sickness, sorrow, and death will never be present in the Holy City. God "will wipe away every tear from their eyes, and death shall be no more, neither shall there be mourning nor crying nor pain any more, for the former things have passed away" (Revelation 21:4). When Jesus brought Lazarus back from the grave, Lazarus returned to this world of sickness and sorrow and death. But this is not so in the City of God. No crippled children will limp in its streets, tearing the heartstrings of mothers and fathers. No loved ones will waste away consumed by suffering and disease. There will be no institutions crowded with men and women suffering from mental and nervous disorders. No heartbroken husband and father will lay his beloved wife and newborn baby in the grave. No drunken drivers will race through its streets, and no gangsters will lurk in its shadows; there will not even be shadows, and the gates will never have to be closed. No bombs will burst over the Holy City, and no air-raid sirens will ever wail. There will be no war, for the leaves of the tree of life will be for the healing of the nations (Revelation 22:2).

But before this is possible, there must be a final judgment. "Do not seal up the words of the prophecy of this book, for the time is near. Let the evildoer still do evil, and the filthy still be filthy, and the righteous still do right, and the holy still be holy. Behold, I am coming soon, bringing my recompense, to repay every one for what he has done" (Revelation 22:10-12). Here is the awfulness of the final judgment: it is so terribly final! While it is the day of grace, the evildoer can repent of his evil, and the filthy can turn for cleansing. Men can be changed! But when the last judgment is finished, there is no further day of grace. From that moment forever, men will be what they are. Inside the Holy City are those who have washed their robes, "that they may have the right to the tree of life." Outside are "the dogs and sorcerers and fornicators and murderers and idolaters, and every one who loves and practices falsehood" (Revelation 22:14-15).

Today it is still the day of grace. "The Spirit and the Bride say, 'Come.' And let him who hears say, 'Come.' And let him who is thirsty come, let him who desires take the water of life without price" (Revelation 22:17).

Bibliography

(A number of titles in my *Great Personalities of the Old Testament* are likewise pertinent to the New Testament, such as Bible Dictionaries, Atlases, etc. I have not repeated them here in the interest of space.)

BIBLE DICTIONARIES (articles on persons, places, terms, etc.)

A Dictionary of the Bible, edited by James Hastings. New York: Charles Scribner's Sons, 1898 ff. 4 vols. and extra volume. [In spite of need of revision in many places, plus presuppositions that are questionable, this work is still valuable for its many excellent articles on New Testament subjects.]

A Dictionary of Christ and the Gospels, edited by James Hastings. New York: Charles Scribner's Sons, 1924. 2 vols. [Not so well known as the previous work, but in many respects superior for work in the Gospels. Some of the articles are the finest treatments of their respective subjects that I have found.]

A Dictionary of the Apostolic Church, edited by James Hastings. New York: Charles Scribner's Sons, 1915. 2 vols. [Probably the least known of the three titles given here and of somewhat lower quality. Still, when I was teaching The Beginnings of Christianity I combed it thoroughly and found it amply rewarding.]

Baker's Dictionary of Theology, edited by Everett F. Harrison, Geoffrey W. Bromiley, and Carl F. H. Henry. Grand Rapids, Mich.: Baker Book House, 1960. 566 pp. [A very useful volume for ready reference on any subject included by the broad term Theology. The viewpoint is conservative but the scholarship is fully aware of competing views.]

(See also *The Westminster Dictionary of the Bible, Harper's Bible Dictionary,* and *The International Standard Bible Encyclopaedia,* full bibliography for which is in my previous volume.)

BIBLE GEOGRAPHIES, ATLASES, AND SIMILAR HELPS

Gustaf Dalman, *Sacred Sites and Ways.* Translated from 3d edition by Paul P. Levertoff. London: Society for Promoting Christian Knowledge, 1935. 397 pp. [Background material for studying the Gospels, based on the land, language, literature, and tradition.]

Paul Bruin and Philipp Giegel, *Jesus Lived Here.* Translated by William Neil. New York: William Morrow and Company, 1958. 239 pp. [A splendid collection of photographs to help you visualize the Holy Land.]

Asia Minor, with 160 pictures in photogravure, 8 colour plates, and introduction by Maxim Osward. Translated by Norma Deane. London: Thames and Hudson, 1957. 32 pp. + 160 plates. [A magnificent volume of pictures, not all of which pertain to Biblical backgrounds.]

Nelson Beecher Keyes, *Story of the Bible World*. Maplewood, N. J.: C. S. Hammond & Company, 1959. 192 pp. [Descriptive text, many pictures, also many maps in color.]

Henri Metzger, *Les routes de saint Paul dans l'Orient grec*. (Cahiers d'archéologie biblique, No. 4.) Paris & Neuchâtel: Delachaux & Niestlé S.A., 1954. 62 pp. [A useful study in the light of modern discovery.]

L. H. Grollenberg, *Shorter Atlas of the Bible*. Translated by Mary F. Hedlund. New York: Thomas Nelson & Sons, 1960. 195 pp. [This is a condensed version of the Atlas which I have recommended most highly. Get the larger edition if you can afford it.]

(See also *Westminster Historical Atlas* and George Adam Smith, *The Historical Geography of the Holy Land*, in my previous volume.)

ART AND LITERATURE

George Ferguson, *Signs & Symbols in Christian Art*. 2d edition. New York: Oxford University Press, 1955. 346 pp., 96 plates, XV color plates. [The symbols are illustrated by line drawings alongside the text; arrangement is by subject; the plates provide a general introduction to the great religious art of the Renaissance.]

Cynthia Pearl Maus, *Christ and the Fine Arts*. 5th edition. New York: Harper & Brothers, 1938. 764 pp. [A storehouse of illustrative material in pictures, poetry, music, and stories.]

The Story of Jesus in the World's Literature, edited by Edward Wagenknecht, illustrations by Fritz Kredel. New York: Creative Age Press, Inc., 1946. 479 pp. [A fine selection, arranged by subjects.]

DAILY LIFE IN ANCIENT TIMES

Everyday Life in Ancient Times. Highlights of the Beginnings of Western Civilization in Mesopotamia, Egypt, Greece, and Rome. Washington, D.C.: National Geographic Society, 1958. 368 pp. [Paintings, illustrations, and text illustrating the life and customs in various periods and areas of the Bible world.]

A Dictionary of Life in Bible Times, by W. Corswant, completed and illustrated by Édouard Urech, translated by Arthur Heathcote. New York: Oxford University Press, 1960. 309 pp. [An excellent work to help bring the Biblical characters to life.]

ARCHAEOLOGY

G. Ernest Wright, *Biblical Archaeology*. Abridged edition. Philadelphia: Westminster Press, 1960. 198 pp. [A condensation, in an inexpensive edition, of the larger work by the same title.]

John A. Thompson, *Archaeology and the Pre-Christian Centuries*. Grand Rapids, Mich.: Wm. B. Eerdmans Publishing Co., 1958. 139 pp.

John A. Thompson, *Archaeology and the New Testament*. Grand Rapids, Mich.: Wm. B. Eerdmans Publishing Co., 1960. 151 pp. [This and the preceding title are brief but reliable works.]

William M. Ramsay, *The Bearing of Recent Discovery on the Trustworthiness of the New Testament*. 2d edition. London: Hodder and Stoughton, 1915; reprinted 1953 by Baker Book House, Grand Rapids, Mich. [Sir William Ramsay wrote many books and articles and I cannot begin to list the important ones here. I have selected this title because it gives the author's summary of the results of his life's work. Unfortunately, Ramsay's works lack splendid organization, and the scholar has to roam through many of Ramsay's works to find material on any desired subject. We are indebted to Baker Book House for reprinting several of the more important titles.]

THE BACKGROUND OF JUDAISM

George Foot Moore, *Judaism*. Cambridge, Mass.: Harvard University Press, 1927. 2 vols. [The classic on the subject of Judaism in the first centuries of the Christian era.]

Josephus. Complete Works, translated by William Whiston. Grand Rapids, Mich.: Kregel Publications, 1960 (reprint). [The serious New Testament student should often look into Josephus for insights and sidelights. A bit of a critical approach to Josephus is, of course, necessary.]

Robert H. Pfeiffer, *History of New Testament Times*. New York: Harper & Brothers, 1949. 561 pp. [Valuable for a study of the intertestamental period and its literature; the work contains a magnificent bibliography.]

Floyd V. Filson, *The New Testament Against its Environment*. (Studies in Biblical Theology, No. 3.) London: S C M Press Ltd., 1950. 103 pp. [An excellent summary of the background of the New Testament, with footnote references to the significant publications.]

LIFE OF CHRIST

A Harmony of the Gospels, edited by William Arnold Stevens and Ernest de Witt Burton. Boston: Silver, Burdett & Company, 1897. 237 pp. [I fail to understand how anyone can study the Life of Christ without a harmony of the Gospels. This one uses the text of 1881 (English Revised Version), but in my opinion its arrangement of the events in the four Gospels is superior.]

Ralph D. Heim, *A Harmony of the Gospels for Students*. Philadelphia: Muhlenberg Press, 1947. 209 pp. [Uses the RSV text.]

Alfred Edersheim, *The Life and Times of Jesus the Messiah*. Eleventh impression. London: Longmans, Green and Co., 1901. 2 vols. [In many ways, still the best Life of Christ. There seems to be no inclination in modern scholarship to attempt a synthesis of the subject as Edersheim has done; yet much in Edersheim needs to be revised or rejected.]

William Manson, *Jesus the Messiah*. The Synoptic Tradition of the Revelation of God in Christ, with Special Reference to Form-Criticism. Philadelphia: Westminster Press, 1946. 267 pp. [Useful for an understanding of how the Gospel record is handled by modern Form-critics; Manson is quite a conservative representative of modern scholarship.]

J. Gresham Machen, *The Virgin Birth of Christ*. New York: Harper & Brothers, 1930. 415 pp. [A classic. The scholar who ignores this work lays himself open to the charge either of ignorance or of unwillingness to face the facts as presented by the best of conservative scholarship.]

G. Campbell Morgan, *The Crises of the Christ*. New York: Fleming H. Revell Co., 1903. 477 pp. [One of the finest works by one of the greatest of recent Bible expositors. Everyone who teaches or seriously studies the Life of Christ should read this work not once but often.]

G. Campbell Morgan, *The Teaching of Christ*. New York: Fleming H. Revell Co., 1913. 333 pp. [An excellent study; there are, however, areas of Christ's teachings that are not covered.]

A. B. Bruce, *The Training of the Twelve*. 3d edition. New York: Richard R. Smith, Inc., 1930. 552 pp. [A well-known and highly praised work that is rich in its insights.]

Richard Chenevix Trench, *Notes on the Parables of Our Lord*. 8th edition. New York: D. Appleton & Company, 1856. 425 pp. [A classic, but why has no one given us an up-to-date study of the same proportions?]

Richard Chenevix Trench, *Notes on the Miracles of Our Lord*. Eleventh edition. London: Macmillan and Co., 1878. 515 pp. [Again, a classic, and very rich, but in need of revision.]

A. G. Hebert, *The Throne of David*. London: Faber and Faber, 1941. 277 pp. [A modern effort to deal with Christ in the typology of the Old Testament.]

H. V. Morton, *In the Steps of the Master*. 23d edition. London: Methuen & Co., 1953. 388 pp. [This is a beautiful combination of geography, travelogue, religious devotion, and interesting anecdotes. I have carried it with me in the steps of the Master, and the opinion I had previously formed about the work was not dimished.]

THE BEGINNINGS OF CHRISTIANITY

F. J. Foakes Jackson and Kirsopp Lake, editors, *The Beginnings of Christianity*. London: Macmillan and Co., 1922. 5 vols. [A masterful work, at some places based on presuppositions which I not only cannot accept but which I feel are unwarranted. Nevertheless, it must be studied—particularly the first volume—by anyone working in Acts.]

F. F. Bruce, *A Commentary on the Book of Acts.* (The New International Commentary on the New Testament.) Grand Rapids, Mich.: Wm. B. Eerdmans Publishing Co., 1956. 555 pp. [Of all the commentaries on Acts that I have used, this is in many ways the most satisfactory. The scholarship is massive; the viewpoint is conservative; the application is devotional and helpful.]

J. Gresham Machen, *The Origin of Paul's Religion.* London: Hodder & Stoughton, 1921. 329 pp. [A thorough work on a subject that perhaps does not claim the attention today that it did formerly. Nevertheless, many of the points in this book are still valid and need to be repeated for the problems of Pauline study that are raised today.]

Bernard Ramm, *The Witness of the Spirit.* Grand Rapids, Mich.: Wm. B. Eerdmans Publishing Co., 1960. 140 pp. [A fine study of the Holy Spirit and His place in the believer's life.]

Daniel J. Theron, *Evidence of Tradition.* Grand Rapids, Mich.: Baker Book House, 1958. 135 pp. [Selections of source material, in the original languages, with English translation, for the study of the New Testament canon, the history of the Early Church, and other matters that require a knowledge of the earliest non-Biblical evidence.]

F. F. Bruce, *The New Testament Documents: Are They Reliable?* 5th revised edition. Grand Rapids, Mich.: Wm. B. Eerdmans Publishing Co., 1960. 120 pp. [A useful handbook on the basic problems of New Testament Introduction, from a conservative and scholarly viewpoint.]

H. V. Morton, *In the Steps of St. Paul.* New York: Dodd, Mead & Company, 1955. 499 pp. [Originally published in 1936, this work, like Morton's companion volume on the Master, is charming. It contains quantities of background material, unforunately without documentation—which annoys the scholar who wants to know where he got some of his material.]

WORD STUDIES

Leon Morris, *The Apostolic Preaching of the Cross.* Grand Rapids, Mich.: Wm. B. Eerdmans Publishing Co., 1955. 296 pp. [A splendid work, combining thoroughly scholarly word studies, well-rounded theology, and deep devotion. Highly recommended!]

J.-J. von Allmen, *Vocabulary of the Bible.* English translation by a group of scholars, edited by Hilda A. Wilson. London: Lutterworth Press, 1958. 479 pp. [Contains a breadth of scholarship. When studying words we need to be reminded that the context governs the meaning of words at least as much as the reverse. Always study words in context!]

Index